CREDITS

LEAD DESIGN AND DEVELOPMENT
Ian Lemke

WRITING
Keith Garrett, Jack Houser, Michelle Klein Houser,
Ian lemkeBrandes Stoddard, Lee Thommock

EDITING
Skyler Mannen

ART DIRECTION
Ian Lemke, Alida Saxon

LAYOUT AND GRAPHIC DESIGN
Thomas Shook

COVER ART
Aaron Riley

INTERIOR ART
William Thomas Arnold, Ryan Barger,
Nora Briscotti, Felicia Cano, J.B. Casacop, Chris
Casciano, Anna Christenson, Vince Conn,
Caroline Eade, Anna Ignatieva, Mitchell Malloy,
Sam Manley, Ricardo Robles Oritz, John Silva,
Lee Smith, Florian Stitz, Nicholas Stohlman,
Frank Walls, Dallas Williams, Qipeng Zhang,
Allen Geneta, Alexander Yakovlev,
Dimitar Spasov, Cristian C. Otazu, Olivia Rea,
Margarita Bourkova

www.pegasusna.com

OFFICIAL LICENSED PRODUCT

3D6 ADVENTURES SYSTEM

Pegasus Spiele

THE MERCHANT AND HIS CHILDREN

Once upon a time, in a land far away, in a city called the City, there lived a wealthy merchant who had three children. This merchant was a widower, and sad to say, his heart and business had both suffered since his good wife died. He had not told his children that his (and his family's) hopes now resided in the success of one precious caravan that was even now making its way back from the village of Villedoc on the other side of the Realm. He had not told his children that the caravan was delayed and overdue, and that if it did not come in before the week was out, the Taxman's Overdue Collections Division would be paying him a visit.

If one is not familiar with the inner workings of the City, one might wonder why this unfortunate merchant was so in fear of the Taxman. After all, he had committed no crimes other than financial insecurity, and he fully intended to pay his debt once his caravan arrived. This reckoning, however, fails to account for the nature of the Taxman himself, one Verrenid Iglac. Iglac was known for his merciless tenacity in collecting accounts, and his Overdue Collections Division's nickname, the "Leg Breakers", was not merely a figure of speech. If the merchant did not pay his taxes, he knew his limbs—and perhaps even his life—would be forfeit.

Next, one might wonder why this merchant did not go to the authorities in the City, to the Sheriff or the Magistrate, throw himself on their mercy, and beg for a less brutal payment plan. One might wonder this if one didn't know the City and how the Sheriff and the Magistrate buttered their bread. The merchant did know, and he was desperate, so he took himself to the Soothsayer to see if she could ask the stars to aid him.

Chimes rang softly as he entered the Soothsayer's small and comfortable shop. She beckoned him to sit across from her at her reading table. He sat, crossed her palm with one of his few remaining gold pieces, and asked, "How can I save my family from ruin?"

The Soothsayer looked at the lines on his palm, tracing them gently with a pointy fingernail. She breathed in and prophesied, "You can't."

"That's all?" asked the merchant. "No details, no maybes, no … nothing?"

The Soothsayer held out her hand, and the merchant irritably paid for his second question.

She pulled out a thick deck of cards, worn at the edges. She held the deck, closed her eyes, and then handed them to the merchant. "Shuffle. Cut."

After he did so, she turned over the top card to reveal a picture of a mature woman in a field of wheat. The woman looked happy and healthy. She reminded him of his dear wife.

"Loss," said the Soothsayer. "You are thinking of your past. Shuffle again and think of your future. Cut." Once more, he shuffled the cards, cut them, and she turned over the top card. This time it was a picture of a gentle youth holding an oversized gold piece in his hands.

"Ah," she said, pointing to the card. "This is good news for you. One of your children can save your family." She turned over the next card, a blindfolded woman holding two swords. She frowned.

"What does it mean?" the merchant demanded.

"I like you," said the Soothsayer, "and this is a very important reading, so I will tell you exactly what it means. The blindfold means you have a very hard choice ahead. The swords mean that you must choose correctly. I can flip more cards to console you, but the choice must be yours. No one else can guide you, not even me."

* * *

The next day, the merchant summoned his children and confessed everything: the caravan, the Taxman, and the Soothsayer's prediction. His older daughter, Donella, and his son, Elgin, each argued in their own favour, but their father was not swayed by either arguments.

"We have a week to find a way to keep the Leg Breakers from our door," he said. "Go out into the City, children, even beyond the walls if you must, and come home to me with a plan. Whichever of you presents the best solution will save my legs, save our fortune, and become my heir. Now go!"

Donella and Elgin both ran for the door, almost trampling each other in an effort to get going. The merchant's youngest child, his daughter Gisela, remained quiet, sitting in her chair and petting the stray cat who always seemed to find a way inside, no matter how many doors were shut and windows barred.

"Why do you sit when your sister and brother are already busily working to save our family?" asked her father.

"I am not clever like my sister or charming like my brother," Gisela said, "but perhaps if I sit and think a while, an idea will come to me."

"Foolish girl," muttered her father, leaving her alone to her musings.

Gisela continued to pet the cat, a fluffy Ragdoll that she had named "Whiskers".

"What do you think I should do?" she asked it, and to her astonishment, the furry feline answered.

"Go to the dockyard and get me some fish."

"You can talk?" Gisela was amazed.

"When I choose to," said the cat, delicately licking its paw.

"I wish I could get you fish today," said Gisela, "but I need to figure out how to save my family. I only have a week, and I don't know where to start."

"Follow my instructions, and all will be well," replied the cat. It jumped up to the windowsill, and before it vanished, it meowed in a way that sounded suspiciously like, "Now!"

Gisela didn't have any fish in the pantry, and Whiskers had been looking bonier of late, even under all that fur. She sighed, put on her cloak, and left for the dockyard.

* * *

The week was almost out, and the merchant was beginning to worry. None of his efforts to extend his credit or to sell his properties or possessions had been successful, and he wondered if all his colleagues in the Avenue of Numbers were waiting for the Taxman to ruin him so they could buy his property cheaply when it was auctioned off. Perhaps he should have cut his losses, packed up his children, and left the City for a simpler life.

Just then, his daughter Donella returned home, wearing a shiny gold vest and an excited smile.

"Dear Papa," she said, "I will save this family from ruin, as well as your own dear legs. I have taken a position with the City government. I am going to be an auditor and work for the Taxman."

"Have you come to collect from your own father?" asked the merchant in horror.

"No Papa," said Donella. "I convinced Mr. Iglac not to send the Overdue Collections Division to collect our debt. He will garnish my wages until your debt is paid, and he promised me that no one will harm you."

"Dear daughter," said the merchant, "did you sign your contract of employment?"

"I have signed nothing yet, Papa. Mr. Iglac said it could wait until I begin work tomorrow."

"Thank heavens!" he said. "I implore you, do not sign. My debt is great, and with an auditor's pay... that horrid man would own you for the rest of your life."

"But I must sign, Papa. I know it is a sacrifice, but when Mr. Iglac sees how clever I am and what an excellent worker I will be, he will surely give me raises and promotions, and your debt will be cleared in no time."

"Sweet daughter, you underestimate the wickedness of a man like Verrenid Iglac. Why would he ever promote you, no matter how excellent you are, if he could retain you as his indebted servant?"

"Nevertheless, I have to sign, Papa. It's the only way I can save you."

"Wait a bit," said her father. "Perhaps one of your siblings will come up with a better solution."

"I doubt it," said Donella.

Just then, Elgin, the merchant's second child, returned.

"Papa," he said, "I have the solution to all of your troubles! I have charmed my way into the good graces of a member of the Golden Rule, one of the master merchants of the City. I speak of Deagle Fallcrest. I know he has a bad reputation, but he assures me it is undeserved. He will help us."

Donella rolled her eyes. Her brother had inherited their mother's beauty, but she wished he'd gotten just a pinch of brains to go with it. The merchant held back the harsh words on the tip of his tongue.

"Tell me more, son. How will Deagle Fallcrest help us, and what does he want in exchange?"

"He'll pay off our debt for practically nothing," said Elgin. "All he wants is to know our secret caravan routes so he can avoid getting robbed when he sends out his traders. Actually, Papa, this is not my first conversation with him. Lord Fallcrest is a good friend of mine."

"You fool!" exclaimed Donella. "Fallcrest may be your friend, but he won't give you money for nothing. He doesn't plan to use our routes to avoid getting robbed; he plans to rob our last caravan!"

"I suppose you have a better idea, big sister? Is that why you're wearing that ugly vest?" The two fell to squabbling so loudly and bitterly that neither of them noticed when their younger sister entered the house holding Whiskers, the stray cat. Whiskers purred, butting Gisela's head with its own. Behind them, towering over tiny Gisela, stood a troll, and his presence, quiet as he was, caused the siblings to stop quarreling.

"What trouble have you brought home, Gisela?" asked the merchant. "Haven't we enough worries?"

"Peace, Papa," said Gisela. "I have brought salvation."

Immediately her siblings began to argue and protest, but the troll, who had to duck through the doorway, took a step forward, and his mere presence silenced them once again.

"Let your sister speak," said the merchant.

"First of all, Papa, Donella, Elgin, I would like to introduce you to my friend, Barok Grimskin. I met him at the dockyards when I was looking for fish."

Her family remembered their manners and greeted Barok politely. Then, they invited him to join them for tea, which he accepted, also politely. In his huge hands, the teacup looked like a doll's teacup, but he held it gingerly as Gisela continued her tale.

"I know you won't believe me, but when I was trying to think of what to do, Whiskers spoke to me."

"She's crazy," said Donella.

"She's making up stories," said Elgin.

"We'll see," said their father. "Hold your tongues, or we'll be here all day."

"What did the cat say to you?" asked Donella, failing to keep the mockery from her tone.

"Whiskers said to go to the dockyard to get her some fish and that all would be well. She was looking rather skinny, and a talking cat seemed magical to me, so I followed her instructions. I got her some fresh fish and fed her. While she was licking her whiskers, Barok, my new friend…" Gisela blushed prettily, then looked away from the troll, who almost crushed his teacup in his attempt to act unmoved.

"Barok and Whiskers are friends. I mean, she visits him, and he pets her and feeds her, just like I do. So we started talking about Whiskers and how she… oh, never mind, that is not the part you want to know. We both love animals, you see, and he began telling me a story about some stray horses he found, and then… sorry Papa, I will get to the point. Maybe… oh forget it, just go to the window and look outside!"

The merchant did as his daughter bid him, and when he looked out the window, he was astonished to see his lost caravan, wagon after wagon, blocking the street. No one dared to move the wagons nor steal from them, for they were guarded by a group of large trolls, none of whom appeared a stranger to violence.

"Gisela! My darling! How on earth …" The merchant was speechless.

"Barok's family found them in a warehouse by the wharf when they were rounding up the loose horses. Our horses. They didn't know whose goods they were, but then they met me and I told them our story, and they kindly returned the lot."

"We wouldn't mind a finder's fee," rumbled the troll.

"Of course, my boy," said the ecstatic merchant. "Of course you shall have it!"

"Also," said Barok, "if you could possibly, please give me permission to court your younger daughter."

The troll was enormous, green-skinned, and smelled like fish. His teeth looked clean, but two of them emerged menacingly from his lower jaw. His dockyard worker's pants were filthy, his shirt not much cleaner. He wore no shoes, and his toenails seemed to have collected all the road dirt between the docks and the merchant's home.

"Ah … um …" mumbled the merchant. "That is to say …"

"Please, Papa," said Gisela.

"You want… him… to court you?"

"A troll?" said her brother.

"A dockworker?" said her sister.

"Stop being snobs," said Gisela. "I like him."

"If she likes you, I have no objections," said the merchant. "But I am curious, not about the courting, but did you happen to notice who owned the warehouse where you found my caravan?"

"Heraldry on the door was Fallcrest," said Barok, "but I saw some gold vests patrolling outside. They scattered when my family all showed up together, sir."

Donella ripped off her golden vest and threw it on the ground.

Elgin groaned, "I hate it when you're right about my friends. Ugh."

"More fish," said Whiskers. She strutted to the middle of the table and daintily extracted some from one of the tea sandwiches. None of the family had the heart to remove her from the table or even speak a harsh word, not on that day or any day of her long, happy life. And, like Whiskers, they all lived happily ever after.

CHAPTER 1: SETTLEMENTS OF THE REALM

Dozens, or perhaps hundreds, of towns, villages, and hamlets cover the outer lands of the Realm. Each has its own unique character, secrets, and opportunity for adventure. The chapter is divided into two parts.

First, you'll find more detailed information on the towns described in the core rulebook. These are the largest towns in the Realm. Although none of them rival the size of the City, or even Villedoc, their names are known by most civilized folk. Each entry offers a little more information about the town itself as well as descriptions of a few notable locations and important people.

Second, you'll find listings for a number of the smaller villages and hamlets a party of heroes might come across during their travels. These descriptions are shorter, but they should give you plenty to work with should you find yourself in need of a village. Each of these also has story hooks as a springboard for new adventures.

TOWNS OF THE REALM

The following towns were previously featured in the core rulebook, but here we take a closer look, sometimes offering a different perspective or new insights. You'll also find story hooks for each of them. The descriptions provided here are meant to supplement those in core rulebook, not replace them.

CHAPELBELL

The lively town of Chapelbell lies at the base of landward side of a mesa that overlooks the sea. Visible from everywhere in town, the towering edifice of the Chapel can be seen rising against the sky. A narrow walkway carved into the rock of the mesa weaves its way from the bottom to the top. The only other access to the Chapel is a large basket, large enough to hold four humans (or two trolls), raised using a large winch. This conveyance provides access for those unable to make the long, steep climb. Once, sometimes twice a day, the people of Chapelbell make the long climb to attend services.

The cobblestone streets in Chapelbell are open and wide and even have sidewalks. Some have described its look as more of a small version of the City than a town. At each of the crossroads is a small square that contains a fountain and statues of various saints revered by the Light. Flowering trees and green shrubbery line the streets, and almost every building has flowers pots out front. In the springtime, white and pink petals from the trees rain down and cover the streets. And at the rate it is growing, it may indeed come to rival the City in size.

Chapelbell has a robust town guard and militia who call themselves the Shield of Light, and each member is called a Shield. The Shield of Light does not tolerate Evil people or beings of any kind in Chapelbell, and even petty crimes are punished harshly. Shields are easily recognizable by silver-trimmed white tunics with a yellow shield on the chest. They can be found patrolling almost anywhere in town or around the perimeter. They will not hesitate to stop newcomers or anyone who looks even remotely suspicious to question them about their business in town. Ghouls, trolls, goblins, and even leywalkers are eyed with suspicion and may well be followed or even encouraged to leave.

Notable Locations

Chapelbell is made up of a mixture of whitewashed wood and stone buildings with red clay rooftops.

The Chapel

The most prominent feature of Chapelbell, the Chapel looks down on the town proper from its position high on the mesa. The Chapel itself is constructed of grey stone, and the outbuildings have the same red clay shingles as can be found in the town. Its position on the mesa affords an incredible view of both the White Horse Hills and the sea. When the Chapel bells ring, they can be heard for kilometres around.

Monk's Barrel Tavern

Chapelbell is not well known for its taverns, but the ale and beer sold at the Monk's Barrel is renowned throughout the Realm. The

The Cells

The Chapel is served by an order of monks who reside in caves, called the cells. These monks go about their daily tasks of farming, tending their beehives, and producing their delicious ale, beer, and mead.

Residents

The population of Chapelbell is predominantly human, with a fair number of dwarves and a few elves who have distanced themselves from their connection to the fey. Other ancestries are looked upon with varying degrees of suspicion.

The Abbess

The Abbess is a true believer and evangelical of On High and the head of the Order of Josephine. She leads the services during the festival of Triumphant Daybreak, and her sermons are renowned for their fire and brimstone eulogies.

The Abbot

In contrast to the Abbess, the Abbot of the Chapel is considerably more laid back and personable. He prefers a lighter touch with his adherents, seeking to bring people to the Light with love rather than fear.

Shield Mistress Glorana

Glorana is the leader of the Shields of Light: a militant faction of the Order of Josephine that acts as the town guard in Chapelbell. Along with the recent rise in the incidences of monsters in the Realm, membership in

the Shield of Light has grown in recent years. As the Shields increase in size, Glorana, in conjunction with the Abbess, has been working on expanding their sphere of influence beyond simply guarding the town. As of late, they have begun offering their services to merchants and others who are in need of an escort. She has also become somewhat obsessed with locating relics of the Light.

Story Hook: Lost Relic

The PCs are approached by Shieldmistress Glorana who requests their aid in recovering a relic of St. Josephine. Several members of the Shield of Light were ambushed on their way back to Chapelbell while transporting the relic. Glorana is too busy dealing with a recent goblin incursion to intervene and asks the PCs to track the attackers and recover the relic.

Greymist

Greymist is a dangerous and desperate place. Once quite prosperous, benefiting from its easy access to the sea and one of the few sources of seafood, increasingly inclement weather and the arrival of the notorious bandit leader Dugan the Red and his crew have hastened the town's decline. Depending on who you ask, the most profitable trades in Greymist are either fishing, distilling liquor, or smuggling ill-gotten goods. Shellfish and even some varieties of fish are dried or magically preserved and shipped to the City. There are several distilleries and brewers in Greymist, although none of them is particularly notable. Still, the fishgut whiskey is notorious throughout the Realm, and many taverns and pubs keep a few bottles on hand for the truly adventurous (or the occasional troll or ghoul who claim to like the stuff).

The town has its share of crafters and artisans, although the high taxes, imposed by the Burgomaster, make for steep prices. Most items purchased in Greymist cost at least an additional gold due to the high taxes. A single human priest named Lenna ministers to the minimal number of faithful villagers from a dilapidated wooden church.

A branch of the Royal Road heads north out of Greymist and leads towards the City. The terrain here quickly becomes less swampy and soon turns to open plains, remaining this way until it reaches the vast farmlands that surround the City. To the west is a sparse, swampy forest that stretches for several miles before becoming the rocky plains that lead to the Hollow Hills. Local children, and some adults, believe this forest to be haunted, which is likely because a small cemetery is maintained here on a hill that is drier than the surrounding swamp. Of

course, any families of note keep a crypt in the larger (and somewhat nicer) cemetery outside Fishburg to the east. A narrow road, not much more than a walking path, leads to the east, connecting Greymist with the small villages and hamlets that dot the coastline throughout the Storm River Delta. At first, the road passes under twisting live oaks that grow out of the spongy ground. This area has become increasingly dangerous with the arrival of Dugan the Red and his band of outlaws. Further on, the live oaks disappear, leaving only barren saltmarsh. And, of course, to the south is the inlet that leads to the open sea.

Notable Locations

Greymist a ramshackle collection of grey, weathered wooden buildings, half of which are built on stilts to keep them safe when the waters rise. The buildings on solid land are mostly residences, while those closer to the water and built on stilts are mostly businesses of various sorts.

The Wilting Lilly

The Wilting Lily is built upon barnacle-encrusted stilts right along the water's edge. The stairs creak as you make your ascent to the entrance, a full two metres off the ground. The exterior is ramshackle and appears uneven and unstable since some of the poles have sunk deeper into the ground, as if the entire building might

slide into the sea at any moment. The Lily is the only inn and by far the nicest tavern to be found in Greymist, so it's where visitors are most likely to be directed, and despite its unsteady appearance, it is perfectly secure.

The interior of the inn is surprisingly warm and cosy. Fishnets, barnacle-encrusted anchors, colourful lures, and other sailing and fishing paraphernalia hang from the rafters, and well-worn wooden tables are scattered haphazardly about. Herbs and other aromatics are occasionally burned in the large hearth fire, almost but not quite covering the pungent smell of fish and marsh.

The Wharf Rat

The Wharf Rat Tavern, or just the Rat, as it's called by locals, is situated right on the riverbank. The building is raised high above the water on stout poles made of whole trees sunk into the bedrock below. The interior is rather light and airy for a tavern of this sort. It smells more of rank seaweed and rotten fish than the usual tavern smells of old beer and smoke. The owner is a scurrilous old troll named Cuthbert who watches over his establishment with a wary eye. Eye, singular, because he wears a patch over his left eye. The Rat is a notorious hangout for smugglers and pirates as well as the occasional brave fisherperson. Cuthbert makes it a point to know all the pirates, smugglers, and fences who pass through his doors and is happy to make connections or introductions—for the right price.

The Fisher's Knot Supply

Located on a pier that extends out over the river, this establishment is run by a young ghoul named Fallow. It carries all manner of maritime supplies and offers custom-made sails and mastheads for those who can pay. The shelves are filled with coiled rope of all lengths and thicknesses, piles of canvas, anchors, nets, fishing gear, and even bait.

Fountain Square

Located in the centre of town is a remnant of Greymists former, more prosperous days. Clear, clean water bubbles up from the centre of this marble fountain. A figure, long worn and chipped so that its original shape of a mermaid is difficult to discern, sits in the middle of the decaying structure. Tossing a coin into the fountain is said to grant luck or even fulfil wishes, so there is always a scattering of copper and even a few silver coins in the basin. The fountain is emptied once a year, and the proceeds are supposedly used for town improvements, although mostly, they end up lining the Burgomaster's pockets. No one dares steal the coins because of the legends of a terrible curse. Additionally, the town guard keeps a close watch at the bequest of the Burgomaster.

Residents

The population of Greymist is predominantly human with a few trolls and even fewer ghouls.

Burgomaster Gorund

The current Burgomaster is a fat, greedy, gluttonous man named Gorund who gorges himself on the best cakes and pies his money can buy (which isn't saying much given the quality of food in Greymist). He has a talent for finding new methods of taxation, but when those don't work out, he taxes the town guard, eager to get his share of the bribes and protection fees they extort from the local populace.

Hettie the Fishmonger

Old Hettie can be found walking the streets selling her wares in the late morning after the first fishing boats come in. Besides fish, she is also a seller of information. Wandering the beaches in the early mornings digging for cockles and oysters, Hettie sees and hears a great deal. She always knows what ships are nearby and who is smuggling and who is pirating.

Lenna

Lenna is a young priestess of the Light who recently took over the small, dilapidated church in Greymist. She has begun fixing up the church and spends many days wandering the town working earnestly to increase her flock. She has chosen to take a light touch in her approach, insisting that people call her Lenna rather than by any formal title.

Story Hook: Politics as Usual

An election for Burgomaster is coming up soon. Gorund has won every election for the past 20 years through a combination of bribery, blackmail, and outright threats. The priestess, Lenna, believes it is high time for Gorund's reign to end and hopes to get someone fairer installed as Burgomaster. Being a priestess, she prefers not to be actively involved in politics, but she makes an exception and asks the PCs to look into a few matters. Several influential members of the town are being threatened and blackmailed into supporting Gorund, so she's hoping that the PCs can free them from the yoke of the current Burgomaster, allowing them to express themselves and vote without fear.

INNSVIEW

The town of Innsview is mostly known for the nearby inn called the Tavern at Innsview. However, despite its name, the town is located almost a full day's ride from the Tavern. In fact, Innsview has been here since long before the Tavern was built, so its name is purely coincidental.

It is a busy and bustling town that grows even busier during market days. During the spring, summer, and fall, Innsview hosts a huge monthly market where people travel from kilometres around to buy and sell livestock, produce, prepared foods, crafts, furnishings, potions, and much more. Almost anything you might want or need can be found at the Innsview market, which lasts for about two days, but people often arrive several days early to beat the crowd. Largely due to its renowned market, Innsview has become a centre for crafters of all kinds: smiths, tinkerers, carpenters, and artisans abound, and the main street is filled with a wondrous variety of shops for a town of this size.

Innsview is situated upon a large hill that overlooks the surrounding region. One can see for kilometres in every direction, and it is said that on a clear day, you can just make out the roof of The Tavern to the north.

The lands surrounding Innsview are mostly flat plains with a few hills, copses of trees, and meandering streams to break up the landscape. Located upon a smaller hill just to the south is a small stone chapel and well-maintained graveyard. The massive fairgrounds are located several miles to the north of town. The grounds rest in a low, flat plain to the west of the Royal Road. There are several permanent structures here that are in use only during market days, including a large stable for horses and livestock, several covered pavilions, a stage, and a long building where workers stay during the market. There is also a separate pavilion surrounded by multiple outdoor ovens and stoves.

NOTABLE LOCATIONS

The buildings off Innsview are mostly made of white and yellow stucco-covered stone with thatched rooftops. The Royal Road runs right through the middle of town and is lined with shops, restaurants, and pubs.

THE CLOCK TOWER

One of Innsview's claims to fame is the magnificent clock tower located right in the centre of town. The clock tower rises almost 20-metres high and is of dwarven and troll manufacture. The stone is cut from white and pink marble, and the numbers and hands on the clock are solid bronze. When it catches the light of the setting sun, the glow can be seen from far around. A curmudgeonly old dwarf named Stela maintains the clock tower and lives inside the base.

RESIDENTS

The residents of Innsview are mostly human, with a few dwarves and elves. Of course, people of all ancestries can be found here during market days.

MAYOR FOGUN

The mayor of Innsview is an elderly dwarf named Fogun. He began his days as an armoursmith of some renown but eventually settled into politics. He has a shrewd wit and an even shrewder business sense and always has the town's interests at heart. There are rumours that he amassed quite a fortune during his smithing days and that he has quite a few impressive pieces of armour in his collection.

STORY HOOK: MISSING CARAVANS

Several caravans have on their way to and leaving Innsview have gone missing—someone or something must be responsible, and the mayor wants to find out who. The PCs are hired to investigate the disappearances, possibly acting as caravan guards for a particularly wealthy convoy hoping to draw out the perpetrators.

LEYRUIN

Although located along the Royal Road, Leyruin does not receive many visitors and merchants and other passersby tend to spend only the night before moving on quickly the next morning. It is not that there is anything intrinsically wrong with this aesthetically pleasing settlement, but its surroundings cause most to leave as quickly as possible. Leyruin lies in a hollow shaded by the nearby trees and ruins. The trees on the western side of Fallen Giant Wood are mostly massive redwoods that cast long shadows over the town until well past noon. But it is the presence of the nearby ruins that give most visitors pause. The ruins to the north of Leyruin are ancient beyond knowing and rumoured to be amongst the most haunted in the Realm. Indeed, there are stories that the Lord of Darkness himself dwells in an underground maze beneath the ruins.

The town itself is a cluster of wood and stone buildings of mostly elven design. Thick moss adorns the rooftops and even the outer walls of some of the homes. Rubble from the nearby ruins was used in the construction of many of the buildings and the streets. As a result, some of the rocks bear ancient runes and strange sigils, which only adds to the mystical feel of Leyruin.

The town is primarily an elven settlement, but almost every ancestry can be found living here. Its access to the sea makes it a common stopover for smugglers. It is a common meeting spot for fences from the City and those with illicit goods to sell, and shady deals occur daily in Leyruin's many inns and taverns.

Leyruin is located high above the seas, but a long series of wooden stairs allow access to the Docks that line the base of the cliffs. Two winch and pulley systems raise large platforms from the docks to the top of the cliffs, raising and lowering cargo as well as the occasional brave passenger. The cliffs themselves are riddled with a maze of sea caves, which further adds to the city's mysterious and dangerous aesthetic.

NOTABLE LOCATIONS

Almost all of the buildings look like something out of a fairytale. The homes are mostly single-story, with stone foundations and walls made of the local redwoods and tall shingle rooftops. Many of the businesses are two-story stone works. The ever-present moss clings to everything, and in the summer, the moss spouts small white and yellow flowers. Plants and flowers are also very common, with most homes having a small flower bed or garden out front.

Sculpture Garden

The sculpture garden is actually a hedge maze that is located in the center of town. The sculptures are located at intersections and cul-de-sacs within the maze. Many

of the sculptures are made of wood and stone and are crafted by local artisans. Others have been salvaged from the ruins that surround the town, however.

Nepenthe Inn

The Nepenthe Inn is the source of many of Leyruin's most powerful and exotic spirits. These alcohols are known to have unique effects, and the proprietor, a human named Eldgar, keeps his recipes quite secret. Besides himself, only a couple of trusted assistants know the exact ingredients—a sprite named Anna Lellia and a pale woman (who some believe to be a vampire) named Lennir. It is known that Eldgar and his assistants gather many of the herbal components for their concoctions from the Fallen Giant Woods. The most expensive and sought-after draught is said to be as sweet as ambrosia and allows the drinker to forget a memory of their choosing.

Built almost entirely of stone salvaged from the nearby ruins, the inn itself is rather dark and sombre, with an air of mystery. Ancient engravings and writings are on almost every piece of stone in the building, and loremasters have travelled from all over the Realm to examine the walls of the Nepenthe Inn.

Sea Caves

The sea caves along the coast are an endless source of mystery, but the fact that some of the caves are used by smugglers is something of an open secret in Leyruin. A few of the sea caves are large enough for a small ship to enter and remain out of sight, and several routes connecting these caves to the surface have been discovered. Notably, one of the tunnels leads to the basement of the Nepenthe Inn, but at least two more lead to locations not far outside of town. To date, there are still vast areas that remain unexplored. Recently, there people have reported seeing things moving on the darkness of the caves, although there have been no reported attacks. However, more than one adventurer has sought to explore the caves only to never been heard from again.

Residents

The population of Leyruin is mostly elvish, but it is truly multicultural in that any ancestry can usually be found here at any given time.

Captain Reynard

Reynard is a tall elven man who captains a sailing vessel called the Black Fox. He often works as a merchant, but his ship and crew are not unfamiliar to smuggling and piracy. In fact, one could argue that merchanting is mostly a cover since most of Reynard's wealth comes from his more illicit activities. Long ago, he left behind the forests and the fey for a life on the sea. Despite his darker proclivities, he is a friendly and generous soul, often sharing his bounty with the less fortunate—much to the dismay of some of his crew. When pressed on the matter, and well into his cups, Reynard will admit that he took to this life for the excitement and adventure rather than any great desire for wealth.

Eldgar

Eldgar is the proprietor of the Nepenthe Inn and perhaps one of the most talented alchemists in the Realm. He is a tall, thin human with dark hair and a wispy moustache. His eyes are sunken with perpetual dark circles under them that make him appear as if he has not had much sleep. Despite his somewhat morose appearance, he keeps his customers happy by continually whipping up new concoctions to serve at the inn and telling tall tales of piracy and forbidden magic.

Story Hook: Cave-In

One night, the entire town is shaken as a section of the cliff near Leyruin tumbles into the sea. Fortunately, the docks are undamaged, but the collapse revealed the entrance to a new cave that now opens directly to the tumultuous waters. Curiously, there are signs that this cave is not entirely natural. Parts of statuary and other worked stone emerge from the new cliff face. This new cave is ripe for exploration, and the PCs are lucky enough to be here when it's exposed. Who knows what dangers (and treasures) lie just beneath Leyruin…

Whitestable

Whitestable appears more like a fortress than a town on approach. Low stone walls that back up against the steep hillside and a stout oak door and portcullis protect the town from intrusion. Inside the walls are neat rows of stone buildings. The famed stables are just beyond the gates, made of wood and painted white using chalk obtained from the hills. It is a matter of pride for the people of Whitestable to keep the fences pristine. The sounds and smells of dozens of horses fills the air. As you proceed into the town, it quickly becomes apparent that these buildings and the stables are only a portion of the town, as the rest is burrowed into the side of the hill.

The entrances to the under-hill part of the town are protected by gates that can be closed, if needed, although they remain open most of the time. Inside, the main halls are so large that you can easily forget you're underground.

Most of the businesses and smelting operations are here, while smaller tunnels lead to residential districts and the mines themselves.

The primary businesses of Whitestable are mining and capturing, training, and selling the horses that roam the White Horse Hills. Rich veins of ore, tin, and silver beneath the hills have become fewer and far between, and the townsfolk are gravely concerned about the potential loss of revenue. The leadership of the town has tried to keep the depletion of the mines a secret, but it has been impossible to keep the rumor mill under control. The Overseer has recently ordered the opening of new shafts deeper in the ground, and several expeditions have begun exploring the possibility of sinking mines elsewhere in the hills. Meanwhile, there is discussion about expanding the horse-selling operations.

NOTABLE LOCATIONS

The buildings in Whitestable are all stout and sturdy of dwarven design. Except for some barns and outbuildings, they are all uniformly stone with slate rooftops.

THE STABLES

The stables at Whitestable rival any to be found in the Realm, even those found in the City. The whitewashed corrals take up nearly half the usable space within the walls. Just beyond those are the stables which are constructed of solid granite just like the rest of the buildings in town.

People come from far and wide to purchase a horse from Whitestable. Almost any color or variety of horse can be found here, but they are famous for the snow-white stallions and mares that they catch and tame.

THE WHITE HORSE INN

The inn is located not far inside the entrance to the underground region of Whitestable. The entire edifice is covered in gold-shot white marble both inside and out. The horse motif can be found carved into the marble everywhere. There are several inns in Whitestable, but the White Horse is the most popular and by far the most expensive.

RESIDENTS

The residents of Whitestable are primarily dwarves with a good mix of trolls. There is also a small population of humans and even a few goblins.

HILL LORD LOTHAR

The position of Hill Lord is much the same as mayor and is an elected position. The position has almost always been filled by a dwarf but the current Hill Lord is a troll. Lothar is tall like most trolls but walks with a noticeable stoop, an affectation he has acquired living so long amongst dwarves and working in the deep mines. Lothar won over the taciturn dwarves in part due to his gregarious personality but also due to his remarkable ability to find new veins of ore.

Overseer Gorgo

The overseer has been in charge of the mines for over twenty years and is a notoriously hard taskmaster. He was in contention against Lothar to be Hill Lord, and he's still bitter about the loss, finding it hard to believe that a troll could possibly know more about mining. He has recently started embezzling from the mines, in part due to his own greed but also out of spite for Lothar.

Horsemaster Shaela

Shaela is a young human woman in her early twenties who has a remarkable way with horses. She is renowned for being able to train even the unruliest horse. She often spends her days walking the hills and observing the roaming herds.

Story Hook: Unicorn Sighting

One of the horse-catchers of Whitestable spotted a unicorn on the White Horse Hills during their last expedition. The hunt is now on, with people of all sorts setting out to catch the unicorn. Some hope to tame and sell it, and others have more nefarious purposes. Will the PCs join the hunt, or will they try to save the unicorn from those who would do it harm?

WOODBINE

The elven town of Woodbine is nestled in a valley of the Split Oak Forest not far from the Royal Road. It has a much more cosmopolitan feel than other elven settlements, which may be due to its close proximity to the City.

The elves of Woodbine are consumed with scholarly pursuits and have lost some of the connection to nature and the fae realms that is common to most of their kind. The primary focus of these scholars is to assemble a true history of the Realm. They discount many of the beliefs and superstitions surrounding the history of the Realm and seek the "true" stories. This strict adherence to truth

and fact goes so far as to discredit the powers of the fey of the Great Forest or even the Ancient Ones of the woods.

No matter how much they turn their backs on the magical history of the Realm, there is no denying that ever since the destruction of the Ancient One at the heart of the forest, there has been a rise in encounters with terrible beasts, monsters, and even spirits in Split Oak Woods. So much so that a faction of townsfolk who still believe in the power of the Ancient Ones have organized and begun pushing for the town to do more to solve the mystery of why the woods are suddenly more dangerous. However, the council of archons, made up entirely of elven scholars, refuses to listen or to devote resources to what they consider to be a trivial matter.

NOTABLE LOCATIONS

The town is a mixture of elven, human, and even some dwarven styles. Nestled under the eaves of the woods, there are more traditional elven tree homes, while more typically, human and dwarven styles of both wood and stone can be found toward the centre of town. Many of the houses incorporate wood from the remains of the Ancient One, which was destroyed around a century ago. Even in the human and dwarvish part of town, elvish accents and flourishes can be seen throughout the architecture.

Hall of Knowledge

The Hall of Knowledge is the tallest and most grandiose building in Woodbine. It's located almost exactly in the centre of town where it is visible to all. It is reminiscent more of a church or a library or university. Tall spires of marble and gold inlay make it quite a sight to behold. The Hall doubles as something of a townhall since the ruling council of archons also gathers here for business. Vast chambers of the hall are devoted to nothing but shelf

upon shelf of books and scrolls. Indeed, it is likely the largest library in the Outer Realm outside the City. Other chambers are devoted to scholars carefully preserving, reconstructing, and copying ancient texts. Rumors persist of a secret chamber, only accessible by the archons, where books of forbidden knowledge are stored.

Kepplepot's Curios

The proprietor of this shop is a gregarious old dwarf tinkerer named Ordo Kepplepot. When no one is in his shop, he can often be found sitting on his stoop blowing smoke rings with a long clay pipe. The inside of the shop is cramped and cluttered. Tall shelves are overflowing with a wide variety of strange items and devices. Kepplepot himself makes many of the tinkered items and toys, including dolls and toys that walk and move on their own. Some of them even speak.

Residents

Although officially an elven settlement, there are fewer sprites than one would expect and a large contingent of humans, dwarves, and even a few trolls. A few leywalkers are known to reside in the nearby forest.

Elestia the Carver

Elestia is an elven woman who is renowned throughout the Realm as a woodcarver of incomparable skill. She carves her works only from heartwood from the remains of the Ancient One of Split Oak Woods. She claims that the wood speaks to her, which provides much of her inspiration. Nobles and art aficionados covet her works, and with good reason, as they stand on display at no less than the Castle itself. She is also a skilled bowyer; her bows are much sought after by the best archers in the Realm. Not only are they extremely well made, but each has custom carvings and designs up and down the length of the bow.

Herga, Captain of the Town Guard

Herga is a tall troll woman and is the current captain of the town guard. She has served the town well for over a decade, but recently, she has found herself in conflict with the archons, and many of her supporters fear that she may not hold her position much longer. Herga is among those who are concerned about the rising monster activity in the Split Oak Woods. She is in regular communication with the leywalkers who reside outside the town and has been convinced that the destruction of the Ancient One is the cause of the rise of evil in the wood. Every request for more resources to investigate further has been denied, and she is becoming increasingly frustrated.

Story Hook: The Ancient One

Since the destruction of the Ancient One, Split Oak Forest has continued to grow darker and more dangerous. Some folks, especially amongst the Leywalkers, believe that the worst is yet to come. Legend holds that before an Ancient One dies, it leaves behind a seed even if it is killed. However, now one has been able to find the seed of Split Oak Forest. The druids, leywalkers, and other allies of the forest are organizing a search for the seed and offering a great reward for anyone who can find it.

Villages and Hamlets

Small villages and hamlets dot the countryside throughout the Realm. Most are located on or near the Royal Road, but some can be found in unexpected places, far from other settlements. Some of those far separated from civilization still have strange customs and worship ancient gods.

Naerendil

Located just off the Royal Road on the eastern edge of the Great Forest, Naerendil is a pleasant village comprising mainly elves, humans, and sprites. Half of the village is built in the boughs of the trees, with each cluster of buildings connected by narrow swinging walkways. These treetop dwellings are inhabited mostly by elves and sprites. The other half, located on the ground, is a small cluster of wooden buildings with thatched rooftops and is home to most of the settlement's human population, as well as a few elves.

The settlement's most notable structure is the Golden Leaf Inn, built amongst the branches of a massive oak tree. The building is circular and surrounds the entire tree, with an outside deck that provides a magnificent view. On a clear day, one can just make out the sparking of the Storm River. The village has a thriving basket-making industry, and Naerendil baskets are known even in The City. They are decorative, lightweight, and extremely sturdy. The basket weavers have recently started to weave pouches and backpacks in much the same manner as their baskets. These have become so popular that they are not able to keep up with demand, and people travel from Villedoc and beyond to obtain them.

BRAKWATER

Brakwater is located on the southern edge of the Craven Idol Woods along the Royal Road. A winding stream of dark water flows sluggishly not far to the west of the village where it emerges from the woods and eventually empties into the Storm River. The locals generally avoid these waters, for there are legends of strange creatures emerging from its depths. Every now and again, an adventurous soul tries to fish the waters, and sometimes they don't return. The reason for the murkiness is uncertain, although there are many stories. Some claim it to be a result of a curse of a witch who resides in the forest. Others blame the goblins and say that the stream turned black when they carved their idol into the Ancient One in the centre of the woods. And others still believe the water of the stream to be coloured black by the blood of an ancient god who lies dying at its source.

The goblins of Craven Idol have become bolder and recent years and are now a perpetual danger for the people of Brakwater. In response, they've constructed a tall wooden wall around the perimeter of the town. The main gate remains open from sunrise to sunset, but it remains closed tight after sundown for fear of goblins. The guards direct anyone wishing admittance after sunset to a smaller postern gate. The buildings inside the walls are mostly wooden with shingled rooftops. A few buildings of import, such as the town hall, are constructed of stone.

HELLEM'S REST

No one knows exactly why this small settlement is called Hellem's Rest, but every settlement member has a different story. No matter the truth of its origins, they have taken its namesake seriously, and the village has become a welcome stop for merchants and travelers on their way to the City. Located about a half-day's ride from the City's gates, many travelers stop here to rest and relax before entering the city proper.

The village is located amongst the rolling hills of farmland on the Royal Road west of the City. The building are all stone covered in brightly coloured stucco, many of which are painted with murals or intricate designs. The village features a large open square around its central well. The most enticing offering of Hellem's Rest, however, is the bathhouses. The village is located above natural hot springs, and several establishments have taken advantage of this fact and feature warm baths, both private and public.

They say that every day is market day in Hellem's Rest. Situated amongst the many kilometre's of farmland surrounding the City, there is always fresh meat and produce available. Additionally, merchants and traders of all kinds stop here every day, and some take advantage to make their wares available to interested buyers. In fact, some shop owners from the City send scouts to Hellem's Rest to make deals and spot the best merchandise before these travelling merchants reach the City. This has become a brisk trade and sometimes involves skullduggery as City vendors compete with one another.

FISHBURG

The foul-smelling, ill-fated Fishburg is known for more than its colourful cuisine: It's a short walk away from a well-maintained ghoul necropolis. Anyone bold enough to climb to the second story of one of the local buildings would see a vast array of meticulously cleaned tombstones and tastefully ornamented mausoleums. Only a few wealthy noble families can pay for one of those marble edifices, however, since the majority of the bodies interred were buried without names or histories. Instead of dates of birth and death, each tombstone has a clever couplet offering a vague guess of who is buried below.

The town is located on the coast to the east of Greymist within the borders of the Grey Swamp. It consists of a dozen or so buildings that are a stone's throw from the beach, though these crumbling structures are in a state of disrepair. Decrepit edifices slant away from the sea, doing their best to slouch an inch or two further away with each passing year. Gambrel roofs are missing tiles, and spindly chimneys look as though they are about to collapse.

The inhabitants of Fishburg are primarily ghouls, with a few humans and trolls. The ghouls occupy themselves mostly with maintaining the nearby cemetery and the funerary trade, while the humans and trolls are involved mostly in fishing and curing and drying fish, which lends to the village's pungent odour.

DEWBERRY

Dewberry is a small mining village that's home to about twenty families. It's located at the foot of Moonbreak Tor, south of the crags and just north of the Great Forest. The town is nestled at the base of the southern side. A track winds from the village up the side of the tor, and about halfway to the top, a winding series of switchbacks ends at the entrance to a mine.

The village gets its name from the large number of dewberries growing in the region. These small plants bloom throughout the spring and summer months on dewy mornings. The flowers are white with tiny red spots. They produce small, translucent berries known for their alleged healing properties and usefulness as a sleep aid. Dewberries are sweet and have a slightly minty flavor.

Most of the villagers, who are comprised of dwarves, humans, trolls, and even a few goblins and minotaurs, work in the mines, but the village also offers a variety of stores and businesses around the village square. Some cater to visitors; others are reliable suppliers for the locals. The general store carries a wide array of durable gear, a small tavern lets rooms to travelers, and three local blacksmiths are hard at work throughout the day producing arms, armor, and tools. The most prominent blacksmith is an old, one-eyed minotaur named Gareth who specializes in making two-handed weapons, although all of his weapons are of excellent quality.

HAVEN

The modest village of Haven lies in the eaves of the Whispering Wood, and the boughs of the massive oak trees loom over the buildings closest to the wood. The centre of the town consists of a cluster of a dozen homes or so that surround an outdoor tavern called the Broken Mule and a small shop known as Curious & Sundries. A large wood mill lies at the edge of the village alongside a large rushing stream. The populace of the settlement is almost entirely human with just a few elves and sprites.

The primary industry of Haven is woodcutting since the Whispering Wood is known to be the only place in the Realm where harmony oaks are found. The wood of these oaks resonates with sound and music in a way like no other, making instruments fashioned from harmony oaks cherished by bards and minstrels alike. The wood is also coveted by crafters building music halls and theatres. Unfortunately, the supply of harmony oaks has been dwindling, requiring the lumberjacks to venture further and further into the ancient wood.

Halfrid, the de facto mayor of Haven, is over a hundred years old but still sharp as a tack. She spends much of her days sitting on her front stoop, smoking a pipe and discussing the pleasantness of the day or the settlement's

current woes with any who care to stop and talk. She insists on speaking to any newcomers, as Haven does not receive many visitors.

GRELDEN

Located on the eastern edge of Craven Idol Woods, this small settlement is hardly known to even the most well-traveled. It's camouflaged by earthen berms that surround the entire settlement. The ground has been dug within these berms so that "street level" is below the ground. The homes are all built of sod blocks with grass-covered rooftops so that they blend in even if you are right above them.

Most of the population are goblins from the Craven Idol Woods who did not fit in with their own society yet do not feel comfortable enough to venture into more civilized places of the Realm. A few minotaurs and trolls can be found living here as well, and even a few humans who don't feel welcome elsewhere have made Grelden their home.

There is little in the way of industry here, and the residents of Grelden struggle for survival every day. Most of their food comes from fishing, foraging, and hunting, or from the vegetable gardens a few residents maintain on their rooftops. Although it is discouraged, when things get desperate, some of the residents resort to banditry or conduct nighttime raids on other villages.

CHAPTER 2: THE CITY AND VILLEDOC

While there are countless little towns, hamlets and villages scattered across the Realm, there is only one City, which resides in the south, and one larger, well-known village called Villedoc, which lies in the north. When it comes to 'civilization' in the Realm, these two places top the list—but civilization can be a funny word. The following chapter expands on the general information presented in the *Talisman Adventures* book: locations, personalities, cultural details, and more. GMs are encouraged to add their own entries or change the details of anything in this chapter as needed to suit their stories.

THE CITY

"We call it simply "the City" because there is nothing in the Realm to compare. If civilization is what you seek in the Realm, this is where you come. The word "city" is not a commonplace concept to most of these folk, so their one and only urban cluster is the pinnacle of society in this place. Just wait until they eventually learn how much larger the world truly is…"

—Professor Tom, Academic Council of Wisdom

It is the largest, most complex, most evolved settlement in the Realm. Located in the south where the Storm River meets the Greensnake River, its walls and towers can be seen from miles away. Most people across the Realm hear tales from the City, but they don't dare dream of ever seeing it. Many, however, grow up with a burning ambition in their hearts to one day move to the great City, discover themselves, and carve out their own destiny, but only a small percentage ever actually do it.

Neighbourhoods and Districts

Over decades upon decades of expansion and evolution, the City developed different sections with their own unique characteristics: several related to professions, some attracting certain types of citizens, some devoted to different faiths, and many more. Each of these neighbourhoods is easily identified today, even by first-time visitors to the City. The types of businesses, styles of architecture, the food and drink, the smells, the sounds, the kind of people commonly found on the streets, the level of care put into upkeep—all of these vary between neighbourhoods.

Government District

While there are many government offices and resources spread around the entire City, the bulk of the main offices, courts, and high-ranking officials who populate them are found in a cluster that dominates the central area. The Magistrate's Tower, the tallest peak in the City, stands in the centre and provides a sweeping view in all directions. Sprawling outwards from there, most of the higher offices of the bureaucracy can be found closest to the Tower, with less critical government buildings loosely forming a ring around those, and so on. The City's two largest avenues cross at the Magistrate's Tower, turning into a massive roundabout, and traffic—both horse-drawn and on foot—is always heavier the closer you get to the centre.

The Spirit Quarter

The religious district of the City occupies the northeastern section, near the merging of the two rivers. The massive and elaborately carved edifice of the High Temple dominates the cityscape here, but temples of different shapes and size can be found on practically every block. Although most are welcoming to any devout soul of the proper denomination, each humanoid ancestry has places of worship that cater more to their cultural nuances and styles, appealing to those who wish to worship alongside their own kind. Across the City, benevolent monks seek out lost souls in need of guidance, food, and care and bring them back to the Spirit Quarter to give them aid and help them find the right path. Similarly spread throughout the streets are

less gentle, more fiery-tempered street preachers who proselytize from atop stacks of crates, informing those on different paths that their souls are in danger. Depending on which part of town, these aggressive clergymen are sometimes met with jeers, thrown produce, offal, and even the occasional manky boot.

The Avenue of Numbers

On the west side of the City sits the financial district, full of counting houses, gambling houses, private accountants, and moneylenders with varying levels of scruples and interest rates. The streets in this section rival the order and cleanliness of the Rosewater neighbourhood. The building façades are swept, sponged down, and polished daily along the main roads, but even the smaller back streets are better lit, less garbage-strewn, and its denizens more polite and better dressed than other corners of the City. The entire district shares the same name as its biggest road, a vital artery of commerce and power within the City, not to mention the entire Realm. Money often translates to power, so many of the most powerful personalities of the Realm can be found tending to their accounts on the Avenue of Numbers.

The Arts Quarter

The southwest quarter of the City is largely dominated by creative pursuits and vendors of artistic wares. Along the broader streets, one can find all manner of galleries and tents dedicated to showing off the talents of painters, potters, sculptors, poets, dancers, theatrical performers, and more. A handful of indoor and outdoor theatres host a constant cycle of performances to entertain the masses. The walls and cobblestones of this neighbourhood are splashed with paint, chalk, hanging lights, strings of beads and jewels, murals dedicated to heroes of legend, or simply bathed in wide swathes of colour to stand out from the monochromatic slurry of the rest of the City. The crown jewel of this quarter is the College of the Arts, the Realm's dominant institution for the education and training of the creative arts.

Rosewater

This high-rent district of the City, located in the northwest quarter, is where the upper echelons of society call home. High-ranking government officials, powerful merchant lords, highborn families, criminal kingpins, they live side-by-side here, giving each other's properties side-eye glances, one-upping their neighbours by updating their estates with the latest trends in architecture, landscaping, and colour palettes. The Rosewater district would seem like a much juicier target for burglars were it not for the Rosewater Regulars, a small force of skilled defenders draped in very distinctive dusky pink cloaks who patrol the affluent neighbourhood day and night, protecting the lush properties from those who would seek to steal from the rich. As much as the criminal element of the City wishes to avoid falling into the hands of the City Watch, the whispered tales of what happens at the hands of the "Pinks" is far more chilling—*if* the tales are to be believed.

Red Lanterns

Veterans of City travel are well-acquainted with the knowledge that the south side, a neighbourhood known as Red Lanterns, is best to be avoided at all hours—unless you have specific business there and know what you're doing. This district, named after the red-shaded lanterns hung in the windows of its numerous brothels, is the worst section of the City to be caught walking around alone. The shadowy alleys and locked doors of this area hide the hub of criminal activity in the City and surrounding regions. The Red Lanterns district is subdivided into a dozen smaller territories, each controlled by a different criminal outfit. Even the City Patrol steps lightly here, commonly accepting regular bribes to look away.

Fishtown

In the east-southeast quarter of the City, one knows how close they are to the Adelai Bridge by the potency of the smell of fish in the air. Aside from the bridge, the defining feature of this neighbourhood is the Underbridge Wharf, which deals with boat traffic to and from the Greensnake River that leads to southern waters. This is where the City gets roughly three-quarters of its fish and other seafood. Fishtown can be a rough neighbourhood for people who get in the way of the wharf trade or the sailors and dock workers who dominate the population, but it serves as a good buffer between Red Lanterns and the more civilized sections of town; the people are gruff but generally good-hearted.

Merchant's Cross

The strongest arteries of business and shopping are not in any one quarter of the City, instead located along the wide, central, north-south axis from the City Gate at the south end to the Storm Gate at the north end, by the Storm River Docks. This broad and busy street is ostentatiously called The Avenue of the Realm. The second strongest avenue of commerce is along the central east-west axis of the City, called Bridge Street, as its east end feeds directly into the famous Bridge. These two main roads combined are referred to as the Merchant's Cross, which is considered its own neighbourhood despite its layout in comparison to the other major neighbourhoods of the City. Telling people, "Meet me at the Cross, southwest," means you want them to meet you at the intersection of the two great avenues, the 'Cross', and which corner. This is because the Magistrate's Tower, the tallest building in the City, dominates the intersection of the two axes and is encircled by a large roundabout. Not specifying which corner of the Cross to meet at could send people on a mad chase running around the giant intersection looking for each other on the wrong side of the giant tower.

Government

"Oh, of course, the government is always an easy target for scorn, mockery, harsh criticism, death threats, what have you—we're low-hanging fruit for unhappy citizens to swipe at. But to anyone who openly challenges me in public, decrying the government of our fair City as an entirely corrupt and useless body, I like to ask them this: Who sweeps up your horse's leavings in the streets? For that matter, who laid those streets that make life easier for all of us? Who removes the piles of trash you leave on every street corner? Who builds and maintains the docks that welcome in the goods that you all seem to enjoy on a daily basis? Who employs the dock workers to unload the ships? Who built our great bridge to help you so easily traverse the river and reach the lands to the east of us? But please, tell me more about how useless and awful we all are. Tell me who will step up and do all the things I just listed—and a thousand more that I haven't—when you spoiled, ignorant, miserable sots bring the torches and hangman's ropes to tear the government down. Good luck, I say. And good day."

—*Magistrate Branthes Eventide*

The City government is far larger and more complex than anywhere else in the Realm, evolving as the City and its needs evolved. As with all organizations formed by humanoids, a certain amount of expected corruption has found its way into the various branches, but the Magistrate is not oblivious to it and is even susceptible to a certain mild degree of it himself—but he tries to contain the corruption to manageable levels and known quantities.

The City Gate

While the City's main gate has fallen into cosmetic disrepair over the years, its underlying architecture remains relatively solid. The archway above the City's

main entrance sits a lofty ten metres above the ground and hosts "the Roost". This covered fortification of stone and wood serves as a lookout post where eagle-eyed archers can snipe troublemakers and threats from above, as well as alert the appropriate authorities of any urgent updates. They send these alerts through a limited network of "message lines"—thin but sturdy ropes that fan out from the Roost to various key points around the City. The gate lookouts have the ability to write a note, insert the rolled-up message into a leather scroll tube that is attached by loops to the line, then fire an arrow attached to message case so that the arrow and case safely zip directly into the straw bale at the other end, ringing a loud bell to alert the recipient that they have a message. As the arrow is specially designed as part of the message case, it will always slide along its dedicated line and hit its intended mark, avoiding any accidental wayward arrows flying off randomly into the City.

The Post, aka "The Money Tree"

The "Money Tree", as bounty hunters are fond of calling it, is a thick wooden post that sits just a dozen metres outside the threshold of the City Gate. The post stands over two metres high and over a metre in diameter, but on any given day, it is barely visible through all the active bounties, leaflets, personal messages and miscellaneous articles posted to its hole-riddled surface. Gate Lieutenant Erin Fulbore and her people serve as gatekeepers for the Post as well as the City Gate, being the only ones who are allowed to put up or take down any kind of notices in order to avoid utter chaos and Post abuse.

Bountiful Harvest

On the first block of the City, on the left side of those entering through the main gate, the Bountiful Harvest is a favourite watering hole and networking venue for bounty hunters as well as merchants who aren't afraid to share in some rough company. Many deals are made here between merchant caravan leaders and bounty hunters who are between marks and looking to earn some gold serving as a merchant's armed escort. Mags Morbier, gutter-mouthed proprietor of the *Harvest*, used to be a renowned bounty hunter herself until an unfortunate run-in with a dragon left her with only one good foot. Despite the injury, it is a widely known fact among her patrons that she is not a woman to be trifled with. She can throw a blade accurately enough to pin a hornet to a beam at ten paces, even if those paces are made on a wooden foot.

Bar the Gate

Directly across the street from Bountiful Harvest sits Bar the Gate, a slightly more upscale-looking tavern whose patrons lend more towards off-duty guards, government officials, and first-time visitors to the City, fresh off the

road, looking for a good meal and comfortable chair to park their weary rear-end—and ask for directions and pointers to help guide them around the City. Bar the Gate is run by Gruden Tankersley, a jovial grizzly bear of a dwarf whose hair looks to have entirely slid down from his head and come to rest around his face.

The Jail

The City's one and only prison is a heavily fortified, unattractive stone block standing two stories high. The upper floor houses offices and a small barracks where guards take turns catching some shut-eye between shifts. The ground floor houses public-facing offices for walk-ins who require help, as well as medical facilities, an armoury, and some short-term drunk tank cells for town rowdies to sleep it off and be released within 24 hours. Beneath street level, however, is the labyrinth prison for more long-term offenders and the occasional captured monster. The labyrinth is divided into sections based on the nature of the prisoner, including one section reserved for the magically talented whose ensorcelled cells maintain a magic-dampening field to nullify the arcane energies of the prisoners. The Jail's exterior perimeter wall and other fortifications paint a foreboding picture for anyone thinking about planning a jail break or any other kind of assault. The Jail has several layers of active and passive defenses, both magical and conventional, that can be triggered with a moment's notice.

City Patrol

For the regular patrollers, the City is divided into four quarters along the four cardinal directions. These quarters are walked for 4-hour shifts by two pairs of patrollers per quarter, so there are 16 patrollers walking the beat at any given time. They change shifts at the Jail to give their feet a rest, where they spend their next four hours writing up reports, checking on the current prisoners on both ground level and down in the labyrinth, and remaining alert and on call in case something goes sideways in the City and backup is called for via the ear-splitting and very recognizable tin whistle each patroller wears on a cord around their neck. In addition to the 16 patrollers stationed at the Jail at any time of day or night, there are another dozen or so additional employees on staff for administrative, medical, and other functions.

City Watch

Whereas the Patrol minds the interior of the City, the Watch mainly focuses their attention outward in all directions. The City Watch is stationed along the walkways atop the City's outer walls and at four tall lookout towers at the four corners. Like the Patrol, the Watch takes 4-hour shifts walking their assigned beat on the walls before swapping out with the rested teams in the corner towers, each of which comes with a small break room and provisions. The entire shift changes out every 8 hours. Like the Roost above the City Gate, each of the four corner towers has a number of message lines tethered to key points around the City in case something newsworthy is spotted on the horizon.

Night Guard

A little different than the Patrol and the Watch, the notorious Night Guard are nastier, sneakier, more clever and generally much more skilled than the "Regulars" (a somewhat condescending term they reserve for the City Patrol and Watch combined). Some of the Night Watch are ex-criminals who went with the Magistrate's offer of a better paycheck and forgiveness for previous crimes in exchange for worthwhile service to the City. The primary mandate of the Night Watch is to monitor, track down, and deal with the more destructive criminal elements of the City, making sure things don't get out of hand. The second critical function of this group is to deal with the occasional nighttime monster dangers within the walls or in the region just beyond the walls. If they have an opportunity to hunt down a threat outside the City before ever letting it get *into* the City, they'll take it; they're known to be a rather proactive bunch.

Dungsweepers

In an effort to keep the ever-present stench far away from the hoi polloi in the pricey homes and offices around the centre of the City, the Dungsweepers' facilities are tucked away in an undesirable corner at the end of Droppings Lane. The 'Sweepers (they prefer to drop the "Dung" part of their name as often as possible, for the obvious reason) have a private campus the locals like to call "the Offal Oval", which includes their own stables, blacksmith, carpenter, much-used bath house, and a 'burn yard' with offal-burning ovens that divert the nauseating smoke upward and outward over the perimeter wall through very tall chimneys—although the effectiveness of this system depends somewhat on which direction the wind is blowing.

Department of the Treasury

The offices of the Treasury sit neatly arranged on the west side of the central government-dominated area of town, appropriately bordering on the edge of the financial district, as Treasury has one foot in each world. The most recognized (and feared) building here is the headquarters of the Taxman. Its stone façade is plain, cold, and impassive—very much like the notorious figure who dwells and operates on its top floor.

Beyond the normal City taxes, the Treasury Department has a plethora of offices for those charged with collecting tolls and fees for all sorts of licenses and privileges: bridge tolls for ships, gate admittance tolls, operator fees for taverns, inns, shops, fees for administrative services, building permits, criminal fines, and repair costs. Agents of the Treasury are recognizable by their golden vests and cravats over crisp white shirts. The "Goldies" or "Dotts" (Department of the Treasury) send people running and/or hiding, especially if it's the leg breaker division. Their official name is the Overdue Collections Division, but even the young children of the City only refer to them as the Leg Breakers.

The Spirit Quarter

"As much as I would love to say that the people visit our section of the City because of their heart-warming faith and devotion to the Higher Powers of our Realm, the hard truth is that people primarily come to the Spirit Quarter because they need something. A change of fortune, forgiveness for some terrible sin, urgent aid for a sick or injured loved one, maybe a quick, easy, divine escape from whatever dire trouble they've landed themselves in, or just some guidance, some direction for a life suddenly and aimlessly set adrift on the ocean of Fate. They need something that they can't obtain anywhere else, and so they come on bended knee in supplication, hoping against hope for a quick and convenient solution to their woes. Some of them even have their prayers answered. Not many, but some."

—the Grey Friar

This district holds most of the temples and purveyors of religious services in the City. Its streets are well-kept and usually fairly quiet and peaceful, and the air tends to smell of various kinds of incense. Taverns are low-priced with modest but nutritious fare, and there are no establishments that encourage rowdy, alcohol-fueled behavior. Only light ale and wine can be found around this part of the City. Adventurers can easily find healers here for a variety of rates, depending on their curative needs.

Sanctuary Square

This wide plaza, the heart of the Spirit Quarter, sits in the northeastern corner of the City. The main feature in this square is of course the High Temple. The remainder of the plaza is dedicated to housing for the High Temple's acolytes as well as various religious shops, services, and discussions. Theological scholars are especially fond of holding deep conversations over a warm meal or a cold pint of ale at a tavern called The Sanctum. At two corners of Sanctuary Square (the two not taken up by arms of the High Temple), a pair of tall, slender lookout towers extend high enough to give people a clear, breathtaking view beyond the City's walls of the gorgeous expanse of water where the Storm River and Greensnake come together.

High Temple

This dominant structure is an elaborate feat of architecture and one of the oldest structures in the City. In addition to the usual features necessary for religious services, the High Temple also contains housing for the three High Priests and a dozen temple stewards, a comprehensive religious library, a private prayer and meditation sanctum only for use by the High Priests, and an expansive subterranean crypt containing the remains of past High Priests and rulers of the City, plus a handful of other notable figures like the legendary paladin, Adelai Arklight. One wing of the High Temple functions as the City's main hospital, and its stores are well stocked with healing elixirs, medicinal herbs, surgical instruments, and more. The three High Priests go through a regular rotation of masses each week, with the Light Priest giving sermons through the morning and afternoon, the Grey Friar taking the pulpit at dawn and again at dusk, and the Dark Prelate proselytizing at night.

The House of Smaller Gods

For those in the minority who do not worship the Balance, a modest building sits as far as can be inside the Spirit Quarter from the High Temple. This less conventional house of worship tries to keep a low profile, so as not to give the High Priests any excuse to banish them from the City. The House of Smaller Gods exists for humanoids with more niche beliefs and allows them to bring in any holy trappings they need to set up a new little shrine if there is no current representation of their deities. The House of Smaller Gods does not have a traditional large nave anywhere, instead having a series of smaller, more private chambers with thick, sound-muffling doors to give each group of worshippers their privacy—and to keep their holy services from becoming one tangled cacophony crashing through every hallway.

Institutions of Learning

The largest learning institution in the Realm is the City's Academy, simply called "the Academy" for lack of any competition. Second to that comes the City's College of the Arts, which draws many creative souls from all corners of the Realm. Besides these two major colleges, the City plays host to a number of much smaller, more private schools catering to a wide variety of niche fields. Many of these smaller schools still have some ties to the Academy as a networking resource if nothing else, but teachers from the smaller schools are granted access to the Academy's expansive library and possibly some other resources in exchange for reasonable fees commensurate with the level of access granted.

The Academy

Long past its heyday, the grand old architecture of the City's once-great Academy has fallen into neglect and disrepair despite the noble efforts of its remaining custodians. Some visiting instructors come and go through the seasons, but the full-time faculty has dwindled down to a mere handful. The facilities are largely dust-covered and underused, but they're intact. The building houses a multitude of different classrooms, insulated laboratories, an expansive library, an astronomy tower that can be seen from all around the City, a massive Maproom that displays the entire Realm painted on the floor of the chamber, and so much more. The City Loremaster and the Academic Council of Wisdom both remain in place, as well as the librarian

and a few other long-time staff, but student enrollment is at an all-time low. The Academy would benefit greatly from the intervention of some kind of saviors if they could find a way to rekindle the thirst for knowledge across the Realm, although such an undertaking is a challenge of epic proportions.

College of the Arts

In the Arts Quarter of the City, one building stands above all the others not only in its height, but in its elaborate architecture as well. Widely considered to be the most beautiful building in the entire City, the College of the Arts is open to all comers who can afford the tuition (or dare to take out a loan). Under its numerous tower peaks and roofs, the College of the Arts houses different schools for just about every branch of the arts: the School of Minstrels, the School of Visual Arts, as well as theatre, dance, writing, and architecture—the list is comprehensive. Most of the Realm's biggest names in any given field of the arts studied here. Its countless hallways and artfully chaotic floorplans leave even seasoned students lost and confused throughout the year, and it is rumoured that one of the highest, most secluded towers contains a 'permanent guest'—a mad sorcerer, a protégé of the paintbrush whose murals had a tendency of driving viewers insane if they stared too long into the picture.

Magic Tutors

If one has a large enough heap of gold—or demonstrates a rare talent, attitude, and drive—there are a few notable wizards who can be found around the City and persuaded to teach their arcane secrets to the right pupil. These wizards are often difficult to find, and cantankerous when they are disturbed from their studies, but the pains undertaken to land one as a magical tutor are well worth the price of admission.

THE GUILDS

"Fear the City Patrol and the Watch if you like. Fear the Night Guard, with their blackened steel blades and silent boots in the dark. Fear the Magistrate in his ivory tower. Fear all the battle-scarred, leering, blustering bounty hunters in the taverns. None of these scare me half so much as the real power here in the City. I'd happily cross any of them before pissing off the Guilds."

—*Rathskeller, Veteran Bounty Hunter*

Three main guilds dominate control of the City, although their control is not overt. While the government is left to manage the day-to-day logistics and upkeep and supposedly uphold the laws of the land, the three major guilds use their deep coffers, their extensive contacts, blackmail, force, and other methods of coercion, if needed, to keep the wheels greased in their favour. This often means that the guilds come to cross-purposes at times, left to sort things out behind closed doors in some amenable arrangement, or they try to outmaneuver one another like some great ongoing game. This section details the three major guilds; several of their major NPCs can be found later in this chapter.

Merchants Guild

The most plentiful and public-facing of the great Guilds of the City, the Merchants Guild is suspected of having enough money and power to rival the City government if they so choose. To date, they have not, although constant rumours abound regarding exactly how much influence the Merchant Guild has on matters of state, new laws and regulations, and the overall direction of the City's future plans. Operating out of opulent, well-fortified estates in the financial district, the Merchants Guild employs a small army of skilled caravan escorts, private house guards, expert lock makers, vault engineers, and coach designers who add new features and defenses to Guild vehicles. Additionally, as regular 'contributors' to the money pouches of the local patrollers, the Merchants Guild could—if they ever had the need—snap their fingers and convert the City Patrol into their own private fighting force. The buildings of this guild have heavily reinforced doors and windows, top quality locks, and highly trained security personnel watching over them day and night, not to mention friendly faces in the judicial system who swiftly and harshly punish anyone caught targeting the merchants.

Over the decades, members of the Merchants Guild have developed a bizarre, singsong slang as a code language they can use in public to disguise their motives and machinations. Not all merchants are privy to this secret language; only those who have paid their dues to become official guild members have earned this right. Any member who is discovered to have shared this secret language with outsiders is immediately banned for life—and their business targeted for ruin. Enough prior examples have been made of those violating this rule that there are very few people who would even think about it these days.

The Merchants Guild is overseen by the Golden Rule, an eccentric name for the seven Master Merchants who determine policy for the guild. The Golden Rule meets once a month in the City, usually somewhere on the Avenue of Numbers, to discuss any relevant business, compare profit/loss numbers, and share news and rumours from around the Realm in order to take advantage of upcoming trends, threats, or any news that will affect the Realm's markets. Members of the Golden Rule serve for life unless a majority vote of no confidence occurs, in which place an elaborate dance of nominations, bribes, negotiations, and votes determine someone's new promotion to Master Merchant and a seat among the Golden Rule.

Rogues Guild

The Rogues Guild's nicely appointed offices on the border between the Spirit Quarter and the central government district are no match for the ostentatious Merchants Guild estates, but they're designed in a way to make visitors exceedingly comfortable and relaxed—and to drop their guard. Claiming to be a division of the Temple, all middle–and higher-ranking officials in the organization have spiritual-sounding titles. In addition to the Rogue's Chaplain—the guild's top "cleric"—there are many so-called friars, deacons, bishops, and the ruling Council of Three. Mirroring the top echelon of the High Temple, the three top-ranking rogues of the guild style themselves as one Light, one Neutral, and one Dark. These High Priests serve a life term. When one dies, the other two discuss replacement nominations. If neither will yield in their preferred nominee, and no compromise candidate can be agreed upon, the tied nominees are put through a series of rogue-related competitions to determine the winner.

The Rogues Guild is fond of hosting joyous street festivals in different parts of the City with all manner of vendors, games, and contests in order to ingratiate themselves with the common folk (and usually to provide cover for some job that needs to be pulled in that area). They are careful not to pick the pockets of the people attending their parties, as they want to keep the commoners coming back for more instead of being scared away. To communicate with one another at a distance, the Rogues Guild developed Whistler's Code—which is exactly what it sounds like. Using different whistled tunes and rhythms, guild members can cover distances in a pinch without shouting their plans to everyone within multiple City blocks. Whistler's Code is also tremendously useful in fleeing a scene before the City Patrol can arrive.

Assassins Guild

While nobody outside the guild knows where the real headquarters of the Assassins Guild is located, there is a narrow back-alley office that serves as the public interface to hire their services. The real headquarters lies underground, in a natural cavern system only reachable by a closed-off branch of the sewers that the Assassins Guild hid behind dead ends and secret doors made decades ago, and now there are no longer any sewer workers alive who even remember the old branch at all. In addition to the secret conjunctions with the sewer system, some tunnels lead from the guild's lair and go under the perimeter walls and out of (and back into) the City undetected. Many go to small, secret locations around the foul-smelling Dungsweepers' campus—a place the City Patrol tends to avoid the most.

The Assassins Guild—by far the smallest of the three most powerful guilds—have their own sign language, a

secret kept under pain of death. Their identities are also kept secret from the public for obvious reasons. Most guild members have a "day job", a public persona in the City, complete with friends, neighbours, even, on some occasions, a family. Guild members with families are expected to keep their membership a secret even from their spouses and children—unless of course the entire family is in the guild, which is very rare. Hiring a Guild Assassin is expensive, but they are the best at what they do. Membership in the Assassins Guild is not given out lightly to anyone who can use a blade in the dark. There are only ever 13 positions in the guild, and membership only ends with death, natural or otherwise (almost always the latter). Replacement members are approached by the guild, never the other way around. Potential candidates are secretly observed and tracked for months before a decision is made to invite them or not. The biggest challenge for the Assassins Guild is and has always been the Night Guard, and the two groups have evolved with a long-standing rivalry like two old chess masters, constantly facing off across a board.

Miscellaneous Features

The City has many features that don't fit into the previous categories. Here are a few of the more notable ones, although GMs are encouraged to add more of their own as needed.

Adelai Bridge

On the east side of the City, spanning the Greensnake River, is a broad stone bridge designed in a graceful arch, lined with artful crenellations along its walls and trellises of flowering vines from strategically placed planters. This bridge is named after a valiant knight, Adelai Arklight, who defended the City when it was on its way to become more than just some little town. She stood on the west bank of the river and, with the help of a few brave farmers and builders, fought off a horde of ogres and goblins who sought to overrun the burgeoning settlement. The creatures came wave after wave, crossing the river on crudely made rafts, but Adelai and her small force of humble townsfolk beat them back time and again until the king of the ogres himself came across. Adelai engaged in single combat and slayed the ogre king, receiving mortal wounds in the process. When the City first became the City and a large stone bridge was planned for construction right on the spot where she died, those who remembered Adelai's stand insisted on naming the bridge after her.

Whether during the Sun's zenith on a dazzling afternoon, or at night with its twin rows of lampposts lit, the Adelei has long been a subject of many painters—especially at sunset, when the last light of the day blazes beneath the arch and across the surface of the Greensnake River. In addition to simply being a valuable resource in crossing the river, it is a major City attraction for an array of reasons. Lovers come to the bridge to propose marriage, pickpockets wander up and down it to make their daily quota from naïve tourists, parents bring their children to fish over the sides, small-time artists set up small stations to entreat new visitors to stop and pose for a charcoal drawing or to buy a souvenir trinket or 'good luck charm'. As such a heavy people magnet, the Adelei Bridge is constantly monitored by the City Patrol at all hours.

The Carousel

A relatively recent addition to the Town Square, the Carousel stands as the top attraction for most children. The line for a ride on one of the lavishly painted, brilliantly carved wooden animals and wondrous creatures usually stretches around the block, especially since the rides are free. The dwarven craftsmen who engineered the hand-cranked, gear-driven pavilion insist that their ride is open to everyone, not just those who can afford it. Their mission in installing the Carousel was to bring joy to all the City's young children. To help the kind Carousel owners with upkeep and repairs, the Light Priest of the High Temple donates a yearly gift of gold. A silly rumour circulates around the City that in the dead of night during a new moon, a few of the carousel creatures come to life and fly around the sky above the City for several hours before returning to their posts.

Emerald Fields

Located right beside the Town Square, the City boasts its one and only real park, a large area of verdant growth and colourful structures where children and their parents come to play and relax. The unspoken but well-known rule of the Emerald Fields is that everyone must leave politics, religion, and other kinds of potentially divisive, firebrand topics outside its borders. When you come into the Emerald Fields, you come to have fun and relax. The park has a few discreet 'stewards' who function in a dual role as both groundskeepers and bouncers, quietly but firmly ejecting anyone who breaks the unspoken compact of tranquility.

The Night Market

After the daytime farmer's markets and other street vendors have closed down for the evening and taken their unsold wares and services home, after the sun has set and the dinner bell has long gone quiet, the Night Market springs up in a different area of the city, ready for business. While its name sounds a bit ominous, the market itself is…well, yes, it actually is a little ominous—but only parts of it. Plenty of innocent, ordinary goods and services can be acquired here, although usually from slightly less respectable purveyors: a carpenter with two missing fingers, an animal handler with teeth mark scars on his cheek, etc. If one knows where to look, or is willing to wander among the shadows, they can find tents and carts with more obscure, stolen, outlawed, and/or damaged offerings, as well as the services of less than savory characters. Naïve and unwary shoppers do, on rare occasions, disappear in the Night Market—so buyers beware.

Storm River Wharf

Through the Storm Gate at the north end of the City, the land between the City walls and the Storm River is entirely claimed by the Storm River Wharf. It has expansive dockyards where new ships are built, damaged ships are repaired, and a bustling port hosts dozens of ships at any given time from all across the Realm. In addition to the numerous trade ships passing through, one can also spot several expensive luxury ships looking to tour the Storm River and see the sights of the Realm. Services can also be bought here for anyone looking to find a ship to sail the Storm River to other parts of the Outer Region. Finding a captain to take anyone through the tempest wall to try and reach the opposite shore and deliver people to the Middle Region is much rarer to find—and much more difficult to afford. Whereas the larger City Gate to the south is considered the "main" entrance and exit for the City, its somewhat smaller sibling on the north side, the Storm Gate, is more tightly controlled. In theory, this gate is only for those who have business with the wharf: dock workers, sailors, merchants, luxury yacht owners, and the families of the aforementioned. In reality, those with the right approach and enough gold to discreetly pass to the gatewatch's hands can buy a pricey entrance or exit, thus avoiding the eagle eyes of Lieutenant Fullbore, her City Watch sharpshooters, and an ever-present mob of bounty hunters at the south gate.

Underbridge Wharf

Though smaller and less busy than its sibling wharf on the north side of the City, this secondary harbour still pulls in a tidy profit from collecting tolls from ships passing north and south under the Adelai Bridge: mostly deep-sea fishing boats and longer-distance merchants looking to skim the outer coast of the Realm to carry trade faster than going over land. Underbridge Wharf is a bit of a rough patch of the City, populated by leather-skinned dock workers, sailors, fishermen—the sort of folk who have no patience for people getting in their way, slowing things down, or generally just being a nuisance. The "Bridge Trolls" (not a nickname they chose for themselves) often have minor clashes with some of the street gangs who slink about the south side of the City. The smaller wharf presents a juicy target for theft on the occasions when loaded merchant ships pull up to

make berth. The Rogues Guild keeps a regular rotation of spotters on top of the Adelai Bridge, keeping a sharp eye out up and down the river for potential incoming prey.

Notable NPCs of the City

"The identity of a place—any little hamlet or village, and especially our great City—doesn't just emerge from its unique buildings, landmarks, and features of the terrain. It is sculpted by, more than anything else, those who dwell there."

—Grey Friar of the High Temple

There are all kinds of interesting and useful personalities in all corners of the City. Here are a few of the more notable ones.

Branthis Eventide, the Magistrate

The position of the Magistrate of the City is an elected position held for a five-year term, with no limits on how many terms a person can retain the office. Branthis Eventide, now serving the last year of his third consecutive term, is currently focused on efforts to secure his fourth. Eventide is a middle-aged human, handsome and charismatic, an excellent orator with a powerful force of personality. He has done right by the City for the most part, although his extended time in office sees him becoming entangled more and more deeply in the webs of other powerful forces and factions who vie for more control over the destiny of the most powerful settlement in the Realm. The Merchants Guild exerts its leverage over him and his body of lawmakers using their domination of coin and trade, without which the City would crumble. They seek to ensure that City policies favour them at every turn so that they can not only retain their power but also continue its expansion. The High Temple holds sway over the minds of the masses who come to worship the Powers, and they use this to gently but firmly influence the City government's position on relevant issues like exemptions from taxation and certain other regulations. And of course, a number of rich and powerful independent personalities from the Rosewater neighbourhood like to flex their coffers and purchase favouritism and influence among the government, and the Magistrate himself is not immune to their machinations. Eventide spends most of his time in the Magistrate's Tower but tries to occasionally venture through the streets of his City to keep his finger on the pulse—although he goes nowhere outside the Tower without a small contingent of his most vigilant and skilled house guards.

BENEFITS

Man in the High Tower: If the Magistrate's attitude towards the PCs is Favourable or better, he helps them through one civil snafu per adventure, so long as it involves something in the City that falls under his dominion. This could be getting released from prison, being sought after by some faction of the government's forces, a comfortable haven in which to hide for a short period of time, access to an institution that the PCs otherwise may not have inroads to—for someone as powerful as the Magistrate, the options are wide open. Attempts to have him perform more than one favour for the PCs per adventure results in lowering his attitude by one level each attempt beyond the first. If the Magistrate's attitude falls below Neutral, the PCs may find themselves on the other side of the fence, with the City's forces on the lookout for them, not to mention bounties placed on their capture, or worse…

Strength: 4   **Craft:** 6
Life: 17

Verrenid Iglac, the Taxman

Arguably the most unpopular single personality in the City, Iglac is also one of the most widely feared. Even his fellow ghouls don't care to share company with him under any context, and Iglac is not bothered by this fact one bit. His only passion and only friend is the almighty G-word: gold. His duty to collect money from every corner of the City is what drives him day and night and forms the core of his being. He has no mercy and rarely puts any effort into social graces, even when dealing with the Magistrate or other powerful entities. His shrewd sensibilities and keen mind are difficult to circumvent, and those who try to dodge or fool the Taxman often end up in much worse shape than they would have been if they'd just paid their taxes in full and on time. His gold-vested auditors prowl the city to present homes and businesses with their biannual tax bill, then return after two weeks to anyone who hasn't paid their share. If taxes are ignored after the second visit, Iglac has a group of brutal, relentless enforcers, officially called the Overdue Collections Division, sent out to extract monies in any way they see fit. His questionable methods are given a great deal of legal leeway from the Sheriff and the Magistrate.

BENEFITS

Two Things in Life Are Inevitable…: If Iglac's attitude towards the PCs is Favourable or better, and if the PCs owe the City government money in any way, Iglac gives them one week's grace period to get their act together and pay what gold they owe. One week. That's all you get. Once.

Strength: 2   **Craft:** 5
Life: 13

Collector Proog, Leg Breaker Captain

The head officer of the Treasury Department's Overdue Collections Division is a massive slab of green-grey muscle with an overhanging shelf of a brow ridge so pronounced that you could set a drink on it. A troll of few words, Proog is the last face people want to see around tax season. Tales of his destructive power and his sadistic streak send chills across the City, thus providing plenty of incentive for citizens and businesses to promptly pay their taxes. Proog may not be the sharpest spoon in the drawer, but he's not nearly as slow-witted as his physical mannerisms would suggest. When pursuing his non-paying quarry, he has an innate sense of how to deploy his forces to anticipate runners and to sniff out hiding places where those who claim to be broke have squirreled away their stashes of coin.

BENEFITS

Kneecap: If Proog's attitude towards the PCs is Favourable or better, he and his leg breakers pay a visit to one person of the party's choosing. If the target is sufficiently high profile and/or difficult to access, the GM may require that Proog's attitude be Liked or Devoted, and even then, the visit may take some time to arrange, waiting for the opportune moment.

Strength: 7   **Craft:** 3
Life: 18

Sheriff Thurston Midge

Thurston Midge continues to find new and innovative ways to be one of the most corrupt people in the City, which is an impressive accomplishment. As the long-running Sheriff (who has no problem exerting his resources to ensure his continued re-election every two years), Midge possesses a good deal of power at the commoner level. While he has no power to direct City laws and policy, he and his forces impose their will on the street day after day, raking in bribe money and other favours from both criminal and innocent civilians alike. The Sheriff is a proud, vain man, with a barely concealed disdain for those with more money and power. Nothing rankles him more than having the higher-ups giving him directions, so he has his sights set on one day finding a way to elevate himself to Magistrate, although he is ignorant to the fact that he is wholly unqualified to hold the office. For the time being, the Sheriff is mostly satisfied with his current position and happy to continually fill his coffers with a healthy percentage of what his guards bring back from their shifts. He can be a powerful ally or enemy for PCs to make, depending on their alignment and their behavior around the City.

BENEFITS

Protect and Serve: If the Sheriff's attitude towards the PCs is Neutral or better, and if he's paid 1d6+4 gold, he offers a variety of services to the party. If the PCs use this service more than once per month, the cost goes up by 4 each time beyond the first. Options for the Sheriff's bribed assistance include (but aren't limited to): sending a goon patrol to track down and beat the daylights out of a target and/or abduct them to a private location of the party's choosing; sweeping the City to locate a particular person, group, item, home, business, or similar quarry; have patrols avoid a particular area of the City for a certain window of time; gain an audience with an otherwise-inaccessible NPC in the City.

"You Know Who I Am?": If the Sheriff's attitude falls below Neutral, the PCs find themselves dogged at every turn by patrols looking to find them and do them harm and/or chase them out of the City. If his attitude reaches Hated, he posts a 10-gold bounty on each PC's head. For each week the bounty goes unresolved, he raises the price by 5, to a max of 25 gold apiece. If his attitude is raised back above Hated, he cancels the bounty (but keep using the above guidelines if his attitude remains below Neutral).

Strength: 5   **Craft:** 5
Life: 17   **Armour:** 3

DEPUTY NUGMET RUNGBELL

Nugmet is Sheriff Midge's top deputy, a loyal follower of orders and general administrator of any tasks the Sheriff deems to be beneath him (which is most tasks). Nugmet is a nervous dwarf who usually comes off as scatterbrained because he's always juggling too many

things at once. When the Sheriff is around, Nugmet is the poster child of a complicit bootlicker. When the Sheriff isn't around, Nugmet puffs out his chest and tries to emulate the belligerent, crafty nature of his boss—an act that the other deputies tend to snicker at behind his back. Deputy Rungbell can be a juicy mark for PCs to manipulate or trick, a potential flaw in the system if they find themselves at odds with the Sheriff and his forces.

BENEFITS

Desperate for Friends: Any PC making a **Persuasion** check (as described in Chapter 2 of *Talisman Adventures*, under the **Strangers** section) gets a +2 to their roll, or +4 if that PC is either a dwarf or an attractive female of any humanoid species.

Greased Wheels: If Deputy Rungbell's attitude is Favourable or higher and paid 1d6 gold, he lends his assistance to getting someone out of jail, putting someone in jail, or getting access to a government official. The PC makes a **Persuasion (Wits)** or **Intimidation (Resolve)** test against **Difficulty 14**.
- **Failure:** Deputy Rungbell takes the money and does nothing.
- **Standard Success:** The desired character is either freed from or put in jail, or the character gets access to the desired official.
- **Great Success:** The desired character is either freed from or put in jail, or the character gets access to the desired official *without* having to pay the bribe.

Strength: 3   **Craft:** 3
Life: 12   **Armour:** 1

MARA CANDLEWYCK, CITY PATROLLER

Born and raised in the City, Patroller Candlewyck serves as the example her fellow patrollers should strive to emulate—but she's in the wrong place for that. Her code of honour and respect for law and order make her a popular figure among many of the common folk on her beat, and she often receives small gifts like a free apple from a fruit vendor, a straw and cloth doll made by a child who looks up to her, a flattering verse or two sung in her honour by a street minstrel as she passes by. She believes the City Patrol does not exist solely to punish those who violate the law, but to help those in need when normal, everyday problems arise, and to protect citizens who require defense. This behavior, however, has earned her a target on her back from less scrupulous patrollers (which is most of them).

BENEFITS

Candle's Light: If Mara's attitude towards the PCs is Favourable or better, she intercedes once per adventure on the PCs' behalf to get them out of trouble with the City Patrol or out of the Sherriff's prison. If Mara is convinced of the PCs' mission to do something to help the City, she is also capable of diverting/distracting some Patrollers' routes for 1d6 hours in a City location and time of their choosing.

Strength: 5   **Craft:** 4
Life: 17   **Armour:** 2

PALTON SACKWORTH, CITY PATROLLER

Patroller Sackworth is widely known as one of the most corrupt guards in the City. He regularly takes bribes not just to look the other way, but for all manner of illegal favours like smashing a rival businessman's storefront, framing a pesky neighbour for a crime they didn't commit, confiscating black market goods from one source and secretly passing them along to another. Sackworth is a cold-blooded, self-serving snake and has no compunctions about putting a dagger into the back of anyone who threatens him or his way of life.

BENEFITS

Sacked: If Sackworth's attitude towards the PCs is Favourable or better, he accepts gold in exchange for some unscrupulous, illegal act on behalf of the PCs, no unnecessary questions asked. The cost is commensurate with the dark deed, however.

Strength: 4   **Craft:** 4
Life: 16   **Armour:** 2

ERIN FULLBORE, GATE LIEUTENANT OF THE CITY WATCH

The most recognizable face to any regulars coming and going through the City Gate is Lieutenant Fullbore, who spends most of her waking hours on duty there. She's a striking human woman, tall and athletic, with an imposing presence and a long scar from her left temple down to her jawline. Fullbore is no stranger to tangling with unruly bounty hunters and, when needed, putting them face-down in the dirt and stepping on their back. She's tough but fair, friendly but vigilant, and suspicious by nature. Her memory for names and faces helps her monitor the comings and goings to and from the City. Most of her Gate Watch fellows respect her even if they don't necessarily like her.

BENEFITS

Master of the Gate: If Lieutenant Fullbore's attitude towards the PCs is Favourable or better, she can offer information to characters about specific comings and goings through the City Gate. If it's a personality or subject known to her even peripherally, she might also offer what neighbourhood the subject in question may possibly be found. A PC assisted by Fullbore gains two bonus dice trying to find a specific person, item, or piece of information in the City.

Strength: 7   **Craft:** 5
Life: 25   **Armour:** 3

JESPAR NETTLES, CITY WATCH

The Sheriff likes to keep at least one or two loyal people in every corner and division of the City's various guards. Jespar Nettles is his best set of eyes and ears at the City Gate. He keeps tabs on the whereabouts of whatever list of people the Sheriff tells him to look out for and sends reports back to the Sheriff while occasionally hiding information from Lieutenant Fullbore.

BENEFITS

Backstabber: If Nettles' or the Sheriff's attitude towards the PCs is Favourable or better, Nettles can offer information to characters about finding something or someone specific in the area or some personal information on any City Gate soldier that could be used to spy on or manipulate them.

Strength: 5 **Craft:** 4
Life: 17 **Armour:** 1

ROOSTER, CITY WATCH

While her real elven name is Sicariel, this member of the Gate Watch is mostly known by her nickname "Rooster" on account of her posting up in the Roost above the City Gate. She is one of the very few elves employed as a City guard and is the unquestioned top sniper among the Gate Watch, possibly among all divisions of the City guard. Good friends with Lieutenant Fullbore, Rooster's keen senses are a great asset in picking out troublemakers trying to pass through the City Gate as well as spotting potential threats in the distance to the south of the City. Her presence in the Roost is a strong incentive for good behavior among the citizenry, as it is well known that her arrows have a habit of painfully taking blades out of hands or pinning people to the ground by their feet if they threaten violence within her line of sight. On a personal level, Rooster is patient, quiet, and shy, able to sit still for hours and engage in zero conversation with her fellow spaRoost-sitters. It's not that she dislikes them or exhibits hostility, she simply doesn't feel the need to speak unless spoken to. The only person who seems to be able to get Rooster to open up is Erin Fullbore. The two have been known to share drinks after their shift from time to time.

BENEFITS

Deadeye: If Rooster's attitude towards the PCs is Favourable or better, Rooster can spend the next 24 hours keeping an eye out for a specific person or group of people coming and/or going through the City Gate and report this information back to the PCs at the next available opportunity. If asked, Rooster will remember any pertinent details like, "Were they with anyone, and if so, what did they look like?" or "Did they appear to be carrying a package?"

Strength: 6   **Craft:** 3
Life: 17   **Armour:** 2

MAGS MORBIER, BOUNTIFUL HARVEST PROPRIETOR

This bawdy owner-operator boasts a cascade of fiery orange hair and a wooden foot and lower leg due to a grievous wound during her final bounty hunt. Too young to face retirement, she turned her attention to opening a tavern that largely caters to the bounty hunter population in the City and has found great success and popularity. Despite the roughness of her typical patrons, Mags takes no guff from anyone and, despite her injury, has no issue using the dangerous skills burned into her muscle memory. Her regulars enjoy exchanging loud taunts and boasts with her but know enough not to truly anger her. A favourite pastime of regulars at the Bountiful Harvest is to see a new face in the tavern who crosses the line with Mags and place quick wagers on the graphic details of the outcome before it unfolds.

BENEFITS

On the House: If Mags' attitude towards the PCs is Favourable or better, she offers information to the PCs about bounty hunters in the **area:** the whereabouts of a specific one (or known cadre), if there are any looking for general work, if there are any who specialize in a specific type of work, etc. She also orders the patrons of her establishments to keep their greasy paws off the PCs.

Strength: 4   **Craft:** 3
Life: 15

GRUDEN TANKERSLEY, BAR THE GATE PROPRIETOR

After retiring from the Night Guard, this jovial dwarf invested his savings in taking over and renovating this tavern across the street from the Bountiful Harvest. His wife, daughter, and son all help him run the business, and he likes to keep things relatively orderly and peaceful— at least compared to the noisy, rowdy place across the street. There are no fights allowed in his establishment, and he personally escorts violators through the back door, to the pile where the day's garbage is left. Tankersley still has many contacts among his former coworkers if he should ever find himself in a pinch, and the door swings both ways. The Night Guard have tasked their ex-member to keep his eyes and ears sharp, picking up valuable tidbits from the ale-loosened tongues of his government employee patrons and passing them back to the Night Guard when one of them stops in for a quick drink and a hello.

BENEFITS

Whispers: If Gruden's attitude towards the PCs is Favourable or better, he can "ask around" to find a piece of rumour or hard-to-find information. After 24 hours (giving Gruden a chance to tap his secret network of contacts), the PCs roll 2d6. On a 7+, he has useful information for the characters. On a roll of 12+, the GM can choose to offer an additional level of useful detail. If the PCs press for information in less than 24 hours, there is a −1 penalty to the roll for every 3 hours early they press Gruden.

Strength: 5   **Craft:** 3
Life: 18

KADIAN ARKLIGHT, CAPTAIN OF THE NIGHT GUARD

For seven years, Kadian Arklight—a descendant of the famous knight Adelai Arklight—has captained the Night Guard. He began his career as a member of the City Watch, walking the walls for a number of years and earning a reputation as a sharp-eyed, cool and collected guardian with a penchant for sniffing out trouble just as it's about to happen. He displayed a knack for spotting, tracking, and slaying monsters, and so attracted the attention of the Night Guard. He eventually switched over to that division and continued his track record of success, this time in discovering and dealing with threats inside the walls rather than outside them. His sixth sense is no mere rumour; he has an uncanny danger sense that he himself cannot fully explain. His demeanour is quiet but intense and full of coiled energy, like a prowling beast ready to strike at any moment. He is crafty and can be underhanded when needed, having zero guilt in using the criminal underworld's own tricks against them to get the job done. His command is unquestioned among his fellows, and his lethal skill in a fight is surpassed by no one in their ranks.

BENEFITS

How the Killing's Done: The Night Guard are particularly knowledgeable about monsters found in the City. If a Night Guard has a Favourable or better attitude towards the PCs, they will share this info if asked, including vulnerabilities, immunities, common hunting grounds, tactics, etc.

Knife in the Dark: If Kadian has a Favourable or better attitude towards the PCs, he can provide extensive detail about specific criminals and/or criminal organizations in the City. If he has a Devoted attitude, he accompanies the PCs on one mission within the City or just outside it, as long as the mission involves taking out monsters or working against the interests of local criminal elements.

Strength: 8   **Craft:** 5
Life: 27   **Armour:** 3

Hadarantham Moonseed, Night Guard Rogue

"Hadar the Hood" used to be a member of the Rogues Guild but left them after one job went badly and Hadarantham's associates left him to die at the hands of a dangerous street gang. After a long vetting process, the leywalker eventually earned the trust of the Night Guard and joined them as a junior member. Having faithfully and effectively served them for several years, he has risen to a full-fledged soldier and is one of Captain Arklight's most trusted people. Hadarantham's experience with the Rogue's Guild, including being fluent in their Whistler's Code and other verbal code phrases, grants him a familiarity with how the guild thinks and how they operate that no outsider can match, which makes him an invaluable asset to the Night Guard.

Benefits

How the Killing's Done: The Night Guard are particularly knowledgeable about monsters found in the City. If a Night Guard has a Favourable or better attitude towards the PCs, they will share this info if asked, including vulnerabilities, immunities, common hunting grounds, tactics, etc.

Ex-Guild: If Hadarantham has a Favourable or better attitude towards the PCs, he can provide detailed knowledge about aspects of the Rogues Guild.

Strength: 6   **Craft:** 6
Life: 22   **Armour:** 1

Lurial, Night Guard Wizard

One of the very few elves ever to join the ranks of the Night Guard, Lurial is its longest-serving member, having been present for the group's original founding. Her elven night sight is a tremendous asset to the mostly nocturnal division, as is her powerful spellcraft. It was she who first noticed a young Kadian Arklight's talents on the City Watch and eventually recruited him. Lurial remembers his famous ancestor, Adelai, and was present for her famous defense on the banks of the Greensnake all those decades ago. In times of great need or a specific kind of assistance, Lurial travels to nearby Woodbine to enlist the aid of her powerful sister, who is the Archon of Dusk there.

Benefits

How the Killing's Done: The Night Guard are particularly knowledgeable about monsters found in the City. If a Night Guard has a Favourable or better attitude towards the PCs, they will share this info if asked, including vulnerabilities, immunities, common hunting grounds, tactics, etc.

Woodbine's Aid: If Lurial has a Favourable or better attitude towards the PCs, she writes them an introductory letter to her sister, the Archon of Dusk in Woodbine. This letter earns the PCs the assistance of the elves of Woodbine in some fashion.

Strength: 4   **Craft:** 8
Life: 20

Light Priestess of the High Temple

The Light Priestess is a stunning figure: a tall, statuesque elven woman in her prime whose powerful presence radiates like the sun. Though surprisingly soft spoken in a smaller, more personal environment, her public sermons are potent and uplifting to her followers.

Eloquent and intelligent, the Light Priestess spends much of her personal time reading. In addition to the expected religious texts, she also enjoys reading histories, biographies, and philosophy. She is rarely seen in public outside the Spirit Quarter, but when approached on the street, she greets her parishioners with a warm smile and is happy to indulge them in short conversations as her time allows. Rumours abound of her life before accepting the mantle of Light Priestess of the High Temple, and those stories tell of her adventures battling hordes of undead that threatened her village, turning them back or destroying them utterly with her divine gifts. When asked about her past, the Light Priestess simply asks the questioners what they feel is the truth and refuses to give the matter any further discussion.

Benefits

Warmth of the Light: If the Light Priestess' attitude towards the PCs is Liked or better *and* the PCs are all of Neutral or Good alignment, she can offer each PC a blessing once per adventure. If her attitude is Favourable or better, she also performs religious/spiritual duties for any of the PCs for no cost such as weddings, funerals, last rites, or similar services.

Strength: 3   **Craft:** 9
Life: 20

Dark Prelate of the High Temple

The Dark Prelate is a charismatic, sharp-witted human woman whose raven black hair is beginning to salt at her temples. Her sparkling green eyes constantly take in the details around her, committing them to her almost supernaturally accurate memory. She seems to know far too much about too many people. This is in part due to her network of acolyte-spies, and in part due to her uncanny ability to deduce details based on her observations of people. In conversation, the Dark Prelate is clever, engaging, and surprisingly funny. She is often seen walking the City streets during the daylight hours, doing her own shopping, sitting at an eatery enjoying a quiet meal with a few friends—'normal people' activities. In her nighttime services, however, she unleashes the full power of her personality, using her booming orator's voice to loudly fire up her congregations with rhetoric about the necessity of the Dark to balance the Light and the roles that she and her followers play in society. She is careful, however, to make sure her followers adhere to keeping the High Temple a peaceful neutral ground since she has to share with her two fellow High Priests; constant altercations between factions would be to everyone's detriment.

Benefits

Coolness of Shade: If the Dark Prelate's attitude towards the PCs is Liked or better *and* the PCs are all of Neutral or Evil alignment, she offers to curse one person of the PCs' choosing. She offers this benefit once per PC per adventure. If her attitude is Favourable or better, she also performs religious/spiritual duties for any of the PCs for no cost such as weddings, funerals, last rites, or similar services.

Strength: 3   **Craft:** 9
Life: 20

Grey Friar of the High Temple

The enigmatic Grey Friar of the City is the most recent of the three High Priests to inherent the mantle, having replaced the previous one two years ago after a hereditary chronic illness claimed his life. The new Grey Friar is a leywalker—the first of his ancestry to fill the role in the history of the City—and after some initial uncertainty among his inherited flock, his presence has been well received. He spends a good deal of his personal time outside the City walls, sometimes riding horseback through the surrounding farmlands to get to know the people of the farming communities, sometimes paddling a boat up and down a stretch of the Greensnake,

occasionally even holding an impromptu sermon with a dozen or two people in the nearby hills. Although there are few of his kind roaming the City, the Grey Friar is especially recognizable by his one broken horn, the details of which he changes with each new person asking about it. Most people find him wise, jovial, and sociable, if a bit odd and aloof. His mind has a tendency to wander down tangential paths during common conversation, as if constantly being distracted by his own thoughts. During his dawn and dusk sermons, the Grey Friar speaks with a rich, sonorous baritone about the importance of the Balance and the danger of extremes and absolutes. He is happy to invite those from the Light and the Dark to attend his services as well, hoping to show them the beauty of the middle ground. In the two years since receiving the mantle of the Grey Friar, he has made more converts to his cause than either the Light Priestess or the Dark Prelate.

Benefits

Comfortably Grey: If the Grey Friar's attitude towards the PCs is Favourable or better *and* the party is at least 50% neutral, he will restore lost life for wounded party members and/or cure them of effects of poison and/or sickness. He is willing to give this kind of aid a reasonable amount of times, but if the PCs abuse his favour, his attitude will be affected or he suddenly becomes notoriously difficult for them to locate. If his attitude is Neutral or better, he also performs religious/spiritual duties for any of the PCs for no cost such as weddings, funerals, last rites, or similar services.

Strength: 3   **Craft:** 9
Life: 20

The Drunk Monk

Outside of the Spirit Quarter, one very recognizable human stumbles around the streets in tattered brown robes, worn out sandals, usually with a jug, bottle, or cup of some kind in his hand and the reek of cheap wine or ale on his breath. His hair is sloppily hacked short on top, but his brown beard is wild and uneven. Nobody knows the true name of the City's famous "drunk monk", but he is something of a celebrity, famous for randomly stepping up on a barrel or statue and delivering an unsolicited sermon about some aspect of life, philosophy, the heart, the mind, the soul, or a big squirrel he saw running down the street just a few minutes ago with an entire loaf of bread. Although his speech is usually slurred with drink, his words are strangely compelling, and it's no surprise that he occasionally accumulates crowds of several dozen onlookers.

Benefits

Drinking Buddies: If the Drunk Monk's attitude towards the PCs is Neutral or better, he offers to provide certain services in exchange for drinks. See the table for services available and the amount of bought drinks (and time spent indulging the sociable monk by drinking with him and making conversation) each will cost the party. Multiple smaller services can be bought over a long sitting with the Drunk Monk instead of one of the more major services.

DRINKING BUDDIES

Drinks and Time Invested	Services Available
1–2 drinks and .5 hours	Heals the party 2d6 life, with the party agreeing on how to divide the points.
3–4 drinks and 1 hour	Performs any basic (common or uncommon) mystic spell for the party.
5–6 drinks and 1.5 hours	Performs a small religious service for the party like a wedding, funeral rites, or giving a public sermon in a place of their choosing within the City. The sermon may include subject matter of the party's direction.
7–8 drinks and 2 hours	Performs any basic mystic spell or any intermediate (common or uncommon) mystic spell for the party.
9 drinks and 2.5 hours	Whips drinking establishment patrons and streetgoers into a collective good-natured frenzy that turns into an impromptu street party throughout the surrounding blocks, drawing the attention of all nearby City Patrol (and pretty much everyone else in the area) for 1d6 hours.
10+ drinks and 3+ hours	Performs any Mystic spell for the party.

Strength: 4   **Craft:** 7
Life: 21

SILMARRA, CITY LOREMASTER

This venerable elven woman remains steadfast in her duties running the City Academy, despite its modern decline. She continues to devote efforts to attracting a new host of worthy instructors, but it has been an uphill climb for the past several years. She tries to hide her emotional fatigue behind a mask of aloofness, but those who know her well realize the toll the school's downward trend is taking on her. Silmarra believes that the erosion of the Academy reflects an erosion of knowledge as well as a decline in the willingness to learn. She frowns heavily upon the current generation for this state of things and believes that society's downfall cannot be far behind if this trend is not reversed, and soon. Secretly, she has begun contemplating whether or not she should begin a search for a new Loremaster, one who may have a better grasp of the dynamics of modern times and who may be able to save the Academy for total obsolescence and rekindle a thirst for learning in the younger generations.

BENEFITS

Master of Lore: If Silmarra's attitude towards the PCs is Favourable or better, she offers up useful information and answers their questions on some obscure piece of lore, or supplies them with books and materials on the requested subject that they can research themselves. She is available to the party for one such conversation per adventure.

Dean of Admissions: If Silmarra's attitude towards the PCs is Favourable or better, the PCs can bring her someone that wishes to enroll in the Academy. A player makes a **Bargain (Wits)** or **Persuasion (Insight)** roll against **Difficulty 15** to plead the candidate's case to her.

- **Failure:** She accepts the new admission but isn't fully convinced they'll be a great student. She expects payment for the first year of classes, room and board, and materials.

- **Standard Success:** She accepts the new admission and waives 25% of the first year's cost.
- **Great Success:** She accepts the new admission and waives 50% of the first year's cost.
- **Extraordinary Success:** She accepts the new admission with a full scholarship at least for the first year, as the PCs have convinced her of this candidate's great promise.

Strength: 2 **Craft:** 7
Life: 15

Arcus Argringrim

This former Master at Arms is an expert in both mathematics and on the military history of the Realm. When he's instructing his handful of remaining pupils on either of these subjects, he's a happy dwarf indeed. When discussing nearly anything else, he adopts a more crotchety, disinterested demeanour. The stump of his missing left hand pains him on a daily basis, and when no one is looking (or he thinks no one is), he undoes the buckles and removes the leather-and-iron armature, massages the puckered end of his arm and downs a pain elixir until he's reached a buzzy numbness. He refuses to admit an addiction to the substance and becomes enraged if approached about it. The battle-scarred veteran still likes to break out his old gear from his glory days, take students out into the Academy's quad, and have them help him re-enact old battles in a more live, interactive way than sitting at desks in a musty classroom. He loves showing off his prowess with his axes, even with just one good hand.

Benefits

Grim Tutor: If Arcus' attitude towards the PCs is Favourable or better, he supplies them with historic lore on a chosen subject and answers whatever follow-up questions the GM sees fit for him to know. This also goes for the field of mathematics, however less likely that need may be. If Arcus' attitude towards the PCs is Favourable or better, he teaches the Melee, Missile Weapon and Throw skills to any PCs looking to learn a new one after gaining a level. These skill lessons take one month and cost 5 gold per character per skill, unless Arcus' attitude is Liked or higher, in which case he waives the cost and holds the lessons in his personal time and not on school grounds. Each character can only learn one new skill from this instructor per month.

Strength: 5 **Craft:** 4
Life: 18

Lady Eisley Fallcrest

Lady Fallcrest has been the Academy's chief financial backer and fundraiser for the past two decades, as well as its Professor of Linguistics. An intelligent, well-read, well-traveled woman now approaching the twilight period of her life, she speaks, reads, and writes five languages fluently and another three passably well. The other few remaining full-time Academy faculty overlook her arrogance and snobbery due to the necessity of keeping in her good graces for her money and her linguistic value. Lady Fallcrest's son Deagle sits upon the Golden Rule as one of the City's wealthiest and most powerful merchant barons, and she loves to regale bored coworkers and students with constant tales of her son's travels and exploits. Her other favourite pastime is throwing elaborate theme parties at her estate in the upscale Rosewater neighbourhood—partly to rub her wealth in certain peoples' faces and partly because she just enjoys a good party every now and then.

Benefits

The Place to Be: If Lady Fallcrest's attitude towards the PCs is Favourable or better, they have a standing invitation to attend most of her parties unless it's a small, private affair.

A Gift for Tongues: If Lady Fallcrest's attitude towards the PCs is Liked or better, she teaches any/all of them a new language in a crash course that takes place over the course of a month, free of charge. It must be the same language for all involved, as this all takes place during the same 'class', and she will only teach one language in between adventures.

Strength: 1 **Craft:** 5
Life: 12

Professor Tom

The Academy's enigmatic resident known only as Professor Tom spends most of his days and nights in reclusive study in the library, his chambers, or in one of the insulated underground laboratory chambers. He rarely takes on students, and those he does instruct are reluctant to divulge any details about what they've learned. The mysterious Professor does hire adventurers periodically to venture out into the Realm to bring him back exotic items for his work. The startling secret behind Tom's identity is that he is a powerful sorcerer and the son of the legendary Warlock. Tom was born in the Middle Region and is familiar with its landscape, but he was cast out by his father after a heated dispute over a difference in their moralities. Tom's ultimate goal is to build up his stores of arcane energy, craft powerful magical items, secure a number of talismans, and one day venture back into the Middle Region and overthrow his father once and for all. His familiar, a grey tabby named Grimalkin, was a gift from Mab after Tom was exiled from his home. Mab guides Tom's efforts through Grimalkin, as she is invested in the Warlock's eventual downfall and the power vacuum that would occur in its wake. Tom has not only seen the Middle Region but is one of the very few people of the Realm who has actually ventured beyond the borders of the Realm to see what lies beyond. He does not speak of this to anyone, including Mab, although he suspects that she knows anyway.

BENEFITS

The Collector: If Tom's attitude towards the PCs is Neutral or better, he is a source of fairly steady work, as he almost always needs some kind of hard-to-get components or items from all corners of the Realm, hiring out adventurers to fetch them for him. He pays well, and successful missions improve his attitude towards the PCs.

The Hermit: If Tom's attitude towards the PCs is Favourable or better, he is willing to offer them magical services, so long as they can be performed within the confines of the Academy—usually in Tom's own tower. Once per adventure, he performs any Arcane spell for the party on the grounds of the Academy. He does not charge a fee for the service, but the party is responsible for any material costs.

Son of the Middle Region: If Tom's attitude towards the PCs is Liked or better, and the circumstances are just right (GM's discretion), he confesses his secret origins to them. This opens the door for the PCs to travel to the Middle Region at some future point if they so desire. Tom is willing to help them get there—or, alternatively, an entire new adventure could be written involving Professor Tom joining the PCs (or them joining him, really) as they venture into the Middle Region to aid Tom in confronting his father, the legendary Warlock. See the entry in this section for **Kalsari Kanni, Fallen Master Wizard** for additional information.
Strength: 4   **Craft:** 10
Life: 25

Taparra, Instructor of the Hunt

The most recent instructor to join the Academy (nearly a decade ago) is an elven scout from the Whispering Wood. Taparra spent many decades earning his reputation as an expert monster hunter and is best known for his longbow fashioned from the prized wood of a harmony oak. When fired, the bow's reverberation makes a unique singing noise, which is the master huntsman's calling card. He instructs his students in the ways of tracking, identifying, and bringing down exotic quarry of the Realm. He currently boasts a larger class of students than any other current instructor at the Academy, perhaps because the Realm has been producing more and more monsters in need of slaying—not to mention the lure of lucrative rewards for certain species and their valuable parts. Taparra is more at home in the wilds than in the City, as most elves are, but he realizes the growing need for more great hunters in the Realm and does not see many of kin as both qualified and willing to take on the role of teacher, so he has stepped up to fill the role. His eerie, ultra-calm demeanour and deadly whisper of a voice gives his students chills, but Taparra is a very capable instructor, so they endure his disquieting presence. Taparra is known to be friendly with just three people in the City: Char Grimskin (the Academy's tanner), Rooster (the Gate Watch sniper), and Lurial (wizard of the Night Guard). Rumours circulate that Taparra and Lurial might perhaps be somewhat more than friends.

BENEFITS

Ways of the Hunt: If Taparra's attitude towards the PCs is Neutral or better, he supplies them with lore on about a specific type of creature and where they might be found in the Realm, and answers whatever follow-up questions the GM sees fit for him to impart to the PCs. If Taparra's attitude towards the PCs is Favourable or better, he teaches the Animal Handling, Athletics, Missile Weapon, Stealth, Survival, and Throw skills to any PCs looking to learn a new one after gaining a level. These skill lessons take one month and cost 5 gold per character per skill, unless Taparra's attitude is Liked or higher, in which case he waives the cost and holds the lessons in his personal time, not on school grounds. Each character can only learn one new skill from this instructor per month.
Strength: 7   **Craft:** 5
Life: 21

Old Dewey, Academy Librarian

The parchment-skinned ancient librarian is jokingly said to be as old as the Academy itself. No one in the City can remember another librarian, though, so the silly joke cannot be disproven. Old Dewey is a sweet, gentle, bumbling soul who spends every day in the Academy's dusty, underused library. Despite his raspy, absent-minded stammering and his shaky, liver spotted hands, the librarian can find any book, scroll, or other miscellaneous reference material among the labyrinthine shelves within a quarter-hour—assuming the library possesses it at all. On the odd night that students spy Old Dewey at a tavern drinking quietly by himself in a corner, they love to approach him, buy him a few rounds, and ply him for stories. The man is a seemingly unending font of interesting and obscure tales, both of his own past and from around the Realm in general. One history student, a young human named Laryssa, repeatedly claims that someday, she's going to assemble his stories into a series of volumes called *The Chronicles of Old Dewey*. To her credit, she already has multiple journals filled with scribbled notes from the wizened librarian's yarn-spinning. Old Dewey seems to be just fine with this idea.

BENEFITS

"Now Let Me See If I Can Find It…": If Dewey's attitude towards the PCs is Neutral or better, he can help them find research materials in the Academy's library pertaining to a lore subject of their choice. He can do this once per character in the party per adventure before he begins to ask if they actually attend the Academy and have a library card. If any of them can supply him with proof that they do, they may continue to use this benefit. If none of them attend the Academy and have no library card to produce, Dewey's attitude will drop to Suspicious, and he immediately ejects them from the library. If they decline to go, he summons one of the other instructors to assist him. The attitude of that instructor will also drop to Suspicious if it is currently higher than that.

Strength: 1   **Craft:** 4
Life: 10

Char Grimskin, Master Tanner

At the rear of the Academy, a slender but well-muscled troll named Char works away at her tannery, turning animals and monsters into useful items like parchment, sheets of leather, bone tools, exotic weapons, armour, and more. If a species has ever been killed and brought to the City within the last 20 years, Char has probably worked it over. Like many trolls, she is a person of few words (except with Taparra, who she considers a coworker, unlike the rest of the Academy staff). Char's cousin Garok runs the Underbridge Wharf, and the two can often be seen around Fishtown sharing a jug of troll grog called *murkh* after hours and getting into street brawls with low-level criminal elements from the South Side.

Benefits

"I Can Work with This…": If Char is presented with the remains of an animal or monster, she can turn it into goods and raw materials for a fair price. Her customers do not need to attend the Academy—she doesn't care, they need the business. If Char's attitude towards the PCs is Favourable or better, she offers them ideas on what products could be made from any given carcass (GM's discretion). If her attitude to the PCs is Liked or better, she offers a small discount on price *or* a faster turnaround time—customer's choice. Costs and turnaround times are at the GM's discretion, but they should be consummate with the rarity of the creature and complexity of the goods being produced by Char.

Strength: 6   **Craft:** 5
Life: 19

Ruegar Gildegrin, Master Merchant

A third-generation merchant, Ruegar Gildegrin is a clever, conniving dwarf and ruthless businessman with an extensive network of contacts placed in every relevant corner of the Realm. His network enables him to adapt his operations to ever-changing markets and environmental factors more quickly than anyone else,

thus retaining his spot as king of the money mountain. Gildegrin is a practiced hand at maneuvering his fellow master merchants, getting them to focus more on one another and less on him. It is this mastery that keeps him as the most influential member of the Golden Rule. Although they officially do not have a single leader and presumably all share the same level of power, Gildegrin is unofficially the top dog, and has been for well over a decade. He is currently grooming his son Lugan in the ways of the wily businessman, with the intention that Lugan will one day inherit his father's place within the Golden Rule. A lesser-known fact about Ruegar is that, in addition to being an expert merchant, he is also deadly in a knife fight, constantly training in private with his top personal guardsman who happens to be a long-time assassin.

Benefits

Loan Shark: If Ruegar's attitude towards the PCs is Favourable or better, he offers monetary loans to them, albeit at high interest rates. Ruegar is open to loans up to 15 gold per PC (or 20 if they are Liked by him), with the expectation they pay him back in a month. Failure to repay the loan in full on time reduces Ruegar's attitude by one, and he demands payment by skill **trade:** the PCs owe him a job consummate to the amount on which they have defaulted, to be called in whenever he wants (usually immediately or in the very near future). Ruegar's attitude does not reach Devoted. The highest he feels for anyone is Liked.

Strength: 5   **Craft:** 5
Life: 22

Deagle Fallcrest, Master Merchant

The eldest child of Lady Eisley Fallcrest is a scheming, backstabbing bastard. This is fairly common knowledge, especially among the master merchant barons who comprise the Golden Rule, but very few people realize just how devious and wicked Deagle is. His intelligence is no match for someone like Ruegar Gildegrin, but his boundless, bloody-minded ambition might just make up for it. The heir to the Fallcrest fortune has his sights set on eventually becoming the unquestioned figurehead of the Golden Rule—the way Gildegrin is now—but Deagle isn't ready to make his move just yet. He bides his time patiently, enjoying a life of luxury and power, riding the coattails of his mother's wealth, drinking and carousing to his black heart's content. One day, however, his patience will begin to wear thin.

Benefits

Bad Friend, Worse Enemy: If Deagle's attitude towards the PCs is Favourable, he becomes a source of employment, offering the PCs a number of shady but lucrative job opportunities over time. Ruegar's attitude does not reach Liked or Devoted. The highest he can feel for anyone is Favourable since he's a sociopath incapable of forging real friendships. If Deagle's attitude towards the PCs falls below Neutral, he actively seeks out ways to attack or interfere with the PCs within the City, and perhaps beyond.

Strength: 3 **Craft:** 4
Life: 17

Leminal Gaunce, Master Merchant

Despite his advancing years, Gaunce's fire burns no less brightly. A deeply pious human who worships the Balance, Gaunce is not shy about loudly and publicly castigating those who he sees as heathens—which is a lot of people. His arrogant, superior, and belligerent personality is off-putting to nearly everyone he comes into contact with, but his domineering will and clever way with words makes him an excellent salesman, and his numbers continue to prove it. One of Gaunce's most trusted advisors is his wife Thessa, a shrewd Prophet whose powers help guide the Gaunce family business in the right directions through an ever-shifting landscape of treacherous competition. If it were not for this prescience, the rest of the Golden Rule would want nothing to do with this unpleasant, judgmental old man.

Benefits

Passage for the Righteous: If Gaunce's attitude towards the PCs is Favourable or better and the party worships the Balance (or convince him they do with successful **Persuasion (Wits or Insight)** roll against a **Difficulty 17**), he offers them free passage alongside one of his merchant caravans to a destination of their choosing anywhere in the Realm that a merchant caravan would reasonably go (the main roads visible on the map of the Realm). While the PCs are travelling with his caravan (and assuming they behave themselves in accordance with Gaunce's demands), the PCs are given free passage in addition to free meals, a covered wagon all to themselves in which to sleep at night, and the full protection of the caravan's escort guard, which always includes at least two priests.

Strength: 3 **Craft:** 7
Life: 13

Mad Maeve the Mauve, Master Merchant

The Golden Rule is currently trying to figure out what to do with this unpredictable dwarf. Mad Maeve has more than earned her self-styled moniker over the last decade by undertaking seemingly insane caravan routes that no other merchant in their right mind would attempt. Nevertheless, year after year, most of Maeve's shipments get to their destinations—and in less time than most other merchants. This enables her to beat others to the punch when competing for business, rocketing her to the upper echelon of the merchant class. The secret to her success is her loyal contingent of dwarven howlers, an equally mad bunch of scouts and warriors who handle all the bandits and hungry wildlife that try to gobble up her wagons. The Golden Rule doesn't want such an eccentric wild card sitting among their council, but they don't want her as an enemy either, thus their current conundrum. The "Mauve" part of Maeve's title comes from her penchant for wearing nothing but shades of pale purple and dark pink, as well as her wild, bushy hair that she dyes to match.

Benefits

Wild Ride: If Maeve's attitude towards the PCs is Favourable or better, she offers passage on one of her caravans to anywhere in the Realm, no matter how out of the way. If the location is remote and/or dangerous enough, a contingent of 1d6 + 2 dwarven fighters breaks off from the caravan and escorts the PCs to their destination with one rickety wagon maximum, if needed.

Strength: 4 **Craft:** 6
Life: 22

Sofillia the Silvertongue, High Priest of Thieves (Light)

Growing up an orphan on the streets of the City, this charming, pretty sprite learned at a young age how to use her wiles to get others to give her what she wanted. This survival technique evolved into the keystone of what would become a decades-long career of high thievery, putting her among the elite of her trade. Sofillia can charm the spots off a cow, can convince a one-legged man to give her his crutch, and can get the wealthy residents of Rosewater to upend their purses. This High Priest of the Thieves Guild is less active these days, however, and is more focused on enjoying her luxurious lifestyle. The time she once put into constructing clever confidence schemes has dwindled; she now mostly spends her days monitoring and guiding her acolytes, trying to keep their crimes lighter and more fun in nature, steering them away from being like the Assassins Guild.

Benefits

Silver Tongue: If Sofillia's attitude towards the PCs is Favourable or better, she makes a visit on behalf of the PCs (with or without them present) to someone in the City and uses her silver tongue to open doors with her charm that might otherwise be shut to the party. This benefit can be used once per adventure.

Strength: 1 **Craft:** 8
Life: 11

Claudiel, High Priest of Thieves (Dark)

Most of the guild thieves around the City know this elven High Priest as "Catpaws" on account of her light-bodied dexterity and soundless footsteps. Claudiel Catpaws has spent many years as the City's best second-story burglar. Her lockpicking skill is surpassed only by her acrobatic ability to silently scale buildings and walls. The Night Guard has had her on their most wanted list for years but has been unable to corner her. Only the elven wizard Lurial has come close.

laudiel's influence over the meaner thieves of the City comes close to encroaching on Assassins Guild territory. She stops just shy of murder, but she encourages her acolytes to get physical with their marks if needed, and there is no target that is morally off-limits in her eyes. She and Sofillia often engage in philosophical debates over the future direction of their guild.

Benefits

Like a Ghost: If Claudiel's attitude towards the PCs is Favourable or better, she aids the party in breaking into a City location without alerting any authorities or triggering any traps. Once inside, Claudiel likely goes back out the way she came, leaving the PCs to fend for themselves on the way out. If her attitude is Liked or Devoted, she stays with the party and assists with their mission for longer.

Strength: 4   **Craft:** 6
Life: 16

Rubber Face Jace, High Priest of Thieves (Neutral)

A consummate performer who rivals even the most talented members of the City's theatre community, Jace has always had a talent for crafting a plethora of personalities. His versatile voice can mimic most people he meets after listening to them speak for just a few minutes. With the right hair, makeup, and prosthetics, his malleable but forgettable face is easily transformed into a host of figures. From a young age, he learned he could use his gifts to pull off creative crimes and quickly disappear into the City, with no one able to recognize who he really was. He impersonates specific members of the City guard, politicians, merchants, and the wealthy elite, with their close friends, family, and coworkers none the wiser. He also invents entirely fictional people for different heists and discards them immediately after making his escape, leaving the City Patrol or the Night Guard looking for a person who will never be seen again. Jace has groomed a number of his favourite acolytes into a troupe of performer-thieves to help him with larger jobs. A funny and mischievous rascal at heart, Jace serves as an excellent buffer between Sofillia and Claudiel's opposing sensibilities and is crucial in keeping the Thieves Guild leadership balanced.

Benefits

Anyone, Anywhere: If Jace's attitude towards the PCs is Favourable or better, he assists them in some kind of effort that requires impersonating others. If multiple impersonators are needed, Jace brings some of his acolytes in on the job. If his attitude is Liked or Devoted, his level of assistance and/or number of acolytes is higher.

Strength: 3   **Craft:** 7
Life: 16

Rogues' Chaplain

Simply referred to as "Chaplain" among the City's thieves, this leywalker is an actual priest (as opposed to the three "High Priests" of the guild). Regardless of a thief's affinity towards light, dark, or middle ground, Chaplain views all of his guild members equally as his "flock". His services are called upon to heal the injured when a job goes wrong, to perform weddings when members within the guild want to get married, and any other ceremonies required among them.

Benefits

A Shepherd to His Flock: If Chaplain's attitude towards the PCs is Favourable or better, he offers to heal them completely of their wounds as well as any sickness and/or poison in exchange for 1 gold per party member receiving these benefits (as a generous donation to the 'clergy'). These services are available to the party once per adventure, plus an additional time for each member of the party in the Thieves Guild.

Strength: 5   **Craft:** 7
Life: 17

Sami Stickyfingers, Pickpocket

This young sprite is a relative newcomer to the big City and has already caught the attention of Sofillia. His area of expertise is in picking pockets. His favoured quarry are clumsy humans staggering home after a night of gambling and drinking. He flutters outside tavern windows to see who the big winners are, then zips in behind them with his light fingers and relieves them of the burden of their heavy coin, deftly swapping the weight out for a pouch full of steel or chips or stones so his inebriated victims don't immediately notice the sudden lightness of their belts. Little does Sami know that Sofillia is close to approaching him about joining the Thieves Guild.

Benefits

Sticky Fingers: If Sami's attitude towards the PCs is Favourable or better, he attempts to pick the pockets of one target of the PCs' at a time and place of their choosing—unless they leave the details to him. His fee for this service is 2 gold in exchange for whatever specific item(s) the PCs have detailed to him to steal. Sami also keeps any gold he finds on the mark, unless the goal was just to clean someone out, in which case he splits the stolen purse 50/50 with the party.

Strength: 1   **Craft:** 4
Life: 12

The Queen Recluse

The current leader of the Assassins Guild is called the Queen Recluse, so named for the fatally venomous spider. Her preferred method of work is poison, obviously, and she has ruled the guild for 19 years. Under her guidance, the guild has flourished both in quality membership and in coin. Every few years, some ambitious up-and-comer tries to unseat the Queen and meets a ghastly end. Most of the guildmembers have both a healthy fear and a healthy respect of their leader and have absolutely no problem letting her continue to run the show indefinitely. While she very rarely appears in clear view of the public, those who meet her in any capacity do not soon forget the encounter. She is tall for a human woman, slight of frame, but burning with a quiet intensity that shines through her differently coloured eyes—one bright green and one dark brown. Her chestnut hair is usually kept woven into an intricate series of braids and twists, which she keeps pinned together by a pair of silver hair sticks which double as poisoned throwing spikes. The Queen has spent her entire adult life building up resistances to most poisons, a successful practice which has left her voice a ragged whisper, but the rest of her otherwise intact.

BENEFITS

"My Mouth Feels All Tingly…": If the Recluse's attitude towards the PCs is Favourable or better, she arranges for a target of the party's choosing to encounter a type of poison in the near future—whether that means a fatal dose, something to temporarily induce nausea, paralysis, or any effect that a poison can create. The timing, location and other details are negotiable, but the Queen Recluse is no fool and will not put herself in unnecessary danger. Targets with more limited access and higher security require more planning and a higher gold cost to the PCs, commensurate with the details of the job.

Strength: 4　**Craft:** 7
Life: 20

THE BLADE

Somewhere in the City, an unassuming elf wanders the streets with his head down, appearing meek and mild-mannered. He dresses like a low-level government employee, a junior acolyte of the High Temple or something similarly anonymous. As his sobriquet suggests, his calling card is knives. He is an unmatched master of the short blade, whether it be in melee combat or thrown. He has a chilling familiarity in the biological designs of all humanoids and knows exactly where to cut to produce any number of desired effects. Sometimes he is not hired to kill quickly, but to make it last. He is a patient, intelligent, thorough assassin who has never botched a kill. To date, he has killed four members of the Night Guard, earning him the top spot on their wanted list. The Blade has no desire to usurp the Queen Recluse, and in fact, he considers her to be one of his very few real friends, but should anything happen to her, he is the most likely candidate to take over leadership of the Assassins Guild.

BENEFITS

Cold Steel, Colder Blood: If the Blade's attitude towards the PCs is Favourable or better, he arranges for a target of the party's choosing to encounter some cold steel in the shadows of the City. The timing, location and other details are negotiable, but the Blade is no fool and will not put himself in unnecessary danger. Targets with more limited access and higher security require more planning and a higher gold cost to the PCs, commensurate with the details of the job.

Strength: 6　**Craft:** 4
Life: 21　**Armour:** 1

THE FIREBUG

This curious, aloof leywalker has always felt a deep, resonating love for fire and has found his place in the Realm as the City's foremost arsonist. He has become an unparalleled expert at manipulating fire—how to lay traps that will ignite at a certain time or under specific conditions, how to direct it, contain it, and accelerate it. For him, fire behaves like a trained animal companion. Socially, this leywalker is awkward and distant, preferring to spend much of his time in books and making charcoal drawings and paintings rather than fraternizing with anyone. The Firebug is responsible for the death of one Night Guard as well as the maiming of two more in his fires. He currently sits near the top of the most wanted list.

BENEFITS

Spark: If the Firebug's attitude towards the PCs is Favourable or better, he arranges for a target of the party's choosing to have a surprise encounter with fire. The timing, location, and other details are negotiable, but the Firebug is no fool and will not put himself in unnecessary danger. Targets with more limited access and higher security require more planning and a higher gold cost to the PCs, commensurate with the details of the job.

Strength: 5　**Craft:** 5
Life: 19

THE ACCIDENTALIST

Upon meeting this joyous, bubbly sprite, no one would have any reason to think she was a deadly assassin. In fact, she doesn't really care for that label. She insists that she has never killed anybody, that all of her marks have fallen victim to accidents. A brilliant and creative engineer, she has mastered the art of making murder look like any number of mishaps, from the everyday to the downright bizarre. A slip-and-fall down some stairs, a bucking horse kick to the noggin, drowning, mistakenly stabbed in a tavern brawl, a collapsed roof on a poorly kept cottage, the list goes on and on. She is so adept at her craft that the Night Guard doesn't have her on their most wanted list—they don't even know about her.

BENEFITS

"WHOOPSIE!": If the Accidentalist's attitude towards the PCs is Favourable or better, she arranges for a target of the party's choosing to meet with an unfortunate accident. The timing, location, and other details are negotiable, but the Accidentalist is no fool and will not put herself in unnecessary danger. Targets with more limited access and higher security require more planning and a higher gold cost to the PCs, commensurate with the details of the job.

Strength: 1　**Craft:** 6
Life: 13

CHIEF DUNGSWEEPER

When the dungsweepers of the City first formed into an official government-funded department, not many people wanted to sign up to be the head of it, knowing it would mean their days and nights for many years would be spent in the company of offal. For a tall, gaunt ghoul called Burgrim, it wasn't a problem. She has been the Chief Dungsweeper since the position's inception, and at this point, she mostly handles administrative duties, dividing up the City routes among her sweepers, and coordinating the efforts of the Sweepers' campus at the end of Droppings Lane. The rest of her time is devoted to another endeavour kept completely secret from the City: she is also the Beggars Boss, the head of the Foundlings Home. See the **Beggars Boss** entry further down in this section.

Benefits:

See the Beggars Boss entry.
Strength: 7   **Craft:** 7
Life: 20

Sloga Narr, Dungsweeper Trainer

Winner of the loudest bellow at the last three straight annual Strange Skills Competitions, this imposing troll takes in new applicants for the City Dungsweepers, runs them through the gauntlet to see if they can handle the job, and trains them how to do it better. She also helps Burgrim decide where to assign new recruits of all types: cart driver, street shoveler, stable hand, burner, carpenter, or administration. Sloga is a stern taskmaster to newcomers but treats her proven employees well once they've earned her respect.

Benefits

Training Day: If Sloga Narr's attitude towards the PCs is Favourable or better, she finds them work on a Dungsweeper crew and trains them in the details of the job. This opportunity can help PCs earn some money if they find themselves in dire financial straits, not to mention putting them in a position to move about the City more or less ignored. Dungsweepers pick up all kinds of street gossip…
Strength: 7   **Craft:** 2
Life: 22

Ferdie Brownshoes, Dungsweeper Gossipmonger

Ferdie signed on to the Dungsweepers five years ago at the young age of 11 after his father died and his mother fell ill. Someone needed to make money for food, medicine, and the Taxman, so he signed on and grabbed a shovel. Today, he is the most popular of the Dungsweeper, cheerful and sociable to people on every block of his routes despite his unenviable job. He has developed a knack for picking up town gossip and trades it with other well-known gossipers, becoming one of the area's greatest spreaders of news—possibly second only to the Speaker of the City. Ferdie is often appointed by Sloga Narr to accompany new Dungsweepers on their first few routes to make sure they're doing the job right.

BENEFITS

The Scoop: If Ferdie's attitude towards the PCs is Favourable or better, and if the PCs pay him 1 gold for his assistance, he tries to glean information from the streets. The GM privately rolls 2d6 for Ferdie when seeking a piece of information and the PCs are told to meet him along his route in 24 hours while he keeps his ears open for significant City chatter.

THE SCOOP

Roll	Result
1–3	He hears absolutely nothing regarding the information the PCs are after.
4–6	He hears loose, conflicting rumours regarding the information the PCs are after. The rumours may be entirely unreliable, or one of them might be somewhat helpful.
7–9	He hears something regarding the information the PCs are after and share helpful info.
10+	He's already heard something useful regarding the information the PCs are after and shares it immediately. No need to wait 24 hours.

Strength: 3 **Craft:** 4
Life: 12

INSPARRA, DEAN OF THE COLLEGE OF THE ARTS

If she had a last name, she abandoned it when she entered the public eye as the Dean for the City's College of the Arts many years ago. Insparra flutters through the halls of her college on her jewel-toned sprite wings, checking in on classes at random, always adding her own little pearls of wisdom and creative inspiration before flitting off to the next destination. Her high, airy voice possesses an almost hypnotic, dreamy quality in addition to its high-society accent and perfect enunciation; she's known to "hold court" at socialite gatherings, enthralling groups of partygoers. Insparra dresses to the hilt every day and sets fashion trends for the Rosewater elites with each new season.

BENEFITS

Magic of the Muse: If Insparra's attitude towards the PCs is Favourable or better, she provides them with safe harbour for up to 8 hours somewhere within her college, perhaps in her private lounge. There, she regales them with an inspiring anecdote or sings a song relating to the party's current situation, and the inspiration of her tale infuses the PCs. Any PC rolling to regain spell points adds 3 to the roll and regains 1 Light Fate.
Strength: 1 **Craft:** 7
Life: 10

UNGER GREYHERRON, HARBOURMASTER OF THE STORM RIVER WHARF

This tall, barrel-chested dwarf runs a tight outfit, containing the chaos of the Realm's busiest wharf and turning it into a profitable enterprise for the City. He excels at logistics and manages the comings and goings of a dozen ships at a time with the expertise of a circus juggler. His dockworkers fear being on the receiving end of one of Unger's full-throated public beratings, which keeps them industrious and careful in their duties. Despite his reputation a s a Taskmaster, though, Greyherron never fails to stand up to the City administrators when it comes to good wages for his labourers and enough gold to keep the wharf in good repair, with some money left over for expansion and improved technologies when they surface.

GAROK GRIMSKIN, DOCKMASTER OF THE UNDERBRIDGE WHARF

Cousin of the Academy's tanner, Char, Garok Grimskin and "his boys" like to have a bit of fun on the waterfront while executing their duties. They skim a little profit here and there—not so much that they draw attention from more powerful authorities, they hassle embarking and debarking passengers for a little more toll money than is actually owed, and the occasional body might disappear under the bridge in the dead of night…for the right price. Garok very much enjoys his drinking, gambling, and street brawling—activities that he often gets his cousin drawn into at night after work is done.

BENEFITS

"What Shipment?": If Garok's attitude towards the PCs is Favourable or better, he helps land them some kind of non-magical and/or non-unique goods that 'somehow got misplaced' in transit around his harbour—in exchange for an equitable amount of gold, of course. The PCs roll 2d6 for each 24-hour period they wait for Garok to try and acquire what they need. On a 7+, he finds something that suits their needs. If the PCs seek something specific that's magical and/or unique and they know it's supposed to be coming in or going out through the Underbridge Wharf, Garok acquires it on a roll of 10+, but his fee is commensurate with the value of the item (or his perception of its value).
Strength: 7 **Craft:** 2
Life: 25

Madame Ferrogot, the Beast Whisperer

The self-styled "Madame" Fergot is a constant source of rumour and speculation around town. She appears in most respects to be a troll but possesses more human features than most; her skin appears less green, more pale, her features smoother, her build more slight, her hair less oily, her voice less rough than most trolls. The prevailing rumour is that she is the byproduct of the mating of both troll and human, although no one dares ask her up front. Ferrogot uses her druid charms and her natural social savvy to lure new creatures into her Menagerie and is very selective about which potential customers may walk away with one of her pets. She treats the animals as well as a loving mother would treat her natural-born children, giving them all names that must be kept by any buyer—most of which come at a very high expense. Unbeknonwst to the City, Ferrogot's assistant zookeepers are also spies of a sort—they keep tabs on her sold animals if they still reside in the City, making sure they are being well treated by their new owners. In cases where the animals are mistreated, Ferrogot and her people will reclaim them. By force if necessary, bringing some of her more… intimidating…pets along for the confrontation.

Benefits

Beastmaster: If Madame Ferrogot's attitude towards the PCs is Neutral or better, she allows the PCs to purchase one of her exotic animals (or more) at a fair market price. If her attitude is below Neutral, she puts the party into her 'black book', meaning they are no longer welcome in her Menagerie. If her attitude hits Hated, the PCs have an unfortunate 'random' encounter with a dangerous creature in some vulnerable place in or around the City one night…

Strength: 5 **Craft:** 5
Life: 17

Rathskeller, Bounty Hunter

Although his spiky hair is going to grey, the man called Rathskeller remains one of the more successful bounty hunters in the region around the City. A dirty, underhanded thief himself, Rathskeller possesses a keen insight into the mindset of people trying to run and hide from the law. As such, he excels at sniffing out hiding places and tracking down bounties both inside the City walls and in the surrounding farmsteads. Always clad in beat-up black leathers, bristling with small blades and leering out of his one good eye from a scarred face, Rathskeller is a very well-known and instantly recognizable figure around the South Side.

Benefits

"I Know How They Think": Rathskeller can be hired by the party for 3 gold per day plus a 10-gold bounty upon completion of a successful retrieval. PCs assisted by him gain a bonus die when tracking prey within the City and surrounding countryside, or when making a Watcher test in the same region. If the PCs leave the tracking and capture of a target entirely to Rathskeller, he takes 1d6 days to locate their quarry and return it to the PCs, usually in the requested condition. Roll 2d6. On a 2, something went sideways and the mark was retrieved, but it was accidentally killed in the process. On a 3–6, the mark was injured. On a 7–10, the mark arrives in the requested condition. On an 11+, the mark arrives in the requested condition in half the time indicated on the 1d6 days for turnaround time. Rathskeller turns down offers to find and retrieve high risk targets. He's not looking to make powerful enemies. GMs should use this knowledge factored with Rathskeller's attitude level to guide their discretion as to which jobs he accepts from the PCs.

Strength: 6 **Craft:** 5
Life: 21 **Armour:** 2

Agdamon Firstscion Shadowseed, Bounty Hunter

This eerie bounty hunter uses his innate leywalker gifts and his sorcery to track down and subdue bounties from all across the Realm. Where many bounty hunters balk at the expenses involved in traveling across the Realm in pursuit of their quarry, Agdamon simply opens a portal to a remote location, nabs his prey, and returns through another portal. While not as constantly active as the other prominent bounty hunters who frequent the City, Agadmon waits for the right high-priced target and snatches them before anyone else can. He then lives off of his big pay day for weeks at a time, sometimes disappearing into the feywilds for extended periods.

BENEFITS

Cheater: Shadowseed can be hired by the party for 3 gold per day, plus a 20-gold bounty upon completion of a successful retrieval. Shadowseed works alone, using magic to aid him in his hunts, but because of his adeptness with teleportation, he can work anywhere across the Realm and return to the City with a speed no other bounty hunter can match. He returns in 1d2 days with or without his quarry because if he can't find them in 2 days, he can't find them at all (and obviously doesn't collect the 20 gold in those cases, which are rare). The likelihood of his success is influenced by how much accurate, detailed information the PCs give him regarding the target.

Strength: 4 **Craft:** 8
Life: 17

Vambria the Treerunner, Bounty Hunter

One of the more feared bounty hunters around the City region is Vambria, a savage elven scout who notoriously uses the treetops to travel and to lay traps and ambushes for her prey. Her strong suit is tracking bounties who have fled into the wilderness, where many other bounty hunters fear to go or are ill-equipped to track prey through dense foliage and deal with the beasts of the wild. While her whip-thin figure, trademark camouflage hunting leathers, and tattooed face make her extremely memorable and recognizable in the South Side, Vambria does not care to spend much time in the City aside from cashing in her bounties and keeping an eye on the Post by the City Gate. She usually sleeps somewhere out in the forested lands beyond the farmsteads that surround the City. It is rumoured that she sometimes overpays struggling farmers in exchange for staying in their hay loft or a spare room in the house when the weather turns cold and snowy.

BENEFITS

Sylvan Stalker: Vambria can be hired by the party for 3 gold per day plus a 10-gold bounty upon completion of a successful retrieval. PCs assisted by her gain a bonus die when tracking prey through forests, hills, or plains, or when making a Watcher test in the same terrains. If the PCs leave the tracking and capture of a target entirely to Vambria, she takes 1d6 days to locate their quarry and return it to the PCs, usually in the requested condition. Roll 2d6. On a 2, something

went sideways; the mark was retrieved, but it was accidentally killed in the process. On a 3–5, the mark was injured. On a 6–9, the mark arrives in the requested condition. On a 10+, the mark arrives in the requested condition in half the time indicated on the 1d6 days for turnaround time. Vambria does not hunt within the City walls. If the PCs include at least one elf, Vambria lowers her fee to 2 gold per day and 8 gold upon retrieval of the quarry.

Strength: 5 **Craft:** 7
Life: 19 **Armour:** 1

Beggars Boss

The head of the City's "Foundlings Home", which is a combination orphanage and underage street thief training ground, is a stooped figure referred to only as "Boss" whose identity and ancestry is always hidden under a hooded cloak and behind a painted leather carnival mask. The Boss brings in young street urchins who have no family and trains them in how to not only survive in the streets, but to thrive on the pity and generosity (or gullibility) of the more fortunate. The Foundlings Home also cleans the urchins up a bit and grooms them for possible adoption by families who have been met by tragedy, are incapable of having children, or simply want a bigger family and have the love and the gold to spare for another child. The Beggars Boss' big secret is that they are also the City's Head Dungsweeper.

BENEFITS

The Queen of Rats and Orphans: If the Beggars Boss' attitude towards the PCs is Favourable or better, she lends 3d6 of her orphans to assist the PCs in some kind of effort within the City that could benefit from a network of street urchins. Her daily fee is an amount of gold equal to twice the amount of orphans lent out, and she will not knowingly send her orphans into any kind of situation that seems more dangerous than the average daily life of an urchin. Depending on the task, GMs may require that the children be given an amount of time to complete their service (1d6 hours, 1d3 days, whatever seems appropriate to the task). If the Head Dungsweeper/Beggars Boss' attitude falls below Suspicious, the PCs suddenly find it very difficult to go anywhere in the City without being shadowed by street urchins, rats, and City dungsweepers. Every task the party tries to complete is likely met by active resistance by these forces until the PCs find a way to make it up to the Beggars Boss and salvage her attitude towards them.

Strength: 7 **Craft:** 7
Life: 20

Wolf Mother

Across the Greensnake, on the outskirts of the settled farmlands to the northeast of the City, there lives an older, worn and thin human woman known to the people of the City as "Wolf Mother". After losing her husband and children to a pox many years ago, this solitary farmer has developed a strange rapport with the wolves of the nearby Split Oak Woods. Unbeknownst to most, Wolf Mother is not just a farmer. Since losing her family, she has become a moderately powerful druid, although she rarely demonstrates her power in front of anyone except for the animals of the woods. Despite her solitary nature, Wolf Mother would take in and lend aid to anyone of good or neutral alignment who stumbled onto her farm from the woods or the Storm River. Those of evil alignment who happened onto her land would likely get to meet her lupine children…

Benefits

Mother's Milk: If the party has no one of Evil alignment, Wolf Mother offers to put them up in her barn for 1d3 days, assuming they behave themselves. She asks for no money but doesn't refuse it if offered by the PCs. If her attitude towards them is Favourable or better, she offers to cure any disease or poison from which the party may be suffering. If the PCs help her around her farm or contribute a generous amount of gold, she provides them with three warm meals a day. If her attitude falls below Neutral, the PCs find themselves being stalked by a pack of 1d6+2 wolves as soon as they leave her farmstead. Any attack on Wolf Mother or her farm instantly summons 2d6+4 wolves to her defense.

Strength: 3   **Craft:** 7
Life: 15

Kalsari Kanni, Fallen Master Wizard

At the end of Rumtumble Row in the Red Lanterns neighbourhood lives an eccentric, washed-up wizard who spends almost every day and night alone, drunk, and clothed in nothing but his underpants. To the locals, he's a neighbourhood fixture and an ongoing joke. They have mocking conversations with him to prod him into one of his wild stories about what lies beyond the edges of the Realm, as the wizard has claimed to have been there and back. The truth is…that it's the truth. Kalsari was once an ambitious, adventurous young man as well as a clever and powerful wizard who trained—and later taught—at the Academy long ago. Some of the things he saw beyond the Realm are what drove him to the bottle, turning him into the picture of a raving madman whose every claim should be discredited and laughed at. The other significant secret Kalsari Kanni possesses is that he is the only person in the City, and possibly the Realm, who knows the true identity of Professor Tom. In his youth, Kalsari's travels took him to the Middle Region, and making the acquaintance of Thomas is what set both of them on tragic paths. Little does Professor Tom realize—however improbable it sounds—this drunk, broken, underwear-clad wizard could be the secret to returning to the Middle Region, if only someone would take him seriously and help get him cleaned up and off the sauce. If he were to be rehabilitated, Kalsari Kanni could potentially return to becoming one of the most powerful wizards in the City—and would even consider taking on pupils once more.

Benefits

"First, Put Some Pants On": Once the PCs have spent a week helping him get cleaned up and looking forward to a brighter future, and assuming Kalsari Kanni's attitude towards the PCs is Favourable or better (it would have to be, after they helped him turn his life around), he casts one arcane spell for them per week. During the first week of his complete sobriety, he can cast common spells. During the second week, assuming the PCs can keep him on the wagon, he can cast up to intermediate spells. During his third week, he can cast up to advanced spells.

"I've Seen Things You People Wouldn't Believe": If Kalsari Kanni's attitude towards the PCs reaches Devoted, he begins to confide in them regarding his adventures in the Middle Region and beyond the borders of the Realm. At the GM's discretion, he may also begin to tell the PCs a little about his past with Professor Tom. This benefit is an opportunity for the campaign to head towards exploring the Middle Region as well as beyond the borders of the Realm—for an ambitious GM who feels ready to create an epic level of exciting new Talisman content entirely of their own imagining!

Strength: 2/5*   **Craft:** 3/9*
Life: 10/19*

*The numbers before the slash indicate Kalsari's poor initial state. If the PCs can get him the help he needs and return him to his former self, the numbers after the slash represent his maximum rehabbed stats. For each week of sobriety, add back 1 Strength, 2 Craft, and 3 Life.

VILLEDOC

A general description is outlined in the *Talisman Adventures* core book, but this chapter expands on that information. GMs are encouraged to add their own entries or change anything in this chapter as needed for their story.

One particular point of interest briefly touched on in *Talisman Adventures* is Villedoc's unique relationship with the shadowed ghoul city of Sepulchre to the north, found at the other end of the Lonely Road that connects the two. Sepulchre has had a long-standing respect for Villedoc, but nobody can quite remember why—it's just always been so. When residents of Villedoc pass away, they are either buried in family plots or cemetaries around town, or they are taken to the cabin of the town's mystic, where they await the arrival of ghoul caretakers who come with a wagon to ferry the dead back to Sepulchre. Nobody is quite sure how the ghouls always know when to send their emissary for a pickup—they just seem to have some supernatural sense of death. Villedoc natives are raised to have a quiet respect for the ghoul city, and any rumblings of people wanting to form up a mob and "clean out" Sepulchre are immediately quashed by the Lord Mayor and the Town Guard, if not by normal townsfolk.

NOTABLE LOCATIONS AND FEATURES OF THE VILLEDOC AREA

While not nearly as busy and complex as the City, Villedoc is still larger and busier than any other settlement around the Realm and has many potential points of interest to adventurers. GMs should feel free to add their own entries or change the ones in this section as needed to suit their stories.

THE LORD MAYOR'S HOUSE

Located on a small rise near the Town Square, the largest, nicest house in Villedoc falls to the Lord Mayor for the duration of their term. From its windows, the entire layout of the town is visible on all sides. The house and its grounds are secured by a high stone wall and guarded day and night by a small contingent of town guard. The Lord Mayor's estate also includes a wing filled with offices where Villedoc's civil officers conduct their daily business of running the town. The town's Treasury is kept safe in a secure vault in the basement of the estate, reachable by a separate, exterior door made of iron, sealed by a high quality, City-made lock and protected both inside and out by multiple guards. The rear lawn of the estate boasts a small swimming pool surrounding by a tranquil garden, providing a place of reflection and serenity for the current Lord Mayor when their duties start to weigh on them. One other notable feature of the house is its safe room, a hidden door located in the study that leads to a reinforced chamber that is kept stocked with food and drink rations, weaponry, potions, other emergency accessories, and an escape tunnel that leads underground to a secret hatch by the fishing piers in case the Lord Mayor and family need to flee down river to safety.

THE TOWN SQUARE

Not nearly as expansive, colourful, or glorious as the town square of the City, Villedoc's town square nonetheless is similarly a centre of activity and the peak opportunity for socialization in the area. The main market for Villedoc extends northward from the square, making it even more of a bustling area from dawn to dusk. Most of the more vital structures are positioned around the town square, like the main tavern—called Second Home—as well as the town's blacksmith, carpenter, temple, clothing shoppe, town guard garrison/jail, toy and game maker, and more. At the centre of the square is a public fountain built over top of a natural spring, constantly being fed fresh water and bubbling with pressure and moderate heat from beneath the earth. The half-metre-deep water is safe for people to walk around in, and children are often found playing in it, but its sanctity is strongly guarded by the townsfolk; no dirty laundry is allowed to be washed here, no stale dregs of ale from the tankards of wandering drinkers are to be dumped here, and any other kind of pollutants are forbidden. Violators of this sanctity are punished the old-fashioned way by any observers who want to enact immediate punishment. At the fountain's centre stands a 3-metre-high statue of an inspiring, heroic figure called Petra. Anyone new to Villedoc asking around about the origins of Petra will be met with shrugs or various conflicting stories that sound more like guesses and three-levels-removed hearsay. The only Villedoc resident who remembers the actual story of the statue's origins and its real-life inspiration is the Mystic—but nobody has thought to ask her about it in recent years.

THE MARKET

Extending northward from the town square, the market bustles with activity from dawn to dusk every day of the week. Goods, services, coins, legitimate news, and spicy gossip are freely traded here, keeping most of the community tightly knit together. Merchant caravans come and go regularly to and from the market, staying for a couple days until their wagons of goods are depleted and/or loaded up for the trip back to the City or other more remote points around the Realm. A handful of street performers, visual artists and hustlers make their daily living here as well, keeping an eagle eye out for any new faces around town. The air around the marketplace is rich with the smells of cooking meat, local spices and perfumes, fresh fish, tanning leather, and more. The cacophony of sounds is equally diverse and interesting, at least to anyone not used to it, and many interesting local personalities can be encountered here at random or by design.

Sorgrin's Trading Post

The most prominent single location in the market, and the hands-down best place for finding more obscure items to purchase in Villedoc, is Sorgrin's Trading Post. This elderly dwarf's massive tent is the northernmost 'cap' at the end of the marketplace, facing southward towards the town square so he can see everyone coming through the market up the town's main avenue, called *Storm Street*. In addition to a stock of normal items, the trading post is owned and operated by a long-time member of the Merchants Guild, which is why it receives regular infusions of inventory that is otherwise extremely hard to find outside of the City. And if the old dwarf doesn't have what you're looking for, he's always happy to place a custom order with his Guild contacts if his customers can stand to wait a bit for it to come in.

The Blacksmiths' Compound

The Galdedar family has owned and operated Villedoc's only blacksmith outfit for several generations and are generally considered humble, unofficial royalty by the locals. The quality of their items is solid and reliable, and their prices fair. They can't compete with the high-end smithies of the City, of course, but the residents of Villedoc have little use for ostentatious ornamentation of their crafted items. A Galdedar blade, for example, will hold up in combat against just about any other non-magical weapon in the Realm, although it may not be as shiny or covered in swirling, artisanal decoration. Galdedar armor will serve its owner well against the many and varied perils found in the wild around the Crags and other dangerous northern regions of the Realm. The Galdedars' family home is located just behind their forge, right off the town square. They have expanded with additions over the decades, and their house now stands as one of the larger structures in Villedoc, now home to well over a dozen family members. Anyone who comes knocking at the door of their home rather than the shop will find the door almost always unlocked, but the interior a dizzying frenzy of activity and usually a good deal of bellowing adults, whining teenagers, and shrieking babies and toddlers—whoever isn't staffing the shop at the time, that is.

The Mystic's Cabin

On the northern edge of the town's main cluster, a dark log cabin sits overlooking the main road into the northern farmlands. On the front porch of this cabin, at most hours of the day, the mystic of Villedoc sits in her rickety wicker chair. From this perch, she and her one-eyed cat Mankins sit and judge passersby, with the

middle-aged woman often making sarcastic comments to her furred partner. The cabin is surrounded by wild, unkempt grass and old trees, giving it a somewhat foreboding atmosphere. The children of Villedoc like to dare one another to run onto the mystic's property late at night and steal an apple from her lone apple tree. For the few people who have seen the inside of the cabin, it appears a chaotic mess, piled high in every corner with books, dried herbs, bones, shelves of oddments. The air is thick and smells earthy, and those who have spent any amount of time here claim to have left the cabin feeling lightheaded. The back room of the cabin shelters a small, round table and four chairs. Here, the mystic will—on rare occasions—entertain visitors seeking favours like sage advice, a fortune reading, a blessing, or the cursing of an enemy.

The Healer's Cottage

Located on the southwestern edge of Villedoc's core, just before the territory of the fishing community, sits the humble but orderly cottage of Jon Kimora. The town's healer is almost always at home, unless he's out gathering supplies from the market, the trading post, or the fertile lands to the west, where many of his healing components grow. The interior of the cottage reveals all the trappings of a single man's home, as well as a large side room capable of hosting up to four people comfortably for whatever type of healing they might need. The air usually smells of pleasant tea leaves and incense. Kimora also keeps several well-tended gardens around his cottage—vegetables, herbs for both healing and eating, useful weeds and flowers, and more. His property is thoroughly fenced off to keep out the local wildlife, which includes townsfolk looking to steal a quick fix. It is also trapped with a clever system of wires and tiny bells to warn him against creatures and townsfolk who exhibit above-average tenacity, and although he is a healer, Kimora is not above hitting thieves with a strong dose of itching powder to teach them a lesson about respecting property.

The Temple

Taking up most of the south side of the town square, Villedoc's only organized temple welcomes worshippers of both the Light and the Balance. Anyone looking to bring the Dark into Villedoc's temple is approached by the town's senior priest for conversion or else encouraged to find a different location in which to express their worship. Predictably, most religious/spiritual ceremonies in Villedoc are performed here. It is a loosely kept 'secret' around Villedoc that the temple has regular contact with ghoulish emissaries from Sepulchre, although the details of those encounters are only known to a select few.

The Gamemaster

A favourite haunt of the town's children, the town square shop called The Gamemaster sits in perennial shadow thanks to the taller, broader buildings that surround it. Within its walls, a wizened old human named Garyx putters around the open, tavern-like setup of tables where he allows the townsfolk to try out his games and puzzles for a short time to see if they'd like to buy them. This shop also contains a fair number of books, making it the closest thing Villedoc has to a public library.

Second Home

Villedoc's only real tavern, this three-story building has rooms to rent on the second floor for visitors passing through. The top floor is the living quarters for the Hearthstone family, who own the establishment. This is the heart of the town after the sun goes down and the day's work is done for most folk. Town gossip is passed around, travelers bring news from the surrounding territories, fantastic tales are told by the large fireplace, and the air is filled with the smells of fine cooking and spilled ale. Adventurers coming to Villedoc would most likely find themselves ending up here to get a room or two, a hot meal, park their horses in the stables behind the building, and get the lay of the land from the locals.

The Ranch

On the eastern edge of the town proper sits a large ranch where one can rent, buy, or sell a variety of riding, pack, or farm animals. Horses, donkeys, and oxen, this ranch hosts the area's best selection of useful beasts at rates that will strain the purse—but not empty it entirely. The ranch employs a handful of regulators who patrol the area, watchful of thieves and predatory animals like wolves. These regulators are skilled with crossbows and melee weapons alike and are unforgiving to anyone caught trying to steal or harm any of the ranch's animals. Adventurers hitching a ride to Villedoc might be interested to stop here to acquire their own transportation—*if* they have the coin.

The Treehouse

Past the northwestern edge of the town proper, beyond the last farms and just across the river, there sits a thicket of old oaks. In this thicket, nestled high up in the thick boughs of three ancient, intertwined trees, sits an elaborately crafted house. The house's sole occupant is an elf named Kyriel, one of the few elves known to make their home around the Villedoc area. Residents of the area know enough to leave the treehouse alone and give the elf his space, lest they find an arrow uncomfortably protruding from the seat of their pants or the toe of their boot. Despite the danger in trespassing, the treehouse is a place where certain insight or resources could be located, if a party figures out how to approach respectfully and showing no threat.

The Westbridge

A long, broad, stoutly constructed stone bridge arches over the river just north of where it forks into the circle that separates the Middle Region. So called the Westbridge because, for Villedoc, it is the gateway to the western half of the Realm. The bridge is always manned by a pair of sentries stationed at each end, plus a toll collector's booth on the eastern end. Each toll collector brings their daily collections to the Lord Mayor's house with their accompanying four sentries when they all swap out for the next 8-hour shift. Locals often fish over the sides of the Westbridge, paying a very small fee to Villedoc on the way home based on the success of their efforts.

The Eastern Fields

Although farmland surrounds Villedoc on all sides, the fertile land to the east constitutes the bulk of the traditional crops that feed Villedoc and get traded across the Realm. The farming community is tight knit, always ready to help out any unfortunate neighbours who may run into a failed crop or some kind of pestilence, knowing that next time, it could be them. The eastern fields' farmsteaders are typically a cautious but friendly sort of folk to passersby, and some are willing to put strangers up for the night in their barn hay lofts and provide a warm meal in exchange for a couple coins.

The Western Fields

In addition to common crops like those found in the eastern farming fields, the land between Villedoc and the Westbridge hosts a more exotic array of herbs and weeds used in medicinal poultices, alchemical endeavours, and cooking. The farmers of the western fields are a bit more wary and brusque, quicker to pick up a sharp farming implement at the approach of strangers. This difference in disposition is due to their closer proximity to the more untamed wilds on the other side of the river. The western fields farming community is known for throwing wild revels around giant, raging bonfires at least once a month.

The Northern Fields

The further one moves north from Villedoc, the rockier the farming soil gets. The farmlands north of Villedoc run heavier on hardier crops like potatoes, peppers, gourds, and a variety of useful fungi in the northeast, closer to Sepulchre. The farmers here are more solitary, each choosing to mostly mind their own business. They will, if asked, help their neighbouring farmsteaders out when needed, but they lack the "big, happy family" kind of social structure possessed by the farmers of the eastern fields.

The Fishing Piers

South of Villedoc, on the banks of the Storm River, the fishing community thrives. Because of the tempestuous nature of the river, Villedoc does not sport a fleet of fishing vessels. Instead, a series of a dozen strong, wooden piers extend from the coastline out into the water up to a few hundred feet. Fishermen begin arriving before the sun has even risen on each morning, staking out the choicest spots on a first come, first served basis, usually staying until the sun has fully set. Although there are very few larger boats docked at these piers, roughly a dozen rowboats can be found tethered to the massive pilings. When the fishermen are feeling bold, they'll take their smaller craft an extra few hundred feet further out with their nets and try to bring in bigger hauls, knowing enough to always keep a weather eye on the river's mood from hour to hour, close enough to shore that they can row back to safety quickly.

Lookout Point

Beyond the southern edge of the town proper, there is a moderate rise near the banks of the Storm River. The highest peak of this little hilly area is known to be the best observation point for locals looking to catch glimpses of the mysterious Castle that lies across the Storm River from Villedoc. Young children and teenagers sometimes sneak away from their homes to climb the hills to Lookout Point, hoping that high winds might blow the river's tempestuous mist out of the way enough to allow them a good look at the Castle's high walls and towering spires. Local artists are also known to set up in this location hoping for the same, waiting for their moment to be able to accurately capture the sight in charcoal or paint. At night, this is also a favourite spot for hormonal young adults to come and exercise their wild urges.

NOTABLE NPCS OF THE VILLEDOC AREA

"We may not be the big, fancy City—but we don't want to be. Too much noise, too much filth. We're fine just where we are."

—Lord Mayor Alysandra Baslo

Some were born and raised in Villedoc, some came later, looking for a fresh start, new opportunities. Here are some of Villedoc's notable personalities, complete with plenty of opportunities to be story hooks.

Alysandra Baslo, Lord Mayor

As Villedoc's first elected female Lord Mayor—she did not inherit the title from her husband's recent passing from illness—Alysandra has kindled a fire that has begun separating Villedoc into two camps: those who think a woman can do any job as well as a man, and those who don't. Lord Mayor Baslo is a firebrand who speaks her mind and deals in a straightforward manner with everyone she encounters, a trait that ultimately earned her the vote to win the office two years ago. In addition to her direct, brusque demeanor, she strikes an imposing, commanding figure. Tall and wiry with muscles that have known hard labour all her life in the carpenter's shop, with a mane of wild auburn hair and a pronounced scar across her left jawline, her physical appearance stands out from the crowd—as does her strong clarion call soprano, a voice smoldering with strength, intelligence, and confidence. Although she came into office with a mission of progress and expansion, her tenure has been fraught with roadblocks. Roughly a third of Villedoc's populace resists her authority at almost every turn, demonstrating their resentment of a woman being the highest power in their hometown. Lord Mayor Baslo maintains a professional demeanor most days, but it has become a well-known fact that a certain amount of bold, public defiance of her edicts might result in a bareknuckle scrap in the street. Alysandra's knuckles are pink with layers of scar tissue, and she has not yet lost a brawl with any of her constituents—a fact that gives the less progressive-minded citizens pause in their judgment of her. Lord Mayor Baslo has two children: Barrith, a boy of 7, and Laithe, a girl of 6. After losing her husband shortly after taking office, Alyssandra has been stretched to her limit in running the town and managing her family life. She has only recently begun considering hiring some kind of housemaid/tutor to help her manage things at home.

BENEFITS

"S'Good to Be the Lord Mayor": If the Lord Mayor's attitude towards the PCs is Favourable or better, she offers a variety of options for favours, limited only by the GM's discretion and the players' imaginations. For the right cause, something that she believes will help her town and not hurt it, Lord Mayor Baslo can be a tremendous asset.

The Carriage House: If the Lord Mayor's attitude towards the PCs is Liked or better, she offers the PCs an open-ended rental of the large carriage house on her property for 5 gold per month, so long as they behave themselves. Bringing danger or property damage to her home and her children will drop Alysandra's attitude two levels and result in a withdrawal of the carriage house offer.

Strength: 4   **Craft:** 6
Life: 15

HARLA AND TOMSIN GALDEDAR, BLACKSMITHS

The Galdedar matriarch and patriarch are among the most well-known icons in Villedoc. Their family has been central to the region since the founding days of what would eventually become the second largest humanoid settlement in the Realm, and metal forged by the Galdedar's previous generations still holds together the most important buildings in the heart of the town. Harla has recently brought up the prospect of herself and Tomsin retiring to a more administrative/clerical role in their shop and letting their eldest son and daughter take the reins. Tomsin has developed a terribly bad back and a constantly aching right shoulder—he says his family calls it "hammer shoulder", an all too familiar ailment in their line of work. Harla is developing a chronic cough and burning in her chest that she secretly fears might turn into something worse but has not shared that with anyone. She plans to visit the mystic at the edge of town to see if she can read Harla's future, and possibly recommend a way to change her fate if the reading seems dire. Tomsin is having a hard time letting go of running the shop but knows in his heart that his wife is right. It's time to pass the torch…and the hammer.

BENEFITS

See the **Armoursmith** and **Weaponsmith** entries in Chapter 2 of the *Talisman Adventures* core book, under the **Stranger Descriptions** section.

HARLA
Strength: 4   **Craft:** 4
Life: 15

TOMSIN
Strength: 5   **Craft:** 3
Life: 15

GREY GALDEDAR, ELDEST SON

As the eldest child of Harla and Tomsin, Grey stands to inherit the shop when his parents retire or pass on. He is hesitant to speak his mind and voice his ardent desire to get out of Villedoc, to go explore the Realm and see what life has to offer other than this same small town he's lived his entire 25 years in. If asked directly by his parents, he knows he'll just comply and accept the mantle, and this leaves a cold stone in his heart every day. He doesn't know how to escape his fate without disappointing his family. To make matters worse, Grey is in love with a girl from the eastern farmlands who shares his desire to escape Villedoc and go adventuring. They regularly sneak away to Lookout Point at night and talk about all the things they could do in the City and in the beautiful, wild places of the Realm.

BENEFITS

See the **Armoursmith** entry in Chapter 2 of the *Talisman Adventures* core book, under the **Stranger Descriptions** section.

Strength: 5   **Craft:** 3
Life: 14

Rikke Galdedar, Eldest Daughter

The second eldest child of Harla and Tomsin, Rikke is as sharp as any of the blades her family forges. She knows that Grey is in line to inherit the shop and see her parents struggling physically with the grueling physical work, and senses that they're contemplating retirement. Rather than boldly speak up and voice her desire to leap the line and take over the family business, she just goes about her day and demonstrates her prowess in every area of the trade. She believes her actions speak for themselves, and while Grey is a good, strong man to have at the anvil and pumping the bellows, he doesn't have the head for business—and despite his silence, she knows Grey wants nothing more than to get out of Villedoc and explore the world around them. She's trying to figure out the best way to encourage her brother to pursue his dreams and move aside for her to take the reins of the family business without being uncouth.

Benefits

See the **Weaponsmith** entry in Chapter 2 of the *Talisman Adventures* core book, under the **Stranger Descriptions** section.

Strength: 3   **Craft:** 5
Life: 13

Jon Kimora, Healer

A central figure of Villedoc, Jon is greeted by smiles and nods wherever he goes around the region. Almost every citizen of Villedoc who has lived there for more than a couple of years can say that if he hasn't helped them directly with some kind of injury or ailment, he has helped a family member or close friend of theirs. A short, awkward-looking rangy man with a messy bird's nest of dark brown hair, a thick beard, and narrow, shrewd, sky-blue eyes, Kimora is not a very social person. Outside of doing direct healing business with the citizens of the region, Kimora spends most of his free time either replenishing his healing stock or talking long walks beyond the outskirts of town. Although he trained for his trade in the City, where he was born and raised, Jon Kimora had the opposite dream of most people in the Realm: he longed to escape the bustling, crowded, nosiy, smelly cacophony of the City and find another place to call home—a settlement big enough to require the regular presence of a good healer but without the constant sensory onslaught of the City. He enjoys wandering the pastoral hills and wild fields outside the settled area of Villedoc, but he also very much loves his quaint, orderly little home on the edge of town, and limited interactions with his fellow townsfolk. He has found his perfect, happy medium and will go to surprising lengths to keep it.

Benefits

See the **Healer** entry in Chapter 2 of the *Talisman Adventures* core book, under the **Stranger Descriptions** section.

Strength: 4   **Craft:** 4
Life: 12

"Auntie" Farrula Strizi, Mystic

As a precocious and curious child, Farrula always wanted to go where she was not allowed to go. Something about being denied access to places lit a fire inside her that drove her to pursue the forbidden. By the age of 18, she had explored every forbidden nook and cranny of the Villedoc region and moved to the City. She spent 5 years there, following the same urges to explore and to learn about hidden things. After she'd had her fill of the City, she spent the next couple of years exploring the wilds of the Outer Region, already knowing in her heart where she would eventually be pulled. Returning home at age 25, she bought herself a small boat and made the bold voyage across the Storm River to see the sights of the Middle Region. What happened over there, she has never said to anyone, but when she returned, she had visibly aged far more years than the amount of time she was gone. She also returned with the Third Eye—the ability to see into the future and bestow blessings and curses upon others. These days, she has had her fill of adventuring and seeking out the unknown, instead spending most of her time sitting on her front porch with her judgmental one-eyed cat, Mankins, and making sarcastic comments regarding passers-by. She entertains the occasional request for a fortune reading, blessing or curse, but is choosy about whom she grants favours.

Benefits

A Visit to Auntie's: If Auntie's attitude towards the PCs is Neutral or better, she grants them access to her cottage for an audience. If the PCs entertain her with their stories and/or convince her to do them a favour—either through great roleplaying or a successful **Entertain** or **Persuasion (Wits or Insight)** roll against **Difficulty 16**—she concedes to performing one or more spells for them in exchange for an amount of gold equal to the total spell points needed for casting plus 1d6. The constraints of her favours are **these:** she is able to cast any mystic spell as well as *Toadify!*, and she does not leave her cottage, so it must be magic that can be cast from within line of sight of her home. If the PCs visit Auntie and her attitude towards them is below Neutral, or falls below Neutral during the course of their audience with her, she casts *Toadify!* on every member of the party, in order of most to least irksome.

Beyond the River: If the PCs also convince Auntie through great roleplaying or a successful **Persuasion (Wits or Insight)** roll against **Difficulty 17**, she shares a little of her adventures in the Middle Region, supplying the PCs with some insight on how they might be able to travel there if they are so determined. She doesn't offer this information without good cause, however, so if the party expresses that they just want to "check it out" for the sake of curiosity and adventure, she immediately throws them out of her home. Any PC refusing to go after being told three times will find Auntie casting *Toadify!* on them.

Strength: 2 **Craft:** 9
Life: 18

Mankins

Strength: 1 **Craft:** 3
Life: 5

Garyx, the Gamemaster

Garyx is a stooped old man in his 60s, suspecting the end is coming for him sometime in the next several years, and welcoming it. He has lived the life he wanted, establishing a place in Villedoc that expands the mind and broadens horizons for the young minds who haven't yet succumbed to the "this is where I will spend my whole life and then die" mentality of the previous generations. He spends his days watching many of the town's children playing his various games and puzzles, buying them when their families could afford it, but Garyx was never a heavy hand in forcing 'his' children to convince their parents to part with their hard-earned money. Secretly, Garyx used to be a member of the Thieves Guild in the City. In his young adulthood, he amassed enough of a fortune to reinvent his identity, move to Villedoc, and build and run his own store without needing to worry about making much of a profit from year to year. His parting with the Guild was unpleasant, to put things mildly. None of his former associates know where he disappeared to, and Garyx intends to keep it that way. His ultimate dream is to find one of the more gifted children he sees mastering all of his games and puzzles and grooming that child into an apprentice—not just as a shopkeeper, but as a master thief, and have his prodigy one day return to the City to pay the Thieves Guild a visit…

Benefits

"I Love Puzzles!": If Garyx's attitude towards the PCs is Favourable or better, and if he sees them struggling with figuring something out around town, he offers his intellectual assistance to help them unravel any kind of puzzle or mystery. This is essentially a GM tool to provide NPC assistance to the players if they're having a hard time figuring out a necessary plot point. Garyx's aid should be delivered in such a way as to lead the players towards the solution, but not spoon-feed it to them.

Strength: 3 **Craft:** 6
Life: 15

Narlibuk, Sepulchre's Emissary

Narlibuk is a tall, slender ghoul who regularly visits Villedoc in the dead of night, coming from Sepulchre with his age-worn, rattling wagon in tow. He stops at the cabin of Farrula Strizi, the mystic, to see if there are any bodies who need to make the journey to Sepulchre. He sometimes tops and visits "Auntie" in her cabin, sharing a cup of tea and swapping stories—one of Narlibuk's few friends with whom he socializes. Normally a very docile and silent person, Narlibuk only exhibits hostility if someone tries to interrupt his duties in ferrying the dead to Sepulchre. In those rare occasions, Narlibuk becomes an entirely different creature. He carries two short, curved, barb-studded blades hidden on his back, beneath his dirty cloak. Any humanoid who has ever tried to hassle him in the wee hours of night ended up being added to the cart and never seen again. Narlibuk is also the only person living who has first-hand memories of Farrula's life before and right after she crossed the Storm River twice and underwent her transformation into an eerily prescient and powerful mystic.

Benefits

Conduit of the Dead: If any of the PCs should die in or near Villedoc and their body is brought to the Mystic or to any of the farmers north of town, Narlibuk comes to ferry them to Sepulchre to provide death rites and a full burial. As 'family' of the deceased, this provides a unique window for the PCs to be invited guests if they choose to accompany the body for the ceremony in the secretive ghoul settlement.

Strength: 7 **Craft:** 4
Life: 23

Baltis Sorgrin, Trading Post Owner/Operator

Baltis Sorgrin is a long-time member of the Merchants Guild who decided to take the plunge and invest his money in establishing a prominent trading outpost in Villedoc. His gamble has paid off in spades, seeing him become one of the wealthiest people in the north, if not the very top of the list. The master trader is a friendly but very shrewd salesman, bringing in rare and enticing goods of both magical and non-magical natures from all corners of the Realm and selling them at premium prices. He is an excellent bargainer and has turned his shop into a place of quiet influence around town, sometime exchanging favours and intelligence in lieu of money. As Villedoc grows—as it inevitably will—Sorgrin intends to remain a central figure in a position of power and influence roughly equal to the Lord Mayor, if not beyond it. He's not an evil man, but he knows what he wants and what he wants is control over his own destiny, including the town he has come to call home.

BENEFITS

"I Don't Do This for Just Anyone…": If Sorgrin's attitude towards the PCs is Favourable or better, he gives them a better deal than he would most customers, taking roughly 10% off the listed price of any basic goods listed in the *Talisman Adventures* core book. If Sorgrin's attitude towards the PCs is Liked or better, he also gives them access to "some items I have in the back", a cache of rare and/or magical items he doesn't make publicly known, instead reserving them for serious buyers. GMs can use this opportunity to allow the players access to some magic items of greater scarcity and power, or an obscure item that would be very difficult to locate by any other means. His 10% discount will not apply to these items, which should be priced accordingly, if not marked up.

Strength: 4   **Craft:** 5
Life: 16

ASJA VALLAR, VISITING TRADER

Asja is a willowy, dark-skinned sprite who makes a circuit of the Realm with her caravan of trusty trolls and one shrewish little human bookkeeper named Palfrey. She is a recognized face in Villedoc, and her arrivals are celebrated by the town's children for her reputation of bringing entertainments for public display/use. She also gives out private little treats like chocolate or cinnamon bars to certain children. Secretly, Asja does this to develop young contacts who will tell her the comings and goings of the town. She trusts the honesty of children over the deceitfulness and conflicting agendas of adults. She is the main supplier for Baltis Sorgin's shop, always bringing him rare, in-demand components and interesting trinkets. He and she exchange news during their visits, usually over drinks at Second Home, and she is his primary lifeline to the Merchants Guild in the City.

BENEFITS

The Latest from the City: If Asja's attitude towards the PCs is Favourable or better, she brings them the latest news and gossip from the City in exchange for any news they may have from other parts of the Realm, or just a good story of their adventures. If they catch her before she offloads her latest caravan of goods to Baltis Sorgrin, she lets them inspect her wagons and is willing to deal with them using the mechanics for either the **Barterer** or **Pedlar** entries in Chapter 2 of the *Talisman Adventures* core book, under the **Stranger Descriptions** section.

Strength: 1   **Craft:** 6
Life: 10

DELL ROWAN, HUNTSMAN

A member of the "westies"—the western farming community—Dell lives with her husband and two children near the eastern base of the Westbridge. She makes a living crossing the bridge to hunt for game in the wilds across the Storm River. The Lord Mayor has given Dell a lifetime pass to cross the bridge in either direction for free, in exchange for a certain amount of game supplied to the city per month—a mark Dell has never missed. She is considered the most skilled hunter in Villedoc. Dell's best friend is Kyriel, the solitary elf who lives in a little house up in the trees just across the Westbridge. Dell and Kyriel often spend extended time in the woods hunting together, and Dell has learned many tips and tricks from his elven friend. A strange, romantic tension has developed between the two of them, something neither of them has ever brought up aloud, and Dell is determined to push it down and ignore it.

BENEFITS

"They Went That Way!": Dell can be hired by the party as a wilderness tracker/hunter for 1 gold per day. PCs assisted by Dell gain a bonus die when tracking prey or when making a Watcher test.

Good References: If Kyriel's attitude towards the PCs is Favourable or better and he communicates this to Dell, her attitude will go up by two levels.

Strength: 4   **Craft:** 4
Life: 17   **Armour:** 1

KYRIEL, ELF IN THE TREEHOUSE

This loner elf remembers a time when there was no Villedoc in his backyard. Always feeling like he never quite fit in with elven society, he had left his homeland and set out to build his own private life somewhere uninhabited by humanoids. It was only a matter of time before some of them realized the strategic value of developing a settlement at that fertile T-juncture of the river and built it up. Over the decades, Kyriel has stood quietly watchful over Villedoc from the other side of the river as the town has grown, mostly keeping to himself. About a decade ago, he struck up an unexpected friendship with a human woman, a hunter named Dell who routinely came to track and bring down game in his neck of the woods. He cherishes their friendship but senses that something about it is changing, something that he doesn't quite understand, so he remains silent about it for the time being.

BENEFITS

The Clubhouse: If Kyriel's attitude towards the PCs is Favourable or better, he offers them the use of his arboreal abode as a sanctuary/safe house. Kyriel's attitude will drop if the PCs abuse his hospitality or bring danger or damage to his home.

Good References: If Dell Rowan's attitude towards the PCs is Favourable or better and she communicates this to Kyriel, his attitude will go up by two levels.

Strength: 5   **Craft:** 6
Life: 20   **Armour:** 2

Ilona Greenthorne, Farmer

Ilona has spent her 20 years digging at the earth, growing and harvesting crops alongside her parents and siblings in the fertile farmlands to the east of Villedoc proper—and she's reached her limit. She wants nothing more than to escape her life and become someone else, somewhere else. Her father, Aric Greenthorne, is the head of the eastern farm families' loose "union", their spokesperson with the town's market, setting prices and working with the Lord Mayor to keep conditions healthy for the eastern farmers. She knows it would be disappointing to her father for her to up-and-leave, but she already has a bag packed, and every night she flirts with the idea of sneaking out through her bedroom window and disappearing down the road to a new beginning. What keeps her in Villedoc (for now) is her love for Grey Galdedar, the eldest son of the town blacksmiths. He wants to flee this life as well, and they want to be together, but his family business weighs more heavily on him. It's an anchor, keeping them both stuck here for the time being—but she's working on that.

Benefits

"I Hope You Like Hay": If Ilona's attitude towards the PCs is Neutral or better, she lets the PCs sleep and store their things in one of the smaller barns on her family's farmland for 1d3 days in exchange for 1 gold.
Strength: 3   **Craft:** 2
Life: 12

Matta Hornsong, Farmer

Matta Hornsong is a tall, barrel-chested figure with long, unkempt brown hair and even wilder beard. He and his massive horses work the largest tract of the western farmlands, and they look to him to represent them in town. Matta is a hard worker, an aggressive negotiator, and a wild party animal. He believes that you should play as hard as you work—that's the balance in a perfect life. Enjoy what you've earned. Earn what you want to enjoy. If not the driving force behind it, he is always found at the centre of every late-night revel held in the westlands. Matta is also a veteran at fighting the occasional creature that encroaches from the wild lands across the river, fearlessly wielding his stout rake and spade in combat when called upon. His namesake comes from the oversized horn he claims came from the graveyard of a family of dragons he found in the Crags when he was younger, which he uses to summon his farmers during emergencies. Its unmistakable sound can be heard clearly for at least a mile away.

Benefits

Blowhard: If Matta's attitude towards the PCs is Favourable or better, and if they plead a convincingly urgent case, he blows his horn to summon the "Westies" together for an emergency meeting for them.
Strength: 7   **Craft:** 2
Life: 18

Boha, Farmer

The mysterious figure known only as Boha is the representative of the anti-social farmers of Villedoc's northlands. A tall, gaunt human who almost resembles a ghoul, Boha is soft-spoken but intense. The prices for the northern crops are not to be negotiated; they simply are what he says they are. Boha has no known family and no strong friendships that anyone is aware of. He works his mushroom farms and his gourd patches and visits with the farm families of the north in a purely logistical manner to keep track of crop status and other pertinent details, but he spends little time or effort socializing with anyone. Despite this seemingly cold demeanor, Boha takes good care of his people. If someone falls ill, he is the first to speed to the healer's cottage to get the needed medicines. If there is a fire, he is in the front row of the water line, throwing buckets on the blaze despite the danger. When asked about his past, Boha always makes an abrupt exit from the conversation.

Benefits

"I Hope You Like Hay": If Boha's attitude towards the PCs is Neutral or better, he lets the PCs sleep and store their things in one of the smaller barns on his farmland for 1d3 days in exchange for 1 gold.
Strength: 4   **Craft:** 4
Life: 15

Raina Lachlan, Ambitious Young Fisher

At the volatile age of 18, Raina Lachlan has no parents—both lost to the sea—and no siblings. She is one of the few people in Villedoc who owns a seafaring vessel, albeit a modest one. She works her own longboat and brings in nets of small fish for a living, making slapdash repairs to the little cottage she grew up in, and dreaming of the deep blue sea. She longs to explore what's further out there, not believing that this "Realm" she knows from her maps is all there is in the whole circle of the world. She inherited her parents' lack of fear (which ended up leading to their demise) but has more of a sense of wonder and ambition to explore than either of them ever possessed. What's holding her back is a crew and a bigger ship. Her little rowboat won't withstand the fury of the sea, and she can't work a bigger boat on her own. She's begun prowling the town proper at night in search of souls who might be willing and have the right skills to join her—and a way to secure or build a larger ship.

BENEFITS

Dare the Sea: If Raina's attitude towards the PCs is Favourable or better, she offers to take them out to sea and pilot them to a coastal point of their choosing—under the condition they help her steal a big enough ship from the harbour (or have one built somehow), and she gets to keep the ship after dropping them off. A successful **Persuasion (Wits)** roll against a **Difficulty 14** will convince Raina to allow the PCs to be her crew—at least for the time being. The PCs' adeptness at taking her orders and helping her handle the ship at sea will determine how long Raina will accommodate this relationship.
Strength: 3   **Craft:** 3
Life: 15

GARSON THE HOOK, OLD FISHERMAN

A stout, loudmouthed figurehead in the Villedoc fishing community, Garson earned his name "the Hook" for his above-average luck in landing big, lucrative catches in his red-painted fishing boat, the *Sea Devil*. Garson is one of the five people making up the fishing community's "Big Boat", meaning their elected representatives to the Lord Mayor and the markets, not just in Villedoc, but for markets around the Realm, including the City. He's a short, stout figure built as solidly as a stone smokehouse, with salt and pepper black hair and beard and skin like tanned leather. Garson feels like the fishermen take a backseat to the farmers in the eyes of Villedoc, a sentiment that leads him to be fiercely protective of his people and prone to getting confrontational at any perceived whiff of offence.

BENEFITS

Big Fish in a Medium Pond: If Garson's attitude towards the PCs is Favourable or better, he summons the fisherfolk of Villedoc together in an emergency meeting for them.
Strength: 6   **Craft:** 2
Life: 19

CORT HILLARD, BUILDER

The most experienced and skilled builder in town (he refuses to let anyone apply the word "architect" to him) is Cort Hillard. His father and grandfather built many of the buildings in Villedoc, and it has fallen to Cort to make repairs on those old timbers and bricks as well as helping to raise up the next generations of buildings as the town continues to slowly expand and develop. He has a natural talent for understanding the physics of building design, although he lacks the vocabulary to articulate it. He sees himself as a common labourer, even if others see him as a rare talent. In between erecting buildings, Cort pays the bills by fixing things the townsfolk bring to him: broken wagons, plows, furniture, and more.

BENEFITS

"Sure, I Can Build That": If Cort's attitude towards the PCs is Neutral or better, he accepts the PCs' request for him to build a house or house-sized structure for them in exchange for a higher-end-of-fair price by Villedoc standards. Cost will depend on the details of the structure being built and how adept the party is at haggling.
Strength: 5   **Craft:** 3
Life: 16

ZENIUS BROCK, TOWN TREASURER

As cold and hard as the coins he's charged with counting and protecting, Zenius Brock is not Villedoc's most popular figure—especially not at tax collection time. Lord Mayor Baslo knows Zenius can be a hard bastard, but he's *her* hard bastard. Despite his off-putting nature and his greasy, rodentlike visage, Baslo knows that Zenius Brock is a man true to his word and uncompromisingly loyal in his duties. Brock attends to his post with as much vigor and professional pride as anyone in any job around Villedoc, even knowing that it makes him one of the more hated people in the region. He secretly pines for the Lord Mayor position, but he understands that even with her husband dead and buried, there is no realistic chance she would ever grow to have romantic thoughts about someone like him. And besides—that would be professionally inappropriate.

BENEFITS

Benefit Name: If Brock's attitude towards the PCs is Favourable or better, he can be persuaded to open Villedoc's vaults for a one-time, short-term monetary loan to the PCs—if they can convince him that the cause is worthy and in Villedoc's best interests. On a successful **Persuasion (Wits or Insight)** roll against **Difficulty 17**, Zenius draws up paperwork for a loan in the amount of up to whatever the successful roll was. The PCs have two weeks to repay the town coffers. Defaulting on this contract lowers the attitudes of Zenius Brock, Lord Mayor Baslo, Captain Druce, and Jamen Windish by two levels. If the adventure demonstrates to the town officials that the PCs did in fact put the money to good use in the service of Villedoc, any part or all of the loan may be forgiven by the Lord Mayor at the GM's discretion.
Strength: 2   **Craft:** 4
Life: 12

THALIA DRUCE, CAPTAIN OF THE TOWN GUARD

While she may not have the imposing size she wished for, Villedoc's Captain of the Town Guard is a wiry-muscled, iron-willed pillar of order in the community. Her eyes are as sharp as a hawk's, and she walks her

patrols day and night, ever vigilant for threats from the wilderness or from any burgeoning criminal enterprises within. She does have a habit of reacting too harshly at times, especially when people give her or her town guards attitude, which is why she relies on the cooler head of her second in command, Jamen Windish. When real danger rears its head, however, Thalia is a force to be feared. She wields her trademark warhammer like a tornado, utilizing a strange, spinning, dance-like technique passed down through the Druce family for generations.

Benefits

"O Captain, My Captain": If Captain Druce's attitude towards the PCs is Favourable or better, and assuming they respect the law and order around Villedoc, Druce offers her assistance in any effort that seems like it will protect the town from mortal danger, corruption, or any other type of negative effect. This could mean she listens to the PCs' advice in constructing additional defenses against a specific threat, doubling the Watch patrols for a short time, organizing an emergency town meeting, putting extra effort into apprehending a criminal offender—the options are up to the imagination of the players and the limits of the GM's discretion.

Strength: 5   **Craft:** 5
Life: 20   **Armour:** 4

Jamen Windish, Town Guard

Mild-mannered and soft-spoken, Jamen is highly regarded around town as a fair and just keeper of the peace and enforcer of the town's laws. He usually resolves conflicts between townsfolk within minutes, rarely needing to use force. During instances where he does need to break a sweat, the large, solidly built guard prefers non-lethal weaponry, like his signature bolos that he uses to entangle criminal offenders. He also carries a stout quarterstaff that he uses to knock people down and keep them pinned there until their temper cools.

While he doesn't command the kind of shock-and-awe respect of Captain Druce, his even-tempered presence is a comfort to the good people of Villedoc.

BENEFITS

Cooler Heads: If Jamen's attitude towards the PCs is Favourable or better, he keeps an eye out on behalf of the party and can be used by the GM as a tool for many **scenarios:** as an early warning system, help in tracking down a particular person around town, breaking up a fight the PCs don't want to engage in (or they're losing), etc.

Strength: 6   **Craft:** 2
Life: 20   **Armour:** 3

KIT CARRIS, BUDDING THIEF

The citizens of Villedoc recognise her as friendly Kit from the market, a skinny, pimply girl of 17 who works her family's fruit carts during the daylight hours and can sometimes be seen at *Second Home*, using her charm and humour to ply the adults to buy her drinks. Kit's dark secret is that she's a thief at heart. The lure of picking people's pockets, of slipping little trinkets into her pockets, of stealing around at night, peeking into peoples' windows to learn about them—she can't resist it. She doesn't seek to hurt anyone and never steals anything that she thinks would derail someone's life, but the need inside her to continue down this path and to improve her skills and take bigger and bigger risks is starting to concern her. She's not sure how to reconcile her growing mischievous cravings in a small town like Villedoc. It's only a matter of time before Captain Druce catches her in the act and brings her secret to light.

BENEFITS

Shady Cravings: If Kit's attitude towards the PCs is Favourable or better, and if they somehow become aware of her 'hobby', she offers her services in exchange for gold. Her price is up to the GM's discretion, commensurate with the task for which she's being hired. If Kit's attitude is Neutral or lower, see the **Cutpurse** entry in Chapter 2 of the *Talisman Adventures* core book, under the **Stranger Descriptions** section.

Strength: 2   **Craft:** 4
Life: 12

ARLEE AND GRAHAM HEARTHSTONE, TAVERN OWNERS/OPERATORS

Graham Hearthstone is a third-generation owner of Villedoc's favourite nighttime social spot, Second Home. His grandparents tore down the previous ramshackle watering hole and built an entirely new three-story building from the ground up. Arlee and Graham live on the top floor with their only child, a daughter of nine years named Mina—although Arlee is currently pregnant with their second. Arlee is a fantastic cook, and Graham tends bar with an affable demeanor as he listens to the townsfolk share stories and swap news. As a result, the Hearthstones are among the most well-informed people in Villedoc. So much so that, on rare occasions, the Lord Mayor has authorized Captain Druce to secretly slip them a few coins in exchange for anything they might know about particularly important subjects that may elude the notice of the authorities.

BENEFITS

The Scoop: If Hearthstones' attitude towards the PCs is Favourable or better (they're counted as one entity for all attitude purposes), and if the PCs are paying customers or pay the Hearthstones 1 gold for their assistance, they try to help glean information from the Villedoc community. The GM privately rolls 2d6 for them when seeking a piece of information and the PCs are told to come back in 24 hours while the Hearthstones keep their ears open around the town chatter.

THE SCOOP	
Roll	**Result**
1–3	They hear absolutely nothing regarding the information the PCs are after.
4–6	They hear loose, conflicting rumours regarding the information the PCs are after. The rumours may be entirely unreliable, or one of them might be somewhat helpful.
7–9	They hear something regarding the information the PCs are after and share helpful info.
10+	They've already heard something useful regarding the information the PCs are after and share it immediately. No need to wait 24 hours.

ARLEE
Strength: 2   **Craft:** 3
Life: 10

GRAHAM
Strength: 3   **Craft:** 2
Life: 10

JOSS JARMIN, BOUNTY HUNTER

One of the most polarizing personalities in Villedoc is Joss Jarmin, the town's most famous and most regular bounty hunter. Joss keeps a sturdy little log cabin on the west edge of town and is considered a permanent resident, although he disappears for stretches of time as is normal for someone in his line of work. Half of the town loves him, and the other half wouldn't be sad to see him fall into the river fully armored. Many of the children like him for his bounty hunter stories, as well as the knowledge that Joss occasionally spreads coins around to them in exchange for being his little eyes and ears throughout the area if he thinks one of his bounties is hiding out locally. The town toughs enjoy his company as a drinking and gambling buddy. The more 'respectable' members of the community see him as a bad element and would prefer to see him pull up stakes and find someplace else to hang his helmet. Despite his buffoonish exterior that he presents to the world, Joss keeps a keen eye out for any new faces to the area, always ready to get the jump on an opportunity to score a new bounty.

BENEFITS

"They Went That Way!": Joss Jarmin can be hired by the party. He tries to charge 2 gold per day but can be talked down to 1 if the PCs haggle (and will complain about it regularly). PCs assisted by Jarmin gain a bonus die when tracking prey or when making a Watcher test.

Dirty Deeds: If Jarmin's attitude towards the PCs is Favourable or better, he charges gold for a variety of services beyond simple tracking. There's very little the man won't do for money. His fees are up to the GM's discretion, commensurate with the task for which he's being hired.

Strength: 4 **Craft:** 4
Life: 16 **Armour:** 3

FATHER ROSEMONT, PRIEST

A long-time pillar of Villedoc, Father Rosemont has been the senior priest at the temple for 20 years. He has a handful of acolytes and other members of his congregation who help with upkeep of the temple and other administrative and logistical duties so that he can focus on writing and delivering sermons and performing other spiritual services around town as needed. He performs marriages and funerals, gives blessings over new child births, delivers last rites, and lends spiritual and moral counseling to those in need. He has no dark secrets, no hidden motivations, no checkered past: he is simply a face-value holy man who understands that he is relatively boring, and he's just fine with that.

BENEFITS

The Only Priest Around: If Father Rosemont's attitude towards the PCs is Neutral or better, he allows them sanctuary in his temple for a short rest once per adventure. Any PC rolling 1d6 to recover life or spell points (as described in Chapter 2 of the *Talisman Adventures* core book under "Resting") adds 2 to their rolls. If Father Rosemont's attitude towards the PCs is Favourable or better, he offers his services to cast any of the following spells (while humbly hinting that the contribution of gold to the temple's coffers goes a long way to sustaining the only temple in Villedoc): Blessed, Cure Poison, Cure Disease, Healing, Greater Healing. Keep in mind Father Rosemont's spell point limit. Once he reaches his limit, he requires rest and is unavailable for any more spells that day. Abuse of this favour will lower Father Rosemont's attitude towards the PCs.

Strength: 3 **Craft:** 5
Life: 14

Mikaela Arzhoun, Horsemaster

The owner of the largest stables in Villedoc, Mikaela rents and sells horses and other beasts of burden. She's a harsh negotiator; her prices are at a premium because her animals are top quality and because there are no other decent, easily accessible stables for dozens of miles in any direction—of which she is quite aware. Mikaela is anti-social, preferring the company of animals to people most days. She has a few hired hands at her ranch, but she does the bulk of the animal purchasing and training herself. She is usually clad in riding leathers, has her dark hair bound up in a frayed, windswept bun, and walks with a pronounced limp (from a riding accident that happened years ago when some raiding goblins spooked her horse). She is also known to turn down a sale every now and then if she suspects a potential buyer would be cruel and unfit to own animals.

Benefits

Saddle Up: If Mikaela's attitude towards the PCs is Favourable or better, she gives them a 1d6 gold discount on any beast of burden they wish to buy from her. If her attitude towards them is below Neutral, she refuses to sell them any animals until her attitude is raised to at least Neutral.

Strength: 3   **Craft:** 3
Life: 13

Hunter, Prince of Cats

Villedoc is home to any number of stray creatures without owners, and one of them is a human boy. Approximately 10 years of age, give or take, this wild child is known only as "Hunter", a name he earned when he was first spotted in the area years ago, prowling and hunting alongside a cadre of feral cats. For some reason, the felines of the area seem to flock to him and serve as his family as he runs around the countryside. Nobody is certain of the boy's origins, but Hunter speaks the Common tongue well enough, and seems to have knowledge of things that suggests he was raised in at least some semblance of civilization before appearing around Villedoc. He stops through the town proper at least once a day most days with his furry entourage to collect scraps from Second Home or wherever else smells good at the moment. Captain Druce has become fond of the child despite the minor element of chaos he tends to generate, and most of the townsfolk enjoy his visits. Hunter spends most of his nights sleeping on hay in some barn around any of the regional farmlands. The farmers don't mind, so long as he doesn't cause trouble with their livestock or crops.

Benefits

Fuzzy, Fanged, Feral Friends: If Hunter's attitude towards the PCs is Favourable or better, or if they are bribed with a warm meal and some fresh milk, he and his friends do a favour for the PCs that is within their capability. The details of what they might be capable of and willing to do is at the GM's discretion, although Hunter will not knowingly put his cats in any real danger.

Strength: 2   **Craft:** 2
Life: 10

CHAPTER 3: ANCESTRIES AND CLASSES

ANCESTRY

Heroes of the Realm have been known to hail from ancestries other than those described in the core rulebook of *Talisman Adventures*. One of these, long considered to be a scourge upon the Realm, has begun to appear more frequently in civilised parts of the world. Although still not accepted by many, goblin heroes have begun to make a name for themselves, and soon, they'll perhaps be walking openly and proudly in the streets of the City and beyond.

Goblin

"What it's like being a goblin? It's great! We can eat everything in sight and still be hungry. We literally don't know the meaning of 'defeat.' In fact, there are a lot of words we don't know. Most of all, we can make a home anywhere, in the small places that other people of the Realm don't notice. Really simplifies things. Who wouldn't want this life?"

—Tylk the Joyful, goblin extraordinaire

Culture

Although goblins can be found almost anywhere in the Realm, most goblins who live above ground call Craven Idol Woods their home. There, they live alongside sinister fey creatures that are their allies, rivals, or bitter enemies. The goblins believe that they were once fey of root and branch, muck, and mire, but pulled themselves up out of the earth and shed that skin. The fey of the Craven Idol Woods are believed to be their shadow-selves, bolstered when the goblins break the rules of kinship or hospitality.

A goblin tribe includes scores or hundreds of goblins. Four major tribes have divided up the Craven Idol Woods, while seven minor tribes are scattered across the rest of the Realm. The tribes mark their territories with fetishes of bone, sticks, and hair. The fetishes around villages ward away the most powerful of fey, while others signal the forest's dangers or mark tribal territory borders. A true war between the goblin tribes is unthinkable, as the elders stop territorial conflicts from escalating beyond harsh words and a few broken bones. Goblins who leave the Craven Idol Woods form a new tribe wherever they settle.

Goblin Perspective

The goblins are confused that many of the Realm's people outside the Craven Idol Woods see them as Evil. The goblin raids that range from the woods toward Villedoc are simple foraging parties—in their eyes, at least. Whatever wrongs they do, they pay back by the hospitality that the goblins show toward lost travelers in the Wood. The Wood's unsavoury reputation is well-earned, but it's no doing of theirs. The carving that turned the Ancient One of the forest toward Evil was made by misguided tribal elders countless moons ago, or by sinister fey masquerading as goblins.

Theft is one of the worst offenses against hospitality, second only to assassination. Even so, many goblins find that they excel as Thieves and Assassins, so they rationalise their work as scouting, foraging, and "shadow-work." Some, of course, reject the morals of goblin society and openly embrace the Ancient One as a representative of the Dark Powers in the Realm.

Goblins who leave the Woods live at the edges of society, subsisting in forgotten or unused spaces and using scraps no one else wants. The ingenuity and tenacity of this life is a source of pride, however, so it both offends and confuses them that others would regard them as scavengers or thieves.

Goblins give little thought to the Wizard or his deeds. They believe their history started when they separated from the fey, a time that came after his rise and fall. A few goblin lore-keepers suggest that the Wizard might be directly responsible for their decision to leave the fey, though how exactly that might have happened, or why, is unclear.

Character Modifiers

Attribute Caps: Increase the maximum for Agility or Wits to 7.

Bonus Skill: Gain the Stealth or Survival skill.

Backgrounds

Roll 1d6 (or choose one):

1–2 Idol-keeper: +1 Wits. Gain the Lore skill. You maintain the fetishes that tell goblins how to survive in the Craven Idol Woods and keep them safe from the most malevolent of its denizens. When you are attacked in Psychic Combat, you gain a bonus die on your Psychic defence test.

3–4 Shadow-worker: +1 Agility. Gain the Notice skill. The canopy of the Craven Idol Woods creates a sheltering dark, where you do such deeds as the tribe prefers not to see. While you are in a forest, you can perceive things in darkness as if you had the elven Night Sight special ability.

5–6 Hidden Villager: +1 Insight. Gain the Survival skill. You survive on next to nothing and live unnoticed in settlements dominated by other peoples of the Realm. You need half as much food as normal, and when you roll a

Survival (Insight) test to avoid notice while camping, you automatically increase your success level by one step.

Special Abilities

Goblins Live Everywhere: While in any settlement outside the Craven Idol Woods, you can make an **Investigation (Insight)** test. The Difficulty is based on the size of the settlement: 8 for the City, 20 for a small hamlet, and somewhere in the range for any other location. On any Success, you can contact goblins (or others) able to help you. Great and Exceptional Successes indicate that they have more applicable resources to aid you.

Choose one:

Danger Sense: The Craven Idol Woods have given goblins a well-honed sense for danger. You gain a bonus die on all checks to surprise enemies or avoid being surprised.

Mark of the Ancient One: You have carved your name into the bark of the Ancient One, and its mark is upon you as well. You learn the basic spell Sacred Offering, which you cast as a Nature spell. You can cast it without expending Spell Points once per day. When you do so, you can choose to roll **Lore (Wits)** instead of **Spellcasting (Nature)** for your Spellcasting test. You cannot choose to burn this spell.

Tribal Bond: The bonds of kinship and friendship are as hard as iron for a goblin. If the influence (magical or nonmagical) of another would cause you to harm your tribe or allies, you can make a free **Fortitude (Resolve)** test to shake off that influence a moment before you cause harm. The Difficulty is 12, or equal to whatever test you failed that put them under their control.

CLASSES

Here you'll find three new classes for the *Talisman Adventures Fantasy RPG*. All of these classes are particularly well suited to city or other civilised environments. The alchemist is skilled at creating potions and other alchemical substances, which are often useful in court intrigue. The gladiator is adept at fighting in close-quarters environments such as city alleyways. And finally, the tinkerer can build, repair, and upgrade cunning inventions and traps.

ALCHEMIST

In the City, an elite group of scholars and artisans have unlocked secrets of transmuting base matter into gold, and gold into power. Some point out that merchants accomplish the former and nobles the latter, but the truth is that every day, merchants, nobles, and others seek out alchemists for their talents. Most alchmists choose the comfort and security of patronage in the City, Villedoc, or another of the larger settlements rather than a life of adventure, but some become heroes of the Realm while learning to refine not just crude metal, but the soul itself.

The Great Work Lies Within

Many alchemists find their purpose as an apothecary, selling medicines or poisons. Others pursue deeper secrets, making more powerful potions or incense, transmuting base matter into gold, or distilling magical power for their own curious ends. They tend to regard themselves as outside the struggle of Light and Dark, believing that pursuing a deeper understanding of the Realm and the soul requires moral neutrality. Even so, their creations shape the fate of the Realm as much as any hero or villain.

Playing an Alchemist

Vast stores of knowledge, investigative ability, and quick wit get an alchemist into and out of danger. Most alchemists prefer to keep their distance in battle, using flasks or envenomed knives, or closing to within a few paces to place a censer or command a homunculus to attack.

The strength of your creations comes from your grasp of secret wisdom, so you'll want to increase your Wits and overall Craft scores as much as possible. Agility helps your aim with envenomed thrown weapons.

Creating an Alchemist

When you choose the alchemist class, you gain the following features:

Strength: 2

Craft: 4

Life: 9 + (Mettle or Resolve) +1 per level

Skills: You gain Artisan, Bargain, Fortitude, Heal, Spellcasting, and Throw. You also gain your choice of Notice or Sleight of Hand. You gain a focus in Spellcasting (Alchemy) and can choose a focus in Heal or Throw.

Core Features

When you choose this class, you gain two features common to all alchemists, Gold Refinement and Unstable Potion-Making.

Gold Refinement

The core of alchemy is transforming base metals into gold, most frequently iron, lead, or steel. You can transform one object made entirely or primarily of metal into Gold, equal to one less than its standard purchase price. This takes one hour for every 2 Gold of value, and it requires both your alchemical tools and unrestricted access to the metal object.

Unstable Potion-Making

At the beginning steps of alchemy, you can create unstable potions or poisons, which hold their efficacy only while you maintain them. At the start of an adventure, or with two hours of work, you can create a total of 5 doses of the following potions and poisons. These doses lose their potency once used, or once they are out of your possession for 1 hour. When you create new unstable potions and poisons, you can replace expended or existing doses, but you are limited to 5 at a time.

- **Antivenom:** A character that drinks this potion, or has it administered to them by another character as an action, reduces the damage it takes from poison by 1d6 for the next hour. They can also make a new **Fortitude (Mettle)** test against the poison's original Difficulty to resist a poison active in their system at the time the antivenom is administered.
- **Basilisk's Blood Poison:** This is an injected poison. When this poison affects a creature, the alchemist rolls a **Spellcasting (Alchemy)** test against the creature's Threat. On a Success, the creature takes 1d6 damage each round on their turn until they die or the poison is cured.
- **Cleansing Potion:** A character who drinks this potion, or has it administered to them by another character as an action, can make a new **Fortitude (Mettle or Resolve)** test against the Difficulty of any curse, disease, or spell currently affecting them. If the character succeeds in that test, the curse, disease, or spell ends. If the recipient of this potion is an NPC, roll 1d6 and add the result to its Threat. If that total is greater than the Difficulty of a curse, disease, or spell affecting that character, the effect ends.
- **Healing Potion:** A character who drinks this potion, or has it administered to them by another character as an action, heals 1d6 Life or one Wound. If the alchemist spends ⬤, it restores 6 Life and one Wound instead. If the recipient is unconscious, they regain 1d6 Life and become conscious.
- **Midnight Poison:** This poison can be mixed into food or drink, causing it to become difficult to detect 1 minute after application. At the next midnight after a creature consumes this poison, the alchemist makes a **Spellcasting (Alchemy)** test.
  - **Failure:** The Midnight Poison has no effect.
  - **Success:** The target takes 2d6 damage from the poison.
  - **Great Success:** The target is unconscious for 2d6 days.
  - **Exceptional Success:** The target dies.

At 3rd, 6th, and 9th level, your maximum carrying capacity of unstable doses increases by 1.

Advancement Features

At 1st, 2nd, 3rd, 5th, and 7th level, you can choose one of the following advancements or choose from the general advancement list in *Talisman Adventures Fantasy RPG*. At 6th, 9th, and 10th level, you can choose the improved version of an advancement you have previously selected.

Practical

Prerequisite: You do not have the Eccentric advancement.

You make a habit of crafting practical goods that you can sell or use in your adventures. You can make a flask of oil, a small vial of ink, or one use of winter oil with half an hour of work and materials equal to half their Gold cost. When you make an item with a listed cost of 1 Gold, you use 1 Gold and can make twice as much of it.

You can purify water that is naturally or magically befouled with 5 minutes of work.

Improved: You can spend 🔘 to make a flask of oil, a small vial of ink, or one use of winter oil with 5 minutes of work, at no material cost.

Eccentric

Prerequisite: You do not have the Practical advancement.

You carry all sorts of oddments with you, whether at home in your laboratory or travelling the Realm. Who knows what's in your pockets, pouches, and bandoliers? Certainly not you. When you spend 1 minute of searching through your backpack, belt pouches, and pockets you don't remember sewing into your clothes, you can spend 🔘 and name one item, worth 5 Gold or less, found in the Tools and Market Goods table in the *Talisman Adventures Fantasy RPG*. Roll 1d3, and if the result is equal to or greater than the Load of the item you named, you find it (if the item is <1 Load it is always successful. Items you "discover" in this way don't have Load for you until you discover them.

Using this feature two or more times in a day increases the cost to 🔘🔘 until sunset.

Improved: As an action, you can spend 🔘 to discover an additional dose of an unstable potion or poison that you can make, and immediately use it.

Incense-Burner

Prerequisite: Craft 5+, and you do not have the Homunculus-Grower advancement.

You have developed alchemy suitable for inhalation as an incense, using a censer and incense cones. Creatures that don't breathe or that are immune to poison, such as spirits and undead, aren't affected by incense.

You can make an incense cone with 5 Gold in materials, 1 hour of work, and access to your alchemical tools. One incense cone burns for 30 minutes or until extinguished.

When you use a censer, you can control the area of the smoke by opening or closing vents on the censer. Choose a 2-metre, 4-metre, 6-metre, or 8-metre radius for the area of the smoke; you can change the area as an action as long as you are within reach of the censer. You can also close all of the vents, which extinguishes the incense cone in 5 rounds. Censers are often carried on long chains, and can be thrown, with a range of 10 metres and a maximum range of 20 metres.

You learn to make the following types of incense.

- **Scouring Cloud Incense:** This incense creates a foul acidic cloud. When you light this incense, make a **Spellcasting (Alchemy)** test. Any creatures within the area of this smoke with Threat equal to or lower than your test result is affected, as is a player character in the area whose **Fortitude (Mettle)** test is a failure against your test result. An affected creature takes 1d6 damage from acid at the start of its turn. A creature mostly or entirely covered in armour takes 1d3 damage, and the armour degrades by 3.
- **Meditation Incense:** This calming scent improves mental clarity, granting a bonus die to **Fortitude (Resolve)** tests to characters within the area of its smoke.
- **Warding Incense:** This incense drives away spirits and undead. When you light this incense, roll a **Spellcasting (Alchemy)** test. A spirit or undead creature with Threat equal to or lower than your test result can't willingly enter the area of this smoke, and all spirits and undead take 1d3 damage if they start their turn in the area of this smoke.

Improved: You can spend 🔘 to choose a character to exclude from the effects of an incense cone you burn, for the duration of that cone. You can spend any amount of 🔘 you want in this way.

Homunculus-Grower

Prerequisite: Strength 4+, and you do not have the Incense-Burner advancement.

Using alchemical procedures and components from your own body, you have created a homunculus, a Follower that is utterly devoted to you. If the homunculus dies, you can create a new one with 8 hours of work, expending 25 Gold in materials and using alchemical tools.

Improved: Your homunculus's Strength and Craft increase by 1, it regains 1d3 Loyalty when you spend 🔘 to restore its Loyalty, and it gains **Internal Alembic:** Spend 1 Loyalty and 1d3 Life from your homunculus to replenish 1 expended dose of an unstable potion or poison.

Lasting Concoctions

Prerequisite: You do not have the Secret of Fire advancement.

You have learned to stabilise your potions and poisons. Stabilising one of your unstable potions or poisons costs materials worth 4 Gold, or 2 Gold if you expend 🔘 in the process to improve your efficiency.

Additionally, your antivenom doses now last for 8 hours rather than 1 when consumed.

Improved: The cost to stabilise one of your unstable potions or poisons now costs 3 Gold, or 🔘 and 1 Gold.

The Secret of Fire

Prerequisite: Craft 6+, and you do not have the Lasting Concoctions advancement.

You have learned to greatly increase the potency of your concoctions while making them stable enough to last a day or so. You can make the following additional concoctions with your Unstable Potion-Making feature.

- **Infernal Flame:** This clay or glass flask explodes into flame when primed and shattered. Make a **Thrown (Agility)** test against your target's Threat.
  - **Failure:** The flask explodes early, dealing 1d6 damage immediately and 1d3 damage for three next rounds to you. 🛡 Damage is increased to 2d6 immediately and 1d6 for the following the rounds.
  - **Success:** You deal 2d6 damage to the target and 1d6 damage for each of the next three rounds, and you or an ally near your target takes 1d6 damage.
  - **Great Success:** You deal 2d6 damage to the target and 1d6 damage for each of the next three rounds.
  - **Extraordinary Success:** You deal 4d6 damage to the target and 2d6 damage for each of the next three rounds. If this reduces a creature or object to 0 Life, it is reduced to ash.
- **Dragonsbreath Potion:** A character that drinks this potion takes 1d3 damage at the end of their next three turns. Within the next minute, they can breathe fire an action on their turn, making a **Fortitude (Mettle)** test for their attack.
  - **Failure:** An ally near you takes 1d6 damage from your fiery belch. 🛡 this damage is increased to 2d6.
  - **Success:** You deal 2d6 damage to one target within 6 metres, and the target can make a ranged or melee attack against you.
  - **Great Success:** You deal 2d6 + your Strength bonus damage to one target within 6 metres.
  - **Extraordinary Success:** You deal 2d6 + your Strength bonus damage to up to three separate targets within 10 metres.

Improved: Your maximum carrying capacity of unstable doses increases by 3, and when you would take damage from any sort of fire, you can spend ⬤ to roll 1d6 + Craft and reduce the damage you would take by the result.

Distilled Power

Prerequisite: Craft 6+, and you do not have the Barrage advancement.

With rare and precious herbs, you have created potions and poisons that affect characters with internal reserves of spell energy, either destroying or restoring it. You can make the following additional potions and poisons with your Unstable Potion-Making feature.

- **Surging Power Potion:** A character who drinks this potion regains 1 Spell Point at the start of each

Homunculus Follower

This small alchemical creature is made from your own body, and grown rapidly to maturity through secret processes. It is unfailingly loyal. A homunculus that survives for a year or more learns to speak.

Benefits

Regrowth: As long as it has at least 1 Life, the homunculus regains 1d6 Life at the start of your turn. Spend 1 Loyalty to deal 1d6 damage to your homunculus and restore the same amount to yourself.

Flight: Spend 1 Loyalty to make your homunculus grow wings, gaining a flying speed equal to your walking speed for 1 hour. At the end of that hour, its wings shrivel up and fall off.

Strength: 2   **Craft:** 2

Life: 10

Max Loyalty: 8. The homunculus does not leave at 0 Loyalty, but it can't use its special abilities that cost Loyalty until it has at least 1 Loyalty again.

Restore Loyalty: Spend ⬤ to restore 1 Loyalty. When you roll 🛡 on a Spellcasting (Alchemy) test, the homunculus regains 1 Loyalty and demonstrates its excitement, in addition to the ⬤ you gain from the 🛡 result.

of their next 10 turns. They cannot exceed their maximim number of Spell Points.

- **Spellburn Poison:** This poison can be made to be injected or ingested, chosen at the time of creation. When it affects a character, Stranger, or Enemy who has Spell Points, you roll a **Spellcasting (Alchemy)** test against their Threat.
  - **Failure:** The Spellburn poison has no effect.
  - **Success:** The target must spend 1 additional Spell Point each time they cast a spell within the next hour. If they can't spend that additional Spell Point, the spell fails.
  - **Great Success:** The target loses 1d6 Spell Points, takes an equal amount of damage, and must spend 2 additional Spell Points each time they cast a spell within the next hour. If they can't spend the additional Spell Points, the spell fails.
  - **Extraordinary Success:** The target loses 2d6 Spell Points, takes an equal amount of damage, loses one Enduring spell, and must spend 3 additional Spell Points each time they cast a spell within the next hour. If they can't spend the additional Spell Points, the spell fails.

Improved: Your maximum carrying capacity of unstable doses increases by 3, and a creature affected by your Surging Power potion can reduce the damage they take from Psychic Assault by 1d6 for the duration of the potion.

Barrage

Prerequisite: Strength 5+, and you do not have the Distilled Power advancement.

As you rely on thrown weapons in many battles, you have become an expert in fast and accurate throws. Once per turn, when you use **Throw (Agility)** to make an attack and roll a ⬛, you can immediately make another attack with a thrown weapon or concoction.

Improved: Once per turn, after you make an attack with a thrown weapon, you can spend ⚫ to make an additional attack with a thrown weapon or concoction or to administer a potion to a willing or unconscious character.

Refinement of the Soul

Prerequisite: Craft 7+, and you do not have the Initiate of the Higher Mysteries advancement.

Through secret processes and the refiner's fire of struggle, you have transmuted the base elements of your soul into something greater. Your alignment can't be changed against your will, and you ignore negative effects from locations and objects based on your alignment.

You gain the Psychic skill and can initiate psychic combat with an Enemy within 10 metres. If you get a Standard success or greater on that attack, you deal 1d6 + Craft damage. This attack uses your action for the round.

Improved: Once per turn after you make a psychic attack, you can spend ⚫ to make one thrown attack with a weapon or concoction, or to administer a potion to a willing or unconscious character.

Initiate of the Higher Mysteries

Prerequisite: Craft 7+, and you do not have the Refinement of the Soul advancement.

You awaken a magical talent for creating the potions and elixirs of legend. You learn to make three types of potions or elixirs from *Talisman Fantasy Adventures RPG*, pages 236–237. With eight hours of work, ⚫⚫, and a Gold cost equal to half the listed value, you can make one of those potions or elixirs. Treat the value of the Phoenix Potion as 100 Gold.

Improved: You learn to make two additional potions or elixirs of your choice.

Gladiator

Whether in the back alleys and seedier side of the City, or in broad daylight during a market fair, some people in the Realm fight for the entertainment of others. They wear distinctive armour that becomes their personal signature, with many donning the armour of the one who trained them. Some take up adventuring to pursue fame through another means, while others seek out trial and danger so that they can prove their mettle and build their name to ever greater heights.

Glory Immortal

It is said that no one is truly dead until their name is spoken for the last time; gladiators strive for immortality through fame. The pure vanity of this drive means that many gladiators are Neutral; Evil gladiators are those most willing to leave any number of broken bodies in their wake as they climb to the top. Good gladiators teach others the ropes and support their fellow gladiators when they're not in the fighting pit. Within an adventuring party, their competitiveness might take the form of a friendly rivalry or a powerful sense of team identity.

Playing a Gladiator

In addition to the physical conditioning needed to wear heavy armour and wield weapons, gladiators need the personal presence to be memorable and exciting. This opens up their options for resolving conflicts without fighting. After all, if you get paid to fight, you can't afford to do it for free. Your reputation may not mean as much out in the wilderness, but the rigors of the arena are as good a preparation for danger as one could want.

Brawn or Agility should be your highest Attribute, followed by Resolve.

Creating a Gladiator

When you choose the gladiator class, you gain the following features.

Strength: 4   **Craft:** 2

Life: 15 + your Mettle score

Skills: You gain Athletics, Entertain, Fortitude, Intimidate, Melee, and Ride and your choice of either Missile Weapon or Throw. You gain a focus in Melee and in either Athletics or Intimidate.

Core Features

When you choose this class, you gain two features common to all gladiators: Armor Training and Glory.

Armour Training

You've learned to wear heavy armor comfortably, such as chainmail or plate armor.

Glory

You thrive on impressing others with your excellence in any task you attempt. Glory is a condition that you can expend and regain; you can't gain it if you currently have it. You gain it at the start of an adventure and when you roll a Great Success or Extraordinary Success on a test with a skill that you have so long as an Ally, Follower, or Stranger observes your action.

When you are reduced to 0 Life, you can expend your Glory to make an immediate attack test against an Enemy that you could normally strike. You ignore penalties from Wounds for this attack. On an Extraordinary Success, you also immediately regain 1d6 Life in addition to the other effects of your attack.

Advancement Features

At 1st, 2nd, 3rd, 5th, and 7th level, you can choose one of the following advancements or choose from the general advancement list in on page 93 of the core rulebook. At 6th, 9th, and 10th level, you can choose the improved version of an advancement you have previously selected.

The Show Must Go On

Prerequisite: You do not have the Showstopper advancement.

You endure every injury to entertain the audience. While you have Glory, you can spend ⚫ to ignore your penalties from Wounds, and instead add +1 per Wound to your tests until the end of your turn.

Improved: When you use this advancement to ignore the penalty from Wounds, you add +2 per Wound to your tests until the end of your turn. You can expend Glory to make a Finishing Blow.

Showstopper

Prerequisite: You do not have the Show Must Go On advancement.

You can bring down the house with a telling blow. When you make an attack against a creature with less than its maximum Life, you can expend Glory to add your Resolve to the damage you deal on a Standard Success, twice your Resolve on a Great Success, and three times your Resolve on an Extraordinary success.

Improved: After you use this advancement in an encounter, when you spend ⚫ to gain a bonus die on an attack, you also gain the damage bonus of this advancement on that attack.

Rally

Prerequisite: You do not have the Demoralize advancement.

You build up your friends, fans, and followers into a frenzy. You can expend Glory to grant a bonus die to the next attack, Defense, or Fortitude test of to up to five characters of your choice who can see or hear you within 20 metres. Your non-animal Followers that can see or hear you within 20 metres regain 1 Loyalty.

Improved: When you expend Glory to use this advancement, you can also spend 1, 2, or 3 ⚫ to give that Light Fate to any character (or characters) that can see or hear you within 20 metres.

Demoralize

Prerequisite: You do not have the Rally advancement.

Your presence gives even hardened warriors pause. You can expend Glory to choose up to five Strangers or Enemies that can see or hear you within 20 metres. The next time they deal damage, reduce the damage by your Resolve, after adjustments for Success level and armour.

Improved: When you expend Glory to use this advancement, you can also roll an Intimidate test against one creature that can see and hear you and that hasn't spent its action for the round. If your test result is a Success against its Threat, it loses one of its actions for the round. A Great Success causes them to lose two actions, and an Extraordinary success three.

Mentor

Prerequisite: Craft 4+, and you do not have the Ruthless Competitor advancement.

You take others under your wing to teach them life-saving skills. At the start of an adventure, one character of your choice gains a skill that you have, and they don't have, for the duration of the adventure. You can spend ⬤ to influence their test, even if you're not present. You can use **Entertain (Resolve)** to Assist them with any test that you can observe.

Improved: When the character that you've granted a skill to for this adventure rolls a Great or Extraordinary Success on a test, you can spend ⬤ to gain Glory.

Ruthless Competitor

Prerequisite: Strength 6+, and you do not have the Mentor advancement.

You have a killer instinct as a competitor, seizing advantages that put others in danger. While you have Glory, the GM can't activate 🛡 features of Enemies from your rolls unless the GM spends an additional ⬤.

When you don't have Glory, you can give the GM ⬤⬤⬤ to gain Glory. This can allow the GM to temporarily exceed their maximum Dark Fate.

Improved: When you gain Glory, you can choose one Neutral or Evil follower that is loyal to you or another character to gain 1 Loyalty.

Encased in Armour

Prerequisite: Strength 7+, and you do not have the Sigils of the Skin advancement.

You customise your suit of armour for your physique so that you're recognisable from every seat in the arena.

- When you own a suit of armour for at least one week and have access to a market or a forge, you add 3 to its Armour Points when you wear it.

- Your Agility penalty for your customised armour is halved (round down).
- The armour has a visor that can cover your face, and most people in the Realm find you highly recognisable by your armour. If someone else is wearing your armour for some reason, they assume it's you until shown strong evidence to the contrary.

Improved: When you repair your customised suit of armour, you can roll **Entertain (Agility)** rather than **Tinker (Agility)**, as it is part of your training as an entertainer. You can spend ⬤ after the test to restore 1d6 armour points, even on a Failure.

Sigils of the Skin

Prerequisite: Craft 5+, and you do not have the Encased in Armour advancement.

Rather than wearing ever more armour, you cover much of your exposed skin with tattoos from your greatest victories.

- While you are wearing light armour or no armour, you can add your Craft to your armour points, and you can reduce the damage you take from Psychic Attack by your Craft score. You can use a shield and wear a helm and still use this benefit. This extra armour fully resets after a short rest.
- When you gain Glory, and your armour value from Craft has been damaged, you can remove an X, or spend ⬤ to remove two Xs.
- When you use a shield or helm to prevent damage, add +2 to your d6 result to determine if the shield or helm are destroyed. If the result is a failure, you can expend Glory to succeed instead.

Improved: Your tattoos tell the story of when the odds against you were at their worst. When the GM spends at least ⬤⬤⬤ in a single round, you gain Glory.

Let There Be Blood

Prerequisite: Strength 8+, and you do not have the Master of the Show advancement.

You have spilled rivers of blood in the fighting pit—yours and your opponents' alike. When you hit with an attack test using an edged weapon, you can expend Glory to make the target take an additional 2d6 damage from bleeding at the start of each round, continuing until it regains at least 3 Life from healing.

When you hit with an attack test using a blunt weapon, you can expend Glory to shatter bone. Your target deals half damage with melee attacks until it regains at least 6 Life from healing.

Improved: You can expend Glory before you roll an attack test. If the attack test is a success, your damage ignores the target's armour.

Master of the Show

Prerequisite: Craft 6+, and you do not have the Let There Be Blood advancement.

You have become an arena master in your own right, whether or not you still compete. At the Game Master's discretion, this might require displacing a previous arena master. You gain one follower, who is your assistant and longtime admirer. Choose either the Apprentice Minstrel or Mercenary follower; if you choose the Apprentice Minstrel, you can use the Backup Band feature even though you are not a minstrel. If this follower dies, you can recruit a new follower in the City with 1 day of work.

Improved: Your follower's maximum Life and Loyalty increase by 5, and your follower automatically gains 1 Loyalty when you expend Glory.

TINKERER

In cluttered workshops of the City and elsewhere, tinkerers build, repair, and continually upgrade their cunning inventions. Brass and steel, clockwork and wire, their devices are useful in anything from a pitched battle to a cooking contest, as many of them are eager to point out. No two tinkerer's devices look the same, even when their function is identical. When put to the test, a tinkerer is an elusive and dangerous enemy, and even the most innocuous item could hold a deadly trap.

Purveyors of Marvels

The people of the Realm love to see a tinkerer's wind-up or clockwork devices on display; requests from a curious public are one of the main barriers to getting that latest upgrade finished. Of course, not all tinkerers are the kindly recluses that people imagine; some are cruel tricksters, driven by revenge or a malicious nature. What unites tinkerers of all kinds is their dedication to craft and the search for improvement—their work is never complete, only abandoned.

Playing a Tinkerer

Preparation and precision are everything to a tinkerer. When in danger, they hope to always have at least one more trick up their sleeve—or else a crossbow stronger than the enemy's armour. Most tinkerers would prefer to avoid combat in favor of more controlled circumstances, though. The chance to test out their inventions calls some tinkerers into a life of adventure. Others long to return to their workshops, just as soon as they recover some dangerous invention that has been stolen from them.

Because a tinkerer lives by precision and invention, Agility and Wits should be your best Aspects.

Creating a Tinkerer

When you choose the tinkerer class, you gain the following features:

Strength: 3

Craft: 3

Life: 12 + (Mettle or Resolve) +2 per level

Skills: You gain Artisan, Evaluate, Investigation, Missile Weapon, Notice, and Tinker. You also gain your choice of Bargain or Entertain. You gain a focus in Tinker and in your choice of Missile Weapon or Notice.

CORE FEATURES

When you choose this class, you gain two Special Abilities common to all tinkerers: Salvage and Tinkered Devices.

SALVAGE

When something no longer serves its purpose, the tinkerer reclaims it for the next project. You can convert one object made mostly or entirely of metal into Salvaged Parts equal to its Gold cost. If its Gold cost isn't clear, roll 1d3 for a small or medium object and 1d6 for a large object. This takes 5 minutes for every Gold of value, and it requires both your tinkerer's tools and unrestricted access to the object.

Furthermore, you can Salvage a construct that has 0 Life. You gain Salvaged Parts equal to 1/4th of its Threat, rounded down. This takes 5 minutes for every Gold of value, and it requires both your tinkerer's tools and unrestricted access to the object.

Salvaged Parts weigh 1 Load per 10 Salvaged Parts.

TINKERED DEVICES

You can combine Salvaged Parts into useful devices. You can spend 3 Salvaged Parts and 15 minutes of work to build any of the following devices. You can keep up to three of these devices in working order at a time.

Noisemaker: This device plays simple music or mechanical noise for 5 minutes; it can be re-wound as a Full Action to play for another 5 minutes. The sound can be soft, loud, or very loud. If you spend ⬤ and 2 additional Salvaged Parts, you can make it record sounds, including voices. You can get improved sound quality with a **Difficulty 14 Tinker (Wits)** test. Use **Tinker (Wits)** in place of Deception to deceive others with a recorded sound. After this device plays sound 2d6 times, it breaks, and you gain half as many Salvaged Parts as you used building it.

Lantern: This device generates light without significant heat for 10 minutes; it can be re-wound as a Full Action to provide another 10 minutes of light. The light is as bright

as a torch. If you spend ⬤ and 2 additional Salvaged Parts, you can overcharge its light to deal damage to a Spirit within 10 metres of you. Make a **Tinker (Wits)** test against its Threat.

- **Failure:** The lantern breaks and the Spirit deals damage to you. You recover half as many Salvaged Parts as you spent on the lantern.
- **Success:** You deal 1d6 damage to the Spirit and the lantern breaks. You recover half as many Salvaged Parts as you spent on the lantern.
- **Great Success:** You deal 1d6 + your Craft damage to the Spirit.
- **Extraordinary Success:** You deal 2d6 + your Craft damage to the Spirit, and it can't willingly get closer to you this turn.

Spider Armature: This tiny spider automaton is your Follower, which you control with verbal commands. It breaks when it has 0 Life, and you regain half as many Salvaged Parts as you used building it.

SPIDER ARMATURE FOLLOWER

This construct is tiny, able to fit through crevices as small as one centimetre. Most tinkerers make them from brass, silver, or steel, though tinkerers intending them as toys or fine art might choose other materials, such as wood or crystal.

BENEFITS

Distract: Spend 1 Loyalty at the end of the player turn to direct the spider armature to distract a creature. You gain a bonus die on your Missile Weapon tests against that target.

Skullduggery: Spend 1 Loyalty to direct the spider armature to pick a lock or steal a small object that you can see, using your Tinker (Agility) test result. The spider armature is immune to poison and takes half damage from traps.

Repair: The spider armature can't be healed by magic. Spend 1 Salvaged Part as a Full Action to restore a spider armature with at least 1 Life remaining to its maximum Life.

Strength: 2   **Craft:** 2

Life: 5

Max Loyalty: 8. The spider armature does not leave at 0 Loyalty, but it can't use its special abilities that cost Loyalty until it has regained at least 1 Loyalty.

Restore Loyalty: Spend ⬤ to restore 1 Loyalty. The spider armature regains 1 Loyalty and chitters with excitement when you roll 🎲 on a Tinker test. (You still get to keep the Light Fate earned.)

ADVANCEMENT FEATURES

At 1st, 2nd, 3rd, 5th, and 7th level, you can choose one of the following advancements or choose from the general advancement list in *Talisman Adventures Fantasy*

Roleplaying Game. At 6th, 9th, and 10th level, you can choose the improved version of an advancement you have previously selected.

Toymaker

Prerequisite: You do not have the Trapmaker advancement.

You believe in the charm and fun of tinkering, using it as a weapon only when you have no other choice. Your spider armature can take the form of any small toy with wheels or legs, giving it an innocuous appearance that makes most foes ignore it. You can use a **Tinker (Agility)** test in place of any Stealth test it would make, and when an Enemy attacks it, you can spend 🔘 to force the attacker to choose a different target.

Improved: You can make spider armatures or other construct toys that other characters can control. They have a maximum of 3 Loyalty and only regain Loyalty with a success or better on a **Difficulty 12 Tinker (Repair)** test. This restores up to 3 expended Loyalty. A spider armature that another character can control generally sells for around 8 Gold.

Trapmaker

Prerequisite: You do not have the Toymaker advancement.

You relish the cunning of tinkering, using traps to kill, disable, or humiliate intruders or enemies. With 5 minutes of unrestricted access to an object and your tinkering tools, you can use 2 Salvaged Parts to install a trap that can trigger one time. The trap's trigger requires your choice of opening a door, stepping into a space, or manipulating the object that holds the trap. When a character does this, roll a **Tinker (Wits)** test against their Notice test or Threat.

- **Failure:** The trap misfires. It is revealed and deals no damage.
- **Success:** The trap activates. The target takes 1d3 damage, falls prone, or loses its next turn to a disabling effect (choose at the time you set the trap).
- **Great Success:** The trap activates. The target takes 1d6 damage, falls prone, or loses its next turn to a disabling effect (choose at the time you set the trap).
- **Extraordinary Success:** The trap activates. The target takes 1d6 + your Craft damage, falls prone, or loses its next 1d3+1 turns to a disabling effect (choose at the time you set the trap).

Improved: When you roll 👹 on your **Tinker (Wits)** test and the result is a success or better, you can choose a second effect for the trap. You can't choose the same effect a second time.

Crossbow Upgrade

Prerequisite: You do not have the Jury-Rig advancement.

Never one to be satisfied with a typical crossbow, you've made a number of improvements to enhance the force and accuracy of each shot. With 1 hour of work and your tinkering tools, you can spend 1 or more Salvaged Parts to improve a crossbow. A character who makes an attack with this crossbow can expend 1 Salvaged Part from it to add 1d6 to the damage it deals.

Improved: If you spend 🔘 while adding Salvaged Parts to the crossbow, a character that makes an attack with it can expend 1 Salvaged Part from it to instantly reload it and fire again. This upgrade wears out after 24 hours.

Jury-Rig

Prerequisite: You do not have the Crossbow Upgrade advancement.

In a desperate spot, your repair work can get you out of a jam. When you roll a Tinker test to repair an object, you can spend 1 Salvaged Part for a bonus die.

- As a Full Action, you can erase 1d3 slashes from the armour of a creature within reach by expending 1 Salvaged Part. This requires your tinkering tools.
- When you refit a suit of armour, you can spend 🔘 and 2 Salvaged Parts to erase an X from the armor.
- You can repair a suit of destroyed armour by spending 🔘🔘 and 3 Salvaged Parts in addition to the normal requirements of repairing armour.

Improved: When you erase slashes from a suit of armour as a Full Action, the armor gains one temporary point of value. This armour value lasts for 8 hours. It is lost first and can't be regained with refitting or repair. A suit of armor can't receive this benefit again until the effect expires.

Sensor Device

Prerequisites: Craft 5+, and you do not have the Battle-Ready advancement.

Driven by curiosity, some tinkerers learn to build devices to sense various forces and signs that are part of life in the Realm. Sensor devices always have a strange and outlandish look, with too many antennae and readouts for anyone else to use effectively. They're at once both delicate and annoying and require a free hand to use.

Choose one of the following forces, energies, or substances that your sensor device can detect within 100 metres; within that area, it can detect approximate direction and distance. At the GM's discretion, other forces, energies, or substances may be added to this list.

- Aligned locations, including which alignment it is
- Invisible living creatures
- Large amounts of iron (a suit of armour or larger)
- Magic items
- Magic portals
- Spells being cast, including whether they are Basic, Intermediate, or Advanced, and whether they are Arcane, Mystic, or Nature
- Talismans
- Tracks or scent trail left by an animal
- Unseen spirits or undead

To use this device, you can use a Full Action to roll a **Tinker (Wits)** test against a Difficulty set by the GM. You can change what your sensor detects by spending 1 minute and 2 Salvaged Parts, or by spending ⬤ and striking the sensor forcefully as a Full Action.

If your sensor is lost or destroyed, you can build a new one with 4 Salvaged Parts and 8 hours of work, requiring access to your tinkering tools. You can't maintain more than one sensor device at a time.

Improved: You can now build the sensor device into a piece of headwear. It positions lenses in front of your eyes (over your spectacles, if necessary) rather than relying on readouts. Further, you can choose three different forces, energies, or substances that it can detect, switching between them as a Minor Action.

Battle-Ready

Prerequisite: Strength 5+, and you do not have the Sensor Device advancement.

Driven by ruthless necessity, some tinkerers develop a bag of dirty tricks for desperate situations. Add the following to the list of Tinkered Devices you can make.

- **Ropecutter:** This blade, tiny but very sharp, is built into bracelets, bracers, or gauntlets. As a Full Action, you can free yourself from ropes, webs, or any other binding that you can cut. If you are engulfed, swallowed, or restrained by a creature, you can deal 1d3 damage to it at the start of your turn without spending an action.
- **Spring-Heels:** These springs can be built into any pair of sturdy boots or shoes or into foot or leg prostheses. Your Speed increases by 4 metres. You can make horizontal leaps equal to your Speed and vertical leaps equal to half your Speed. You can roll **Tinker (Agility)** in place of **Athletics (Agility)** when you Disengage, and if you roll 🛡 on this test, you can kick one enemy with your spring-heels, knocking them prone.

The number of Tinkered Devices you can maintain at a time increases by 1.

Improved: The number of Tinkered Devices you can maintain at a time increases by 1. Add the following to the list of Tinkered Devices you can make.

- **Weight Belt:** This belt modification adds onto the support of a broad leather belt, increasing the weight you can carry. Your maximum Load doubles, and you can roll a **Tinker (Agility)** test in place of any **Athletics (Brawn)** test.
- **Tinkermaster:** This iron bar is covered with close-set grooves, concealing pieces of metal that can be extended or retracted as a Minor Action to form a wide variety of tools, including a screwdriver, a crowbar, a glass cutter, and more. This is a universal tool for tinkering, thieves' tools, and many artisan skills. When you roll an **Artisan (Agility)** or **Tinker (Agility)** check, a 1 or a 2 on a non-Kismet die is treated as a 3 instead.

Tinkered Flight

Prerequisite: Strength 6+, and you do not have the Tinkered Guardian advancement.

Falling can be fun, but only when you do it on your own terms—and you have a device for that. This device weighs 4 Load and is built into a backpack. As a reaction when you begin to fall, gyroscopic balancers in the device cause glider wings made of silk and brass to pop out of the sides of the pack. Spend ⬤ and make a **Tinker (Agility)** test against Difficulty 12 + your current Load, not including the Load of the glider wings.

- **Failure:** You don't arrest your fall, and the glider wings break.
- **Success:** You slow your fall but lose directional control, landing safely in a random empty space near where you would have landed without the glider wings' aid.
- **Great Success:** You slow your fall, and you can move 20 metres horizontally on your turn, descending 4 metres.
- **Extraordinary Success:** You find enough thermals to keep you aloft. You can fly with a Speed of 20 metres for the next 30 minutes, until you land, or until you fall unconscious. You can make a new **Tinker (Agility)** test against Difficulty 12 once at the end of each 30-minute span to keep flying.

If your glider wings break, you can recover 3 Salvaged Parts from them. Making a new set of glider wings requires 8 hours of work and 6 Salvaged Parts.

Improved: Add half of your current Load to your **Tinker (Agility)** tests to use this feature instead of your full Load.

Tinkered Guardian

Prerequisite: Craft 6+, and you do not have the Tinkered Flight advancement.

You have surpassed the spider armature and developed a Tinkered Guardian, a semi-autonomous construct that is your Follower. At the time you construct it, and again when you rebuild it, you can choose for it to have either two legs or any number of legs between four and eight.

Tinkered Guardian

This construct might be built in a wide variety of shapes and any size up to roughly that of a horse.

Benefits

Guardian: Spend 1 Loyalty. When you take damage from an Enemy, you can choose to deflect up to half that damage to your Tinkered Guardian if the Tinkered Guardian is within 4 metres of you. You can't deflect a greater amount than the Tinkered Guardian's current Life.

Repair: The Tinkered Guardian can't be healed by magic. Spend 1 Salvaged Part as a Full Action to restore a Tinkered Guardian with at least 1 Life remaining to its maximum Life.

Strength: 5   **Craft:** 3
Life: 15   **Armour:** 2
Max Loyalty: 8. The Tinkered Guardian does not leave at 0 Loyalty, but it can't use its special abilities that cost Loyalty until it regains at least 1 Loyalty.

Restore Loyalty: Spend  to restore 1 Loyalty. The Tinkered Guardian regains 1 and watches in silent approval when you roll 🎲 on a Tinker test.

Improved: Your Tinkered Guardian now has 6 Strength, 20 Life, and 5 Armour.

Clockwarden

Prerequisite: Craft 7+, and you do not have the I Can Rebuild You advancement.

You've built the greatest device that tinkering will ever invent: a personal temporal destabiliser. It even works! When and how it wants, apparently.

With one hour of work, you can install up to 8 Salvaged Parts in your device. On your turn, you can do one of the following:

- Expend 1 Salvaged Part to gain a second Free Action.
- Expend 2 Salvaged Parts to gain a second Reaction.
- Expend 4 Salvaged Parts and 🪙 to gain a second Full Action.

To use your personal temporal destabiliser, you must hold it in one hand.

Improved: With further improvements, your personal temporal destabiliser can hold up to 16 Salvaged Parts. You can target a character within 10 metres of you with this device, granting them additional actions or reactions.

I Can Rebuild You

Prerequisite: Strength 6+, and you do not have the Clockwarden advancement.

You have developed tinkered devices that diagnose injuries and perform rapid surgery. A spider armature that you build gains an additional Benefit: Stitch Wounds.

Stitch Wounds: Spend 1 Loyalty. The spider armature moves to one Ally or unconscious creature you can see within 10 metres. The target regains your choice of 2d6 Life or 1 Wound.

Improved: You've built the greatest device tinkering will ever invent: the means to reanimate the dead. A spider armature that you build gains Reanimator if you spend 3 additional Salvaged Parts when you build it.

Reanimator: Spend 2 Loyalty and destroy this spider armature. One dead character within 2 metres is restored to life. You can't use this on a player character without the player's agreement. They lose one Special Ability of their choice from their race and gain Tinkered Construct.

Tinkered Construct: Your maximum number of Wounds increases by 3, and you suffer no penalties for your first 3 Wounds. When a character would roll a **Heal (Insight)** test to heal you, they can roll a **Tinker (Wits)** test to repair you instead. You can be Salvaged to gain 6 Salvaged Parts.

CHAPTER 4: STRANGERS AND FOLLOWERS

The City is a vast and teeming metropolis, home to throngs of people of every size, shape, and color. Among this endless mass can be found every type of person, from pauper to lord, healer to soldier, baker to butcher. Each of them is an individual with their own goals and desires, some of which may come into conflict or align with the PCs' goals and desires. The City provides a huge cast of characters to draw from that the PCs can meet, fight with, learn from, befriend, or romance. This chapter will provide a small selection of such individuals.

STRANGERS

The people of the City go about their lives each day, seeing to their own needs and little involved in the activities of so-called heroes. They do their jobs, take care of their families, and do their best to stay out of trouble. Despite these efforts, these folk are sometimes pulled into the orbits of heroes and villains who find themselves in the City or other settlements. These Strangers may be friend or foe or neither, but in any case, they provide a

rich backdrop to populate the civilised areas, from law enforcement to criminals, from scholars to rat catchers.

The Strangers described here are specifically for the City but can easily be adapted to other locales.

City Watchman/woman

City Watchmen are most commonly encountered at the City Gate, the Town Square, lower-and middle-class neighbourhoods, and the Wharves. When out in the City, they can be easily identified by their tabards, quartered silver and black, and their copper badges of office. They patrol and investigate reports of crime or other disturbances in their assigned neighbourhood and will stop and question strangers they encounter while doing so. The Watch usually falls back on arresting any known troublemakers and hoping something shakes loose when out of leads. The City Watchmen treat visitors to the City well and don't practice extortion, but they usually see adventurers and the like as troublemakers who should leave their neighbourhood as quickly as possible. City Watchmen can be an excellent source of local news and information if befriended. They know all the local gossip and often serve as guides in their neighbourhoods, providing directions and helping to find locals.

Benefits

Word on the Street: A City Watchman whose attitude is Favourable or better can offer information to characters about the neighbourhood and any criminals in the area. A PC assisted by a Watchman gains a bonus die trying to find a specific person or piece of information in a neighbourhood.

Strength: 4   **Craft:** 2
Life: 14   **Armour:** 3

City Patrol

The City Patrollers can be found in any part of the City where trade occurs and are easily identifiable by their green tabards and gold-dyed belts. They are rarely concerned with street crime and instead primarily protect those businesses associated with the Merchant's Guild. They will attempt to stop an obvious crime committed in front of them but are more concerned with petty crimes against the Guild. Any visit to a Merchant Guild store of note will be under the keen eye of the City Patrol. Because of this, the City Patrol knows the gossip of the Merchant Guild and has a surprisingly in-depth knowledge of inventories, surpluses, and desperate merchants. If you want to find a deal in the City, the City Patrol are a good place to start—assuming you make it worth their while.

Decades of low-level graft has turned the City Patrol into the private police of the Merchant's Guild, but this isn't the jailbreaking, violent, obvious, widely condemned graft of the Sheriff' Deputies. This is a more insidious, lower-key, long-term graft where rivals of the Guild find their lives slightly more difficult while the crimes of the Guild and its members get overlooked from time to time. The Merchant' Guild is not stupid and knows that the outward appearance of propriety must be maintained.

Benefits

Knows Where the Deals Are: A City Patroller whose attitude toward the PC is Favourable or better, and who has been paid a 1d3 gold bribe, can help the PC find a specific mundane good, elixir, or potion for sale among the merchants of the City. Roll 2d6. On a roll of 7+, the Patroller knows where the item may be obtained at its normal cost. On a roll of 10+, the Patroller knows where the item can be obtained for a 25% discount from its normal price. On a roll of 12, the Patroller knows how the item can be obtained for a 50% discount from its normal price. Items purchased at a discount may be stolen goods or have other issues.

Strength: 4   **Craft:** 3
Life: 12   **Armour:** 3

Night Guard

The most widely feared of the City's law enforcement agencies, the Night Guard can be found in any part of the City since their duties take them everywhere from the Square of Kings to the Wharves. The Night Guard deal with the threats seen as too dangerous or unusual by the Watch, Patrol, or Deputies. This usually means monsters or magic is involved but can also mean normal criminals of sufficient deadliness. The Night Guard shares members with the Assassins Guild, who use the Night Guard as a cover job while putting their skill to use killing for the good of the City.

Night Guards are easy to spot in their grey cloaks and tabards. The people of the City avoid them due to their reputation for being dangerous; indeed, most avoid calling the Night Guard at all costs, instead calling the Watch or Patrol, and letting them call the Nigh Guard as needed. It is well known Night Guards leave bodies in their wake. Thus far, enough of those bodies have been dangerous monsters or rogue magicians that the Mayor leaves them be.

Benefits

How the Killing's Done: The Night Guard are particularly knowledgeable about monsters found in and beneath the City. If a Night Guard has a Favourable or better attitude towards the PCs, they will share this info if asked, including vulnerabilities, immunities, common hunting grounds, tactics, etc.

Strength: 5   **Craft:** 3
Life: 18   **Armour:** 6–9

Sheriff's Deputies

The Sheriff of the City is well known for his corruption such that it is a source of many jokes among the people of the City. His deputies are only slightly less corrupt and can be found across the City, but particularly near the buildings of government on Gold Street and Noble Street. Among their duties are maintaining the City Jail, from which they regularly allow prisoners to escape in exchange for bribes, and guarding the courts and city officials. The Sheriff's Deputies like their work easy and do little actual law enforcement, preferring jail duty or guarding the offices of government and getting bribes for access. The deputies see visitors to the city as being particularly tempting targets for their graft since such people usually aren't familiar with the Deputies' reputation—or who to complain to about them. Anything too egregiously publicly corrupt and the Sheriff will give them a public dressing down and a slap on the wrist, but the corruption among the deputies cannot be excised without removing the Sheriff.

Benefits

Greased Wheels: A Sheriff's deputy whose attitude is Favourable and paid 1d6 gold will lend their assistance to getting someone out of jail, putting someone in jail, or getting access to a governmental official. The character must make a **Persuasion (Wits)** or **Intimidation (Resolve)** test against **Difficulty 14.**
- **Failure:** The Sheriff's Deputy takes the money and does nothing.
- **Standard Success:** The desired character is freed from jail or put in jail, or the character gets access to the desired official.

- **Great Success or Better:** The desired character is freed from jail or put in jail, or the character gets access to the desired official without having to pay the bribe.

Strength: 3   **Craft:** 3
Life: 12   **Armour:** 3

Grifter

A fool and their money are soon parted, but someone must do the parting. The grifters of the City make their coin by tricking others out of theirs, be it through scams, rigged gambling, or other forms of trickery. A grifter is not a thief, for their victims provide their valuables freely. Grifters can be found in every neighbourhood of the City, rooking everyone from peasants to nobles while dressed to blend in with their chosen targets. Grifters are criminals and are arrested when they are caught, but many of their victims are too embarrassed to even report the crime. Similarly, grifters seem to escape jailtime with startling ease.

Benefits

Rigged Game: If a PC chooses to play in a grifter's game of chance, that PC makes a **Notice (Wits)** test against **Difficulty 15.**
- **Failure:** The PC loses the game and 1d6 gold.
- **Standard Success:** The PC loses no gold but also wins none.
- **Great Success or Better:** The PCs wins and uncovers the grifter's entire scam. The PC can either gain 1d6 gold from the grifter or turn them into the City Watch.

Strength: 2   **Craft:** 4
Life: 12

Instructor

Despite the decline of the Academy, once one of the greatest institutions of Higher learning in the Realm, the City remains the home of dozens of instructors specializing in various disciplines. While some still work for the Academy, most are now involved in private tutelage of the upper classes or study in the service of a patron. Those few instructors who are available for hire are in high demand; not just any scholar can teach. Those seeking instruction usually go to the Academy, for there is usually a small swarm of unemployed instructors hoping to pick up work hanging around the side alley of the Academy, casually named Scholar's Dive. Although informal, this is by far the most effective method to quickly find an instructor or a sage willing to work on the cheap.

BENEFITS

Crash Course: If an instructor has a Favourable or better attitude towards a PC, they may attempt to teach the PC. The PC must make a **Notice (Wits)** test against **Difficulty 16**.

- **Failure:** The PC learns nothing and must either pay the instructor 1d6 gold or have their attitude worsen by one level.
- **Success:** The PCs learns one skill from among (Decipher, Evaluate Heal, or Lore) but only retains this knowledge for one week. The PC must either pay the instructor 1d6 gold or have their attitude worsen by one level.
- **Great Success or Better:** The PCs learns one skill from among (Decipher, Evaluate Heal, or Lore) but only retains this knowledge for one month. The PC must either pay the Instructor 1d6 gold or have their attitude worsen by one level.

Strength: 2   **Craft:** 5
Life: 12

PHILOSOPHER

Even in the prosperous and cultured City, philosophers are few and far between. They spend their days contemplating the whys of life and the Realm, debating, discussing, and writing as needed to get their ideas in ideal form. This sort of introspection and conversation doesn't exactly bring in a great deal of coin. Indeed, most philosophers are either effectively beggars, living among the street sages, or benefit from the support of a wealthy patron. Indeed, having an eloquent philosopher in your service is seen as a mark of accomplishment and refinement among the upper crust of the City. While many philosophers are merely students of the universe seeking some sort of greater meaning, some have obtained nuggets of truth they can share. These rare philosophers are in great demand, but not everyone is fit or ready for their truths; they only share this information with those whom they trust most.

BENEFITS

Philosophical Truth: If a philosopher has a Liked or better attitude towards a PC, they may be convinced to share their truths with the PC. The hero must make a **Persuasion (Wits)** test against **Difficulty 15**. If successful, the philosopher will share their truth, but the PC must make a **Decipher (Insight)** test against **Difficulty 16** to understand it. A PC can only attempt to understand a single philosopher's truth once, though they may try to understand the truth of other philosophers.

- **Failure:** The PC misunderstands the truth and is led astray, losing 1d3 Light Fate to a minimum of 0 Light Fate.
- **Standard Success:** The PC understands the truth and how to apply it to their life, gaining 1d3 Light Fate.
- **Great Success or Better:** The PC's worldview is changed by the philosopher's truth so deep is their comprehension of it. The PC may change their alignment and gains 1d6 Light Fate.

Strength: 2   **Craft:** 5
Life: 8

RACKETEER

While the City has sufficient law agents to avoid most woes of banditry, there are still criminals who use threat of force to make their living within its walls. Indeed, you'll still find racketeers: thugs who pretend to be legitimate businessfolk offering protection services to create a weak veneer of respectability over their operation. Claiming to be operating a neighbourhood aid agency or a private club, these racketeers use their "business" to gather a gang of thugs and criminals they can use to threaten local residents and businesses. Those that do not pay find accidents befalling their businesses and homes, from property damage to arson to assault, carried out by the racketeer's minions. The people themselves are roughed up and robbed if they do not pay, and the Watch and Patrol always seem absent when this happens. Racketeers make sure not to target people with enough wealth or power to resist, relying on bribes and threats to keep the law off their back. In every neighbourhood, the racketeer is among the most despised people in the neighbourhood—but only in private, as no one wants to be the target of their wrath.

BENEFITS

It'd Be a Shame if Something Happened: A PC is confronted by a racketeer and their gang, who demand money from the PC in exchange for passage though their neighbourhood. The PC can choose to pay 1d6 gold and pass safely, can start a fight with the racketeer, or can resist the racketeer. If the PC chooses to fight, they'll be forced to combat the racketeer and their 1d6 enforcers (use **Bandits** on page 183 of the core rulebook). If the PC wishes to resist, they must make a **Persuasion (Insight)** or **Intimidate (Resolve)** test against **Difficulty 14**.

- **Failure:** The PC loses their nerve and gives the racketeer 1d6 gold.
- **Standard Success:** The PC intimidates the racketeer into leaving them alone and does not have to pay.
- **Great Success or Better:** The PC forces the racketeer to cower and retreat. The racketeer and their thugs will not bother the PC again and will actively avoid them.

Strength: 4   **Craft:** 4
Life: 12

SHADY DEALER

Many goods in the City change hand through less than legal means, making their sale on a normal market difficult without answering hard questions. The shady dealer asks no such questions; instead, they are merely concerned with the price they pay for the item in question compared to the price they can sell it for once they change its appearance, melt it down, or transport it far from the city. Shady dealers are a mixture of underworld merchants and counterfeiters, knowing both who is buying and selling stolen goods and how to present those goods as legally obtained. Most shady dealers have deals with the Rogues Guild to serve their members without question and work with the Den of Thieves to supply high priced goods of questionable legality. Shady dealers pay bribes as needed to avoid law enforcement, but coin is not always enough if a shady dealer ends up with goods taken via violent crime, goods of very high value, or goods taken from the rich and powerful. More than a few shady dealers have turned informant to the City Watch, City Patrol, or Night Guard in exchange for leniency. Such informants still trade in minor stolen good but report anything of note to the law.

BENEFITS

Fence: If the shady dealer has a Liked or better attitude towards a PC, they may buy stolen goods from the PC. The PC must succeed in a **Bargain (Wits)** test against **Difficulty 16**.

- **Failure:** The Shady Dealer refuses to by stolen goods from the PC. If the player rolls a , the shady dealer is an informant for the law and reports the transaction.
- **Standard Success:** The shady dealer will only pay half the normal value of the stolen items in gold but only has 4d6 gold available to do so.
- **Great Success:** The shady dealer will only pay full value of the stolen items in gold but only has 8d6 gold available to do so.
- **Extraordinary Success:** The shady dealer pays full value for any stolen goods and can buy as much as the characters have to sell.

Questionable Goods: Shady Dealers usually have a selection of unusual goods for sale. If the shady dealer has a Liked or better attitude towards a PC, they may show the PC some of their more unusual items. This requires a **Bargain (Wits)** test against **Difficulty 17**. If the player rolls a , the items are stolen and may attract unwanted attention in addition to costing twice as much as normal.

Failure: the shady dealer refuses to show the PC any special items.

Standard Success: The shady dealer has 1d3 potions or elixirs for sale.

Great Success: The shady dealer has a minor magic item for sale (100 gold or less).

Extraordinary Success: The shady dealer has 1d3 minor magic items or one major magic item (100–500 gold).

Strength: 3   **Craft:** 5
Life: 12

PIED PIPER

A long-standing tradition in the City, the pied pipers of the City have provided pest control for centuries. Decked out in their colourful outfits, the pied pipers can be found throughout the City hawking their skills and drawing attention with their pipes. Using magical skills passed from piper to apprentice, these musicians can enchant rats and other vermin, causing the vermin to follow the piper as long as the piper keeps playing. Using this ability, a pied piper can empty a building of rats and lead them to the wharves to drown en masse. It is rumoured that the first pied piper was given the gift of this magic centuries ago by the Great Wizard in exchange for some service. Some say that the colourful clothes of the pied pipers are part of their gift, and they can only play their enchanting music while wearing ridiculous outfits. Perhaps the first pied piper was cursed by the Wizard to always be a laughingstock and looked down upon, scrambling among the vermin.

BENEFITS

Rat Charming: For 1d6 gold, the pied piper will remove the rats and vermin from a building using their magic, leading them to their doom (or wherever they go). This may help the sick inside recover and can make food supplies last longer. The pied piper need not take their rats to their death; if paid the right price, the pied piper can take them anywhere. If a PC is Liked by a pied piper, the PC may pay the piper 1d6 gold to take the rats and vermin they have charmed to a specific location. This could be the home of a hated rival or perhaps as a distraction while the PCs are up to no good.

Strength: 3   **Craft:** 6
Life: 14

Followers

While many in the City are looking to forge their own path, some are looking for a banner to follow or a master to serve. For whatever reason, their goals line up with the goals of their chosen liege, or they simply fall under the sway of a charismatic leader even as that leader works against the Follower's interests. Followers are many in the City, as there are thousands looking for a cause or a person they can believe in. And the PCs may prove to be just that.

Black Cat

Widely feared for a long-standing association with bad luck and evil magicians in folklore, many peasants avoid black cats. While this is mostly superstition, these stories have a nugget of truth; while black cats can sometimes aid magicians in their arts, any tendency towards the darker side of magic has been grossly exaggerated. Black cats are highly sought after as pets and companions among those wizards and sorcerers. However, they are often treated quite poorly by common folk. Having a black cat at your side is a good way to get blamed by every farmer you meet for their cow giving bad milk.

Benefits

Black Cat's Luck (Average): Spend 1 Loyalty when the GM gains a Dark Fate to gain 1 Light fate.

Familiar's Blessing (Average): Spend 1 Loyalty to add +2 to a Spellcasting test to cast a spell.

Strength: 1   **Craft:** 6

Life: 5

Max Loyalty: 3 (5 for sorcerers or wizards)

Restore Loyalty: Once per day, you may restore 1 Loyalty to the black cat by spending 1 gold on catnip and toys for the cat. You can also restore 1 Loyalty by doing nothing but snuggling and petting the black cat for one hour once a day.

Demagogue

A manipulator of the masses, the demagogue tells the public what they want to hear, whipping them into a frenzy to be directed as needed. A master of mass appeal, the demagogue always wraps themself in the cloak of the common people even when they work against them. They often seek to be in service of charismatic leaders in the hopes that proximity to power will also bring them power. They'll help their chosen leader ascend through counsel of dubious morals and methods, believing that the ends will justify the means.

Benefits

Convincing (Weak): Spend 1 Loyalty. The demagogue grants you a +2 bonus to a Persuasion test to influence an NPC.

Flexible Morality (Average): Spend 3 Loyalty and ○ to change your alignment.

Rabble Rouse (Average): Spend 1 Loyalty. By making a public speech, the demagogue can worsen the crowd's attitude towards a person or group by one level on the attitude chart.

Strength: 2   **Craft:** 4

Life: 10

Max Loyalty: 3

Restore Loyalty: Restore 1 loyalty when you pay them 1 gold or give them an item worth at least 1 gold. Restore 1 Loyalty when you further their political agenda.

Draft Horse

A massive creature, this horse is as big as horses come. Immensely strong, draft horses can pull just about anything on wheels and carry an enormous load. Draft horses are horses that have been trained for work, not warfare, and are commonly used for labour by travellers and farmers.

Benefits

Hauling (Strong): The draft horse can carry up to 50 load in extra items; this benefit does not cost Loyalty. If you spend 1 Loyalty, the draft horse can carry up to 30 extra load for one day.

Riding (Average): The draft horse can carry one character. If you spend 1 Loyalty, the draft horse can carry an additional character. Riding a draft horse at a grueling pace costs an additional 1 Loyalty per day.

Strength: 8   **Craft:** 1

Life: 20

Max Loyalty: 6

Restore Loyalty: Once per day, you may restore 1 Loyalty for this Follower by feeding it 1 ration.

Faithful Hound

Anyone would be lucky to have this sort of dog at their side. Loyal beyond all reason, this hound will follow its master through thick and thin, facing danger and violence as needed. And it gives excellent snuggles on cold nights. Hounds such as this are usually raised from puppies by kind, loving trainers and given to deserving owners, though some are strays in need of a good home after a rough life.

Benefits

Be the Person Your Dog Thinks You Are: Spend 1 Loyalty to add a bonus die to one Resolve test.

Claws and Teeth (Average): Spend 1 Loyalty. You can add the hound's Strength to the damage from your next successful attack.

Guard Dog (Average): Spend 1 Loyalty. Your dog will sit on watch for four hours, growling if anyone comes near that it does not know. During this time, the dog adds its craft to any Perception tests you make.

Scent Tracking (Strong): Spend 1 Loyalty. The Faithful Hound can track a living being with a scent it knows or can detect. When you're attempting to track someone or something, the faithful hound grants you a bonus die to your next relevant test. To use this benefit, the dog must have met the quarry, or you must have an item of clothing that was in the quarry's possession.

Strength: 4   **Craft:** 3

Life: 10

Max Loyalty: 10

Restore Loyalty: Once per day, you may restore 1 Loyalty for this Follower by feeding it 1 ration. Playing fetch or other games with the faithful hound for one hour will also restore 1 Loyalty.

Fortune Teller

Whether reading palms, cards, bones, or entrails, the fortune teller uses their mystic abilities to see into the future and offer advice; their guidance is helpful with surprising regularity. Often, they seek out people with good fortune to help them attain their destiny. Conversely, they'll track down those destined for terrible things to try and help them avoid such a fate.

Benefits:

See the Future (Strong): Spend 1 loyalty and pay 1d6 gold. The fortune teller uses their magic to see the future and if good or ill fate awaits you. Roll 3d6 twice, as if you were rolling a test with a kismet die. Record the totals. You may use these rolls to replace any two rolls you make until you use this ability again. A fortune teller can only do this once a month.

Unassuming (Average): The fortune teller is not targeted by monsters unless there are no other valid targets. If more than one Follower in the party has this ability when there are no valid targets, roll a die to determine which of them is targeted. The Gamemaster may spend ⚫ to nullify this effect.

Strength: 2   **Craft:** 3

Life: 10

Max Loyalty: 3

Restore Loyalty: Restore 1 loyalty when you pay them 1 gold or give them an item worth at least 1 gold. Restore 1 Loyalty if you spend four or more ⚪ in one day.

Gremlin (Cursed)

Gremlins are vicious, mischievous little beasts that take great joy in causing chaos and consternation. They steal, eat vast quantities of food, and generally make a mess of anywhere they are allowed to remain. Most people see them as vermin to be exterminated or removed, though according to some legends, it is possible to befriend gremlins, but it's said to be a long and annoying process that will involve plenty of stolen gold. Gremlin Followers are usually picked up by accident when a gremlin latches onto a particularly wealthy or well fed but poorly defended individual. Once a gremlin begins following you, they're difficult to get rid of, which is only even possible after building some level of good will with the creature.

Benefits

Not Nailed Down (Weak): Spend 1 Loyalty. Roll 2d6 on the table below to see what the gremlin does that day.

2D6	Result
2–3	The gremlin steals a random item from your inventory. This can include a magic item worth up to 200 gold.
4–5	The gremlin steals 1d6 gold from you
6–7	The gremlin steals 1d3 gold from you.
8–9	The gremlin steals 1d6 gold from an NPC and gives it to you
10–11	The gremlin steals a random mundane item from an NPC and gives it to you.
12	The gremlin steals a potion or minor magic item (worth 100 gold or less) from an NPC and gives it to you.

Make a **Stealth (Agility)** test **Difficulty 15** to see if the Gremlin steals from someone else.

- **Failure:** The Gremlin is seen and immediately followed back to you.
- **Success:** The Gremlin is seen but does not attract attention back to you.
- **Great Success or Better:** The Gremlin is not seen, and the victim of the theft has no idea it happened.

CURSE

Hoarding: Once per week, the GM can spend  and restore 1 Loyalty to the gremlin and roll 1d6.

1D6	RESULT
1	The gremlin steals a random magic item or potion worth up to 100 gold from you.
2	The gremlin steals gold or items worth up to 10 gold from you.
3	The gremlin steals gold or items worth 1d6 gold from you.
4	The gremlin steals gold or items worth 1d3 gold from you.
5	The gremlin steals a mundane item worth less than 3 gold from you.
6	In an act of kindness, the gremlin gifts you with 10–60 gold (roll 1d6 × 10) or a mundane or magic item worth up to the rolled amount.

Unwanted Pest: The Gremlin will not leave your side unless you Spend 1 Loyalty and make a **Persuasion (Wits)** test **Difficulty 21** to convince it to leave. The GM can also come up with other means of ridding yourself of the gremlin. If you attack the gremlin, its Loyalty drops to 0, and it turns invisible and hides until you stop, but you cannot force it to leave.

- **Failure:** The Gremlin does not leave, instead stealing 1d6 gold from you.
- **Success:** The Gremlin does leave but steals 2d6 gold or a potion from you.
- **Great Success:** The Gremlin decides to leave.
- **Extraordinary Success:** The gremlin leaves and gifts you 1d6 gold before leaving.

Strength: 2   **Craft:** 3
Life: 8
Max Loyalty: 3
Restore Loyalty: Restore 1 loyalty when you pay them 1 gold or give them an item worth at least 1 gold. Restore 1 Loyalty when you help the gremlin cover up their thievery. If a gremlin's Loyalty is reduced to 0, it does not leave, but none of its benefits can be employed.

HAGGLER

To the haggler, everything has its price; they just need to find out what it is. A master of not just arguing prices, the haggler also knows exchange rates, market rates, and the bigger picture regarding economic concerns. Hagglers often seek to enter the service of travelers, knowing they can benefit from trading while on the road to meet distant vendors whom they've heard are selling high-value goods.

BENEFITS

Bargaining (Average): Spend 1 Loyalty to reduce the price of each item offered by a vendor by 2 gold (to a minimum of 1 gold).

Haggling (Average): Spend 1 Loyalty. You sell an item for 150% value.

Strength: 2 **Craft:** 5

Life: 10

Max Loyalty: 3

Restore Loyalty: Restore 1 loyalty when you pay them 1 gold or give them an item worth at least 1 gold.

PANHANDLER

This poor soul survives in the Realm on the generosity of others. A master of evoking pity either through real or falsified tragedies, they can solicit enough coins from passersby day to day to get by. Panhandlers will often readily take up service with those who can support and protect them—but not at the cost of their freedom. Panhandlers are not interested in lives of strict rules and will simply wander off if badly treated, but if well treated, they can prove a valuable scout or lookout.

BENEFITS

Collecting Alms (Average): Spend 1 Loyalty. The panhandler goes into the nearest settlement to attempt to convince the locals to give them money. The panhandler returns with 1d3 gold, or 1d6 gold if they are in the City.

Distracting (Strong): Spend 1 Loyalty. The panhandler can distract one or more NPCs for you in a crowded setting; each character adds a bonus die to their next Stealth roll in that encounter. Of course, this distraction may place the panhandler in danger, though most people, even criminals, are more likely to have the panhandler arrested or roughed up than seriously injured.

Unassuming (Average): The panhandler is not targeted by monsters unless there are no other valid targets. If more than one Follower in the party has this ability when there are no valid targets, roll a die to determine which of them is targeted. The Gamemaster may spend ⬤ to nullify this effect.

Strength: 2 **Craft:** 4

Life: 10

Max Loyalty: 5

Restore loyalty: Restore 1 Loyalty when you pay them 1 gold or give them an item worth at least 1 gold. Restore 1 Loyalty when you supply lodging for the panhandler overnight.

PHYSICIAN

A student of the body and the ways to heal it, the physician relies on science and knowledge rather than magic to tend wounds. It may not be as fast, but it is very reliable. Physicians seek to put their skills to good use, and tending to the wounds of heroes who generally do the right thing is not the worst way to do so. Plus, it can pay quite well.

BENEFITS

First Aid (Average): Spend 1 Loyalty. Add a bonus die to a Healing test made to perform First Aid or when taking a Recover action during a short rest.

Heal (Weak): Spend 1 Loyalty. The physician heals a character for 1d3 Life.

Long Term Care (Average): Spend 1 Loyalty. The Physician tends to your wounds during a long rest, granting you a bonus die on the **Heal (Insight)** test.

Strength: 2 **Craft:** 4

Life: 10

Max Loyalty: 3

Restore Loyalty: Restore 1 loyalty when you pay them 1 gold or give them an item worth at least 1 gold.

POLTERGEIST (CURSED)

You've somehow attracted an angry spirit that has decided to tag along and make your life difficult. It is sometimes useful, but it's more commonly troublesome, and terribly so. It's appetite for fate seems unquenchable. Poltergeists often follow those who are cursed or have disturbed the dead. They are not sought out.

BENEFITS

Cursed Hunger (Average): Spend 1 Loyalty. Roll 1d6 on the following table. This benefit can only be used once per day.

1D6	RESULT
1	The Game Master gains 1 Dark Fate
2	You lose 1d3 Light Fate
3	You lose 1 Light Fate
4	You gain 1d3 Light Fate
5	You gain 1d6 Light Fate
6	The next time the Game Master should gain ⬤, they do not.

Spirit Strike (Average): Spend 1 Loyalty. You attempt to get the poltergeist to destroy an item. This functions as the Shatter spell. Instead of the normal Spellcasting test, roll Intimidate (Resolve) test.

- **Failure:** The poltergeist breaks a random object nearby and not the one you wanted.
- **Success:** The poltergeist breaks the item you wanted but some other random item as well.
- **Great Success:** The poltergeist breaks the item you wanted.

CURSE

Doom: Once per week, the GM can spend 1  and increase the poltergeist's Loyalty by 1 to roll 1d6.

1D6	RESULT
1	You lose 1d6 Light Fate
2	You lose 1d3 Light Fate
3	You lose 1 Light Fate
4	GM gains 1 Dark Fate
5	GM gains 1d3 Dark Fate
6	You gain 1d3 Light Fate

Breaking Things: Whenever you roll ⚫, the GM can immediately spend the Dark Fate earned to have one item (worth 5 gold or under) on your person break. This is often the item you were using.

Poltergeists' Curse: The poltergeist will not leave your side unless you cross the River or spend 3 Loyalty and make a **Lore (Wits)** test against TN 15 to exorcise it. If you attack the poltergeist, its Loyalty drops to 0, and it turns insubstantial. You cannot force it to leave through violence, however.

Failure: The poltergeist does not leave. It takes 1d3 ⚪ from you, and the Game Master Gains 1 ⚫.

Success: The Poltergeist does leave, but it takes 1d3 ⚪ from you.

Great Success: The poltergeist leaves.

Strength: 3 **Craft:** 3

Life: 14

Max Loyalty: 5

Restore Loyalty: Restore 1 Loyalty by feeding the poltergeist 1 ⚪. If a poltergeist's Loyalty is reduced to 0, it does not leave like other Followers; however, none of its benefits can be used.

SCRIBE

In addition to possessing excellent handwriting, scribes know many different languages and are often astoundingly well read. Using their specialized skills, they can even copy magical texts if given the right resources.

BENEFITS:

Inscription (Average): Spend 1 Loyalty. The scribe can make an extra copy of a spell you possess (typically within a spellbook or on a scroll). You must pay the cost for any materials.

Master of the Written Word (Average): Spend 1 Loyalty. The Scribe grants you a +2 bonus to any Decipher tests.

Transcribing (Average): Spend 1 Loyalty. The scribe can transcribe a scroll into your spell book for you, taking one day.

Strength: 1 **Craft:** 4

Life: 10

Max Loyalty: 4

Restore Loyalty: Restore 1 Loyalty when you pay them 1 gold or give them an item worth at least 1 gold.

SELLSWORD

Not just a thug for hire, a sellsword is a professional soldier with military training and experience. They can lead soldiers into battle and even plan out strategies if ordered to do so. But they know their skills are in demand, so their services do not come cheap. Sellswords are always looking for a fight that can make them a few coins.

BENEFITS:

Combat Boost (Average): Spend 1 Loyalty. You can add this Follower's Strength score to the damage from one successful attack

Defender (Average): Spend 1 Loyalty; this benefit lasts for the duration of one combat. When another Follower takes damage, this Follower takes the damage instead.

Independent (Average): Spend 1 Loyalty. The sellsword makes an Attack (Melee or Ranged) action on their own as if they were a PC. If you gave them orders that include attacking, you do not need to be present to use this ability; if you tell your sellsword to accompany this person and attack anyone who attacks them, you may spend Loyalty to make the sellsword attack even if you are not there. The sellsword attacks with a skill of 5 and inflicts (weapon) +5 damage. The player makes the roll for the sellsword.

Strength: 5 **Craft:** 2

Life: 18 **Armour:** 10

Max Loyalty: When you recruit a mercenary, choose a Max loyalty (up to 7) for that Follower. Then pay twice that amount in gold.

Restore Loyalty: Restore 1 loyalty when you pay them 2 gold or give them an item worth at least 2 gold.

Stinker

This small rodent may not be the best company, but if you need a room cleared or attention diverted, they are the best beast for the job. Stinker is attracted to snacks and warmth; anyone with a warm space with a lot of snacks may find themselves with an unexpected Stinker follower.

Benefits:

Diversion (Strong): Spend  and 1 Loyalty. Stinker prevents an enemy from responding to an attack this round.

Strong Smell (Average): Spend 1 Loyalty. Any creature passing through the area for the next hour has their sense of smell overwhelmed by a powerful smell. The stink makes it impossible to track by scent, and most people will leave the area without a strong reason to stay.

Strength: 2 **Craft:** 2

Life: 6

Max Loyalty: 3

Restore Loyalty: Once per day, you may restore 1 Loyalty for this Follower by feeding it 1 ration.

Taleweaver

Nothing spreads fame and renown like a teller of tales telling your tales. Having a taleweaver in your retinue is one of the best ways to get your name and deeds out into the world. Don't be an unsung hero, be a sung hero. Taleweavers are always looking for heroes from whom they can obtain new stories; the crowds constantly want fresh content.

Benefits:

Reputation Proceeds You (Strong): Spend 1 Loyalty. The NPC you are interacting with has heard tales of you and is starstruck. Their attitude becomes Liked for the next hour unless you give them a reason not to like you.

Announce (Average): Spend 1 Loyalty. On entering a business, party, or other social occasions, your taleweaver announces you, reciting your name, titles, lineage, and deeds. You gain a +1 bonus to your next Persuasion, Deception, or Intimidate check, whichever comes first.

Strength: 2 **Craft:** 4

Max Loyalty: 3

Restore Loyalty: Restore 1 Loyalty when you pay them 1 gold, give them an item worth at least 1 gold, or perform a great deed worthy of a story.

Trophy Hunter

Trophy hunters can always be found loitering around job boards in the major city squares, hungry for the latest wanted posters. Bounty rewards are how trophy hunters make their living, and they are always looking for new prey. They also sell their services as manhunters to any who can pay.

Benefits:

Ambusher (Average): Spend 1 Loyalty. When you're attempting to ambush enemies, partial surprise becomes complete surprise.

Come Quietly (Average): Spend 1 Loyalty. Add a +2 bonus to Intimidate tests to scare an NPC into submitting

Manhunter (Average): Spend 1 Loyalty. Add a bonus die to any Investigation check when you are hunting a person.

Strength: 4 **Craft:** 2

Life: 14 **Armour:** 6

Max Loyalty: 3

Restore Loyalty: Restore 1 loyalty when you pay them 1 gold or give them an item worth at least 1 gold.

Urchin

Urchins can be found on the streets and alleyways of the City and other large settlements. They are usually children who have no family and nowhere to live. They often attach themselves to adventurers as a means of survival.

BENEFITS:

Streetwise (Average): Spend 1 Loyalty. The urchin goes out into the streets to get the lay of the land and collect rumors, reporting back any they find. The exact details provided are up to the GM. This benefit places the Follower at risk. The GM may choose to roll 2d6 to determine the outcome.

2D6	RESULT
2	The urchin leads trouble back to you, such as the law, your rival, etc.—anyone you don't want finding you.
3–4	The urchin makes it back but has stirred up trouble. Your enemies and rivals in the city are looking for you, but the urchin can tell you where they are.
5–9	The urchin knows all the latest news on the streets, what your rivals are up to, what the law is doing, etc. The urchin also brings back 1d3 gold
10–11	The urchin brings back all the major news on the streets: location of fences, what gangs are at war, any good scores to be made, etc. The urchin brings back 1d6 gold as well.
12	The urchin returns with all manner of useful information, from guard schedules to secret passwords to hidden treasure locations, and to top it off, they aroused no suspicion. You get a bonus die on your next test taking advantage of this info. Additionally, the urchin brings back 2d6 gold.

Unassuming (Strong): The urchin is not targeted by monsters unless there are no other valid targets. If more than one Follower in the party has this ability when there are no valid targets, roll a die to determine which of them is targeted. If other followers have a weaker version of this ability, they are targeted, not the urchin. The Gamemaster may spend 🜄 to nullify this effect.

Strength: 2 **Craft:** 3
Life: 10
Max Loyalty: 5
Restore Loyalty: Restore 1 loyalty when you pay them 1 gold or give them an item worth at least 1 gold.

WARHORSE

The product of years of training and generations of breeding, a warhorse is a magnificent beast of a horse. Capable of not only fearlessly carrying its rider into battle but lending aid with the occasional kick.

BENEFITS:

Hauling (Strong): The warhorse can carry up to 50 load in extra items; this benefit does not cost Loyalty. If you spend 1 Loyalty, the warhorse can carry up to 30 extra load for one day.

Riding (Average): The warhorse can carry one character. If you spend 1 Loyalty, the warhorse can carry an additional character. Riding a warhorse at a grueling pace costs an additional 1 Loyalty per day.

Combat Boost (Strong): Spend 1 Loyalty. You can add the warhorse's Strength to the damage of one from one successful melee attack.

Strength: 7 **Craft:** 2
Life: 20
Max Loyalty: 8
Restore Loyalty: Once per day, you may restore 1 Loyalty for this Follower by feeding it 1 ration. Spending an hour caring for the warhorse by brushing its mane or cleaning its shoes, for example, restores 1 Loyalty.

CHAPTER 5: CITY GEAR AND REWARDS

Within the City, a dazzling array of goods can be found, a selection unequaled in the Realm. Not only do merchants come from all over the Realm to sell their goods, but the City is home to numerous craftsmen, including masters of nearly every trade. Here they perfect new methods and designs, pushing their craft ever forward. Whether searching for ancient treasures or unique prototypes, the City is the premier place to find rare goods. Its markets are the envy of the world and are frequented by many adventurers seeking supplies for their next foray or selling their recently acquired loot.

TOOLS

While the tools of many professions can be found for sale throughout the Realm, the City and some other large settlements provide rare and specialized tools that can rarely be found elsewhere. In addition to more portable kits that tradespeople can carry with them, entire workshops can be purchased in the City. While not portable, these workshops allow a dramatic increase in efficiency.

Item	Cost	Load	Features
Artisan Tools	10–25 gold	2	Includes the basic tools needed to practice a single Artisan focus.
Artisan Workshop	25–50 gold	20	Provides an in-depth variety of tools for single Artisan focus. Tests using that focus in the workshop gain a bonus die.
Burglar's Kit	5 gold	2	Includes lockpicks, prybars, and other tools useful for entering somewhere you are not invited. Adds a bonus die to any skill check to bypass the defenses of a structure.
Pickpocket's Tools	5 gold	1	Includes finger knives, resin, and other tools useful for pickpocketing. Grants a bonus die to Sleight of Hand tests to pick pockets but is very suspicious if found on your person.

Alchemy Kit

A large bag of alchemical supplies and tools including beakers, tongs, scales, and common ingredients. It is enough to do many basic alchemical tasks, though additional supplies are sometimes required. Producing an alchemy kit requires the work of several craftsmen: smiths, glaziers, etc., but they are usually found for sale in alchemist shops.

Benefits: Provides a pool of 3 Light Fate that can only be used with Alchemist class abilities while the character has the alchemy kit with them. This Light Fate pool can be refilled by making a **Spellcasting (Alchemy)** test of **Difficulty 14** that takes 8 hours. Restored Light fate can never exceed the pool of 3.

- **Failure:** No Light Fate restored and lose 1d3 gold in ingredients.
- **Success:** 1 Light Fate restored but spend 1 gold on ingredients.
- **Great Success:** 1d3 Light Fate restored but spend 1 gold per Light Fate restored.
- **Extraordinary Success:** Up to 3 Light fate restored for no cost.

Load: 3
Value: 10 gold

Alchemy Lab

A room-sized set of alchemical tools, supplies, and reference books, these labs are usually only found in alchemist shops or the homes of particularly well-off alchemists. A workshop contains the means to produce most alchemical items, but certain rare ingredients will still need to be found. Such a lab can take many months to put together due to the rarity of its tools and reagents.

Benefits: Provides a pool of 10 Light fate that can only be use with Alchemist class abilities if the character is in the same location as the alchemy lab. The lab is large enough that it is usually stationary or in a wagon. This Light Fate pool is refilled with a **Spellcasting (Alchemy)** test of **Difficulty 15** that takes 8 hours. A new attempt can be made once per day.

- **Failure:** No Light Fate restored and lose 1d3 gold in ingredients.
- **Success:** 1 Light Fate restored but spend 1 gold on ingredients.
- **Great Success:** 1d3+1 Light Fate restored but spend 1 gold per Light Fate restored.
- **Extraordinary Success:** Up to 5 Light Fate restored for no cost.

Load: 100
Value: 250 gold

Clipper's Kit

A set of tools for the clipping, smelting, and counter-feiting of coins. Very illegal! Using this kit, the counterfeiter clips the edges off existing coins, just slivers per coin, so it is not noticed, melts those scraps down, and casts them into new coins. Unfortunately, getting the coins to look like real coins is very difficult, though often, the counterfeiter can get close enough to deceive most people who don't look too closely. Such coins will not fool experienced merchants or bankers, however, who have noticed that counterfeiting has become a growing problem in the City.

Benefits: To use a clipper's kit, you must make a **Difficulty 15 Tinker (Wits)** test.
- **Failure:** You lose 1d3 gold.
- **Success:** You gain 1d3 gold, but the coins are not perfect forgeries.
- **Great Success:** You gain 1d6 gold, but the coins are not perfect forgeries.
- **Extraordinary Success:** You gain 1d6 gold that are nearly indistinguishable from the real thing.

Load: 3
Value: 10 gold

Tinkerer's Kit

A collection of tools for working with complex machinery, a tinkerer's kit includes both basic tools, like a hammer and chisel, and tools for more fine work, such as magnifying glasses and tweezers. The tools and parts contained are sufficient for many basic repairs. Building a tinkerer's kit requires a variety of crafts, but most importantly, it requires the skills of a tinkerer, who are usually the ones who sell such kits.

Benefits: If a character has the Tinkerer's Kit with them, reduce the Salvaged Parts cost of Tinkerer class abilities by 1 and gain a pool of 3 Light Fate to be used for Tinkerer class abilities. It is refilled with a **Difficulty 15 Tinker (Wits)** test that takes 8 hours.
- **Failure:** No Light Fate restored and lose 1d3 gold in ingredients.
- **Success:** 1 Light Fate restored but spend 1 gold on ingredients.
- **Great Success:** 1d3 Light Fate restored but spend 1 gold per Light Fate restored.
- **Extraordinary Success:** Up to 3 Light Fate restored for no cost.

Load: 2
Value: 10 gold

Tinkerer's Workshop

This is a stationary workshop that contains just about all the tools and parts a tinkerer could ask for. Such large kits are usually only found in the shops and homes of master tinkerers, though some have managed to build such a workshop into specially made wagons. Creating a tinkerer's workshop can take many months; thus, they can be difficult to find for sale.

Benefits: While a character is in the same location as the tinkerer's workshop, reduce the Salvaged Parts cost of Tinkerer class abilities by 2 and gain a pool of 10 Light Fate that can only be used with Tinkerer class abilities. The shop is large enough it is usually stationary or in a wagon. It is refilled with a **Difficulty 15 Tinker (Wits)** test that takes 8 hours.
- **Failure:** No Light Fate restored and lose 1d3 gold in ingredients.
- **Success:** 1 Light Fate restored but spend 1 gold on ingredients.
- **Great Success:** 1d3+1 Light Fate restored but spend 1 gold per Light Fate restored.
- **Extraordinary Success:** Up to 5 Light Fate restored for no cost.

Load: 100
Value: 250 gold

MAGIC ITEMS

Magical wonders of many kinds can be found throughout the Realm. The magic items detailed here might be discovered in the City, although they might just as well be found anywhere.

MAGIC ARMOUR

Smiths of great skill from all races and cultures can be found in the City. In addition to their more recent masterworks, the products of armourers of ages past can be found for sale in the City. Magic armour is never commonly for sale in the City, however, but it can be found on occasion if one knows the right stores or has contacts in the Merchant's Guild.

Armour of Humility

This armour is said to be cursed, and if one were to look at the list of its previous wearers, that would seem to be the case. From Sir Askiel of Ezenvale to the Margata, every one of them was defeated in battle, yet they survived through some quirk of fate. That is the true magic of this armour; it may doom you to defeat, but you will live to tell the tale.

SPECIAL QUALITIES

The Armour of Humility will doom the wearer when they are close to defeat, but that defeat will never result in the wearer's death, allowing them to escape by some miracle.

⬤ While wearing this armour, if your Life is reduced to half or below, when you take damage from an

attack, you take an additional 1d6 damage, but you gain one ◯.

◯ If you are reduced to 0 Life while wearing this armour, you immediately return to 1 Life but also move to a safe location far enough away from the battle that you cannot rejoin it. This movement should appear incidental, like falling into a river, getting drug away by your horse, or rolling down a hill.

Benefits: 13 Armour, and you have a bonus die on any death tests. This armour can always be refit to full and does not need to be repaired.

Agility Penalty: −3
Load: 8
Value: 100

Golden Gauntlet

This thick-plated gauntlet looks to be made of gold, but it's actually plated steel. Despite the heavy appearance of the Golden Gauntlet, it weighs little and does not inhibit the wearer's movement. This gauntlet is said to be from the armour of the ancient dwarven hero Djar Goldenhair who disappeared in battle with a dragon; this gauntlet was the only piece of her armour that was recovered. It has since travelled the length and breadth of the Realm, worn by various heroes and warriors.

Special Qualities

◯ You may double the value of any worn armour for one round but mark an X in the armour points track.

◯ Your armour protects against psychic damage for 1d3 rounds.

◉ If your armour is more than half damaged, the Golden Gauntlet falls off your arm and is lost. You can spend ◯◯ to prevent this.

Benefits: The value of any armour worn increases by +2. This additional value can always be refit and does not need to be repaired.

Load: 1
Value: 250

Mirror Shield

Said to have been made by the elven craftsmen Elilr the Dawnforger long ago, this shield is crafted of a large piece of crystal, cut and polished to provide a mirror-smooth reflective surface along its face. According to legend, this shield can reflect magic power and images. The mirror shield is rumoured to have been destroyed many times before reforming and reappearing in the hands of a new hero. Or, perhaps, there is simply more than one of these shields.

Special Qualities

◯ On a Great Success or better, with a Defend or Protect action against a spell or magical attack, you can redirect the attack to a new target, using your Defend test as the new attack roll. The new target must be in range of the spell or effect as if you cast it.

⊙⊙ If the mirror shield is destroyed by blocking an attack, it reforms on the next dawn if you have any of its pieces.

⊙ You may return any gaze-based attack back on its user with a Great Success or Extraordinary Success on a Defend or Protect action.

Benefits: Acts as a normal shield. Max Damage Absorbed: 30

Load: 1

Value: 150

MISCELLANEOUS

Not every magic item can be easily categorized. Most shops that deal in magical goods have a sizeable Miscellaneous section for those strange objects that don't fit anywhere else. Such sections are rarely well curated and could contain poorly priced items of great power for the discerning shopper.

BRASS BOTTLE

This small brass bottle has a stopper attached to it by a short chain. Unadorned and plain, the brass bottle gives no outward sign of its power. Said to have been developed by the inhabitants of the Firelands for dealing with dangerous elementals, these items have now spread cross the Realm. Several have passed through the City over the years, often snapped up by adventurers looking for an edge when facing elementals or spirits.

When a brass bottle is found, roll 1d6 to see if it has a being trapped within. On a roll of 5 or 6, a being is already trapped in the brass bottle and must be released before another can be trapped. Such a trapped creature may show thanks for being release or rage at its imprisonment. Spirits are more likely to be hostile toward living beings while elementals are more likely to just leave. To determine the type of creature released roll 2d6 and consult the following chart:

2D6	CREATURE
2–3	Banshee
4–5	Air elemental
6	Fire Elemental
7	Earth Elemental
8	Water Elemental
9–10	Spectre
11–12	Wraith

To determine its attitude, roll 3d6 on the **Attitude Chart** (see page 152 of the core rulebook) with a −2 penalty if an elemental and −4 if a spirit.

SPECIAL QUALITIES

When the brass bottle is empty, you may attempt to use it to trap a single elemental or spirit inside. This requires an action and a **Psychic (Wits)** test against the spirit or elemental's Threat.

- **Failure:** The target is not trapped and strikes you for full damage.
- **Success:** You trap the creature in the bottle until the next sunrise or sunset, and the target strikes you for half damage.
- **Great Success:** You trap the target in the bottle, and it cannot escape until released.
- **Extraordinary Success:** You trap the target in the bottle, and it cannot escape until released. You can use the bottle to drain the creature's power, destroying the creature to regain 1d6 spell points.

Once trapped, the creature may be released as a full action requiring no test.

Load: 1

Value: 150

ORBS

Orbs have long been a favored implement of magicians wishing to project a less combative image than one does with a wand or a staff. Glass or crystal of such quality and size needed to make an orb are very rare, thus they project an image of power and wealth. Orbs are commonly used as focuses for arcane power, amplifying the effects of spells in certain respects. Current fashion leans more towards wands, with orbs being the choice of older magicians.

ORB OF FLAMES

Crafted from volcanic glass, this black obsidian orb glows as if flame is trapped within, pulsing with the heat of a volcano for its master's use. Orbs of Flames are carried by magician who favor fire magic—often to an unhealthy extent. Such pyromancers are commonly seen as unhinged by their fellow magic workers, and thus, the Orb of Flames has become something of a pariah's tool in arcane circles.

Special Qualities

⬤ You learn the spell fireball if you are able.

⬤ You can cause any fire already burning to double in size.

⬤ You suffer a penalty die on defend actions against fire-based attacks.

Benefits: If you cast a spell that inflicts fire damage, the damage increases by +1d6. If you take fire damage from any source, you take an additional +1d3 damage.

The Orb of Flame can produce light on demand, creating full light up to 4 metres and dim light out to 8 metres.

Load: 0
Value: 150

Orb of Knowledge

Orbs of knowledge are popular not just with magicians, but also with scholars and sages of all stripes. The magic of this item allows the user to access a vast storehouse of knowledge within that was accumulated over centuries by the past owners of the Orb of Knowledge. Because this knowledge varies from orb to orb each Orb of Knowledge has its own specialties and quirks.

Special Qualities

⬤ You learn the spell brainwave if you are able.

⬤ You may treat a Great Success in a test using a skill you are proficient in as an Extraordinary Success.

⬤ Recall any event the orb was present for with perfect clarity.

Benefits: You gain a bonus die on any tests using Lore and one other skill of the GM's choice based on the events the orb has recorded.

Load: 0
Value: 100

Orb of Prophecy

The Orb of Prophecy allows fleeting glimpses into the possible futures of the orb's owner. These glimpses are rarely clear and are usually quite cryptic. In addition to these visions, the Orb of Prophecy can guide its owner towards a desired end, advising them through dozens of small choices.

Special Qualities

⬤ You learn the spells *augury* and *divination* if you are able.

⬤ Select one skill. You gain a bonus die on tests with it for one hour.

Load: 0
Value: 65

Orb of Time

Said to be formed of fragments of solidified time energy, these purple crystals are highly sought after by any who wish to escape the ravages of time. By skipping across the timeline, the Orb of Time allows the owners to manipulate time to the point of bending it back on itself. Interestingly, some scholars claim there is only one of this object, which theoretically loops through time repeatedly to appear as several distinct copies.

Special Qualities

⬤ You may take two actions in a single turn, one after the other.

⬤ Double the duration of a single spell or magic item effect.

Benefits: You gain a bonus die on death tests. When you spend ⬤ to reroll a die, you can reroll two dice. Additionally, you do not age so long as you possess the Orb of Time.

Load: 0
Value: 250

Potions and Elixirs

The most common type of magic items, potions and elixirs are available at many merchants in the City. Produced by local magicians or alchemists, these magical concoctions are expensive, but with some footwork, one can find many less powerful potions and elixirs for a fair price. More expensive and rare potions and elixirs may require more effort, and perhaps some greased palms, but if there's somewhere an object might be for sale, the City is the place to find it.

Elixir of Might

Brewed with a combination of rare herbs and fragments of an earth elemental, drinking this potion makes the imbiber as tough as stone for a short time. This potion is favored both by warriors and magicians

who want some security if they are cornered. It can often be found in the alchemist shops of Guild Street and the Merchant's Quarter.

Benefits: Drinking this potion grants +2d6 to max Life and 10 armour. The potion's effects last for 2d6 rounds.

Load: 0
Value: 30

Elixir of Life

One of the rarest potions, its creation requires troll blood, among other difficult and disgusting ingredients. In addition, it must be sealed in a container of silver to maintain potency, requiring significant precious metals to create.

Benefits: For 2d6 hours after drinking this potion you gain 1 Life any time you make a death test, allowing you to quickly recover when reduced to 0 Life.

Load: 0
Value: 50

Elixir of Rage

Brewed using a mixture of the strongest alcohols, hallucinogenic herbs, and lion blood, this potion is only sought out by the most determined warriors. The Elixir of Rage puts the drinker into a terrible, murderous fury that makes them a ferocious combatant while vastly impairing their judgment and perceptions.

Benefits: For 2d6 rounds after drinking this potion, you enter a terrible rage. While in this rage, you inflict +2 damage with melee attacks, gain armour equal to your Mettle, and can continue taking Melee Attack actions while at 0 Life, but any round you do so, you automatically fail your death test. While in the rage, any round you can make a Melee Attack action, you must do so, even if your only target is an ally.

Load: 0
Value: 25

Elixir of Wrath

A rare potion both due to the difficulty of making it and low demand, this potion fills the drinker with unbridled magical power, allowing the imbiber to wreak great destruction if they are a magician. Few magicians find the experience of drinking an Elixir of Wrath enjoyable and want to repeat the experience. It is carried by some as a device of last resort.

Benefits: For 2d6 rounds after drinking this potion, you enter a magical frenzy. While in this frenzy, you gain one spell point per round and inflict +1d6 damage with spells and Psychic Attack actions. Each time you take advantage of this damage bonus, you suffer 1d3 damage (ignores armour). You can continue taking the Psychic Attack action while at 0 Life, but any round you do so, you automatically fail your

death test. If you know no spells and cannot make the Psychic Attack action, drinking this potion inflicts 2d6 damage on you and has no other effects.

Load: 0
Value: 25

Elixir of Wisdom

Sought by magicians of all sorts, this rare potion boosts the spellcasting capacity of the drinker. Made from various products of the Woodland realms, it is most often found in the hands of the fey but can occasionally be found for sale in the City. Unfortunately, mortal magicians often find the Elixir of Wisdom highly addictive and consume them even when the boost of arcane power is not needed.

Benefits: Drinking this potion grants +1d6 to max and current spell points. The potion's effects last for 2d6 rounds.

Load: 0
Value: 35

Unstable Potion

These potions are found for sale across the City, being cast-off mistakes or products of alchemists in training. Every alchemist shop has a box of them stored somewhere awaiting an unwary buyer. Their effects are completely random, so they are only purchased by the desperate.

Benefits: Each time you drink an unstable potion, roll 2d6 on the table below to determine the effect.

2d6	Result
2	You age 1d6 years.
3	Your age decreases 1d3 years.
4	You gain the elven ability of Night Sight (see page 59 of the core rulebook) for 1d6 hours.
5	You pass gas loudly and stink for the next hour. You suffer a penalty die for any social interactions while this is happening.
6	You heal 1d6 Life (can exceed maximum).
7	You are poisoned for 1d6 damage.
8	You gain 1d6 spell points (can exceed maximum) that last for 24 hours.
9	You vomit uncontrollably and are incapable of taking an action aside from Recover until you succeed at a Recover action.
10	You belch fire in a stream in front of you, which acts as the spell *Fireball*.
11	You are cured of any poison or disease.
12	You turn invisible as per the invisibility potion.

Load: 0
Value: 5

WANDS

Wands are ubiquitous among the sorcerers and wizards of the City, though most are merely nonmagical focuses rather than items of arcane power. They are particularly common among the younger magicians, who like the speed and portability of the wand compared to the size of the staff or weight of the orb. This has been further enhanced by the fact the most popular wand dealer in the City, Haseed Oaksong, has turned his family's shop into a popular coffee bar and meeting place for the wizarding community of the City. This store, the Duchess of Oaks, can be found near the Academy by following the smell of coffee and the murmur of constant arguing over arcane theories.

Psionic Wand

This wand allows the user to focus the powers of their mind, transforming them into physical force. The user can use this to lift or manipulate objects at a distance or even make attacks by wielding weapons with their mind. This is favoured among more martial wizards and spellcasters.

Special Qualities

This wand has 10 charges and crumbles to dust when the last charge is used. It can recover 1 charge a day if the owner spends 8 hours of meditation with it.

1 charge: You lift a weapon with the power of your mind, making a Melee or Ranged Attack action using your Craft for your Brawn or Agility. Melee attacks made in such a way have a range of 10 metres.

1 charge: You can make a Psychic Attack as if you had the Sorcerer Core Feature (as described on page 80 of the core rulebook). You gain a +2 to your test and inflict +2 damage. This applies whether you have Psychic Attack or not.

1 charge: You can make a Defend or Protect action using your Psychic or Spellcasting skill.

Load: 0
Value: 150

Skull Wand

In the minds of most mages, skull wands are the tools of villains. Made of human bones, usually a femur, they are distinctively grisly. These wands feed on death and suffering, and their abilities do nothing but bring more death into the world. Anyone caught with such a wand is likely to be ostracized by those who recognize it, and as such, these items are rarely for sale in the City. Even thieves and Shady Dealers are loathe to deal in this sort of item

Special Qualities

This wand has 10 charges. Once these charges are gone, it rots away into nothing. Skull wands can regain 1 charge for every month left in a tomb or crypt.

1 charge: ☠ add +2d6 damage to an attack or spell.
1 charge: Add a bonus die to a Psychic Attack test.
3 charges: Animate a corpse as a putrid zombie under your control. The zombie remains until destroyed. It cannot be healed.
Benefits: Any death tests made in your presence have a penalty die.
Load: 0
Value: 300

Syphoning Sceptre

This crystalline scepter has had every spark of arcane power drained from it, becoming a void that pulls other magic into it. A trained magician can use this to drain magical power from others, however, but at the cost of their own magical abilities. It is often carried by mages who do battle with other magicians, but this raises suspicions about their intentions. Among magesm carrying this wand openly is seen as a declaration you mean to start trouble.

Special Qualities

This wand has 10 charges. Once these charges are gone, it explodes, draining 12d6 spell points from anyone within 5 metres. 1 charge can be restored once per month by spending 5 spell points.

1 charge: ☠ On a Great or Extraordinary success on a Defend or Protect action against a spell, you drain

1d6 spell points from the spellcaster and gain them yourself.

1 charge: Add a bonus die to any Defend or Protection actions against a spell.

2 charges: On a successful Psychic Attack action, you drain 1d6 spell points from the target and gain them yourself. This only work on targets who have spell points.

Load: 0
Value: 300

Wand of Cinders

These charred black wands are the product of ritually prepared trees being hit by lightning under specific conditions. The wands created are sought out by mages who favour fire magic, but they are also feared since so few can control the immense power contained within. Commonly, stories surrounding wands of cinder involve spontaneous lightning, unintended fires, and general havoc wrought against their owner's wishes.

Special Qualities

This wand has 10 charges. Once these charges are gone, it burns away to soot. The wand of cinders regains a charge after spending 1 week in a continuous fire.

2 charges: Fire a bolt of fire as a full action. Choose a target you can see and attempt a Craft test. If the result equals or exceeds the target's Threat rating, the target takes damage equal to 2d6 +Craft.

2 charges: The target of a spell or Psychic Attack takes an additional 2d6 fire damage.

X charges: On a spell or psychic attack action, a random unintended target within 5 metres takes 1d6 fire damage, or a random flammable substance within 5 metres catches on fire.

1 charge: While holding this wand, reduce any damage due to fire (magical or natural) by your Craft.

1 charge: As a full action, this wand may be used to light flammable materials on fire by touch.

Benefits: This wand can produce light on demand, creating full light up to 4 metres and dim light out to 8 metres. This does not require a charge.

Load: 0
Value: 300

Wand of Dragonfire

These extremely rare wands are crafted from the bones of dragons, though a single dragon can have several bones large enough to be used for such. They are favoured by dragon hunters and magicians who want raw destructive power. Unfortunately, those who possess these wands sometimes fall under its sway and seek to build their own dragon hoard.

Special Qualities

This wand has 10 charges. Once these charges are gone, it disappears in a burst of fire, inflicting 1d6 damage on the bearer. The wand of dragon fire regains a charge each month it is left in the ashes of a burned corpse.

1 charge: While holding this wand, gain a bonus die on any test to avoid or resist dragon breath attacks.

1 charge: Destroy a nonmagical item of shield size or smaller by melting it. If it is being carried or wielded, this requires a successful Ranged Attack action using a **Missile Weapon (Agility)** test.

2 charges: Release a gout of flame from the wand at a target within 10 metres. Make a ranged attack using **Missile Weapon (Agility)** test against the target's Threat.

Failure	No effect.
Success	The target and all engaged creatures take 2d6 fire damage.
Great Success or Better	The target and all engaged creatures take 4d6 damage. Any creature killed in this fashion also has all their nonmagical equipment destroyed.

Benefits: You become unreasonably greedy for the next day and seek to hoard all the wealth you can, sleeping on it if allowed.

Load: 0
Value: 150

CHAPTER 6: THE NIGHTMARE INVASION

"The Nightmare Invasion" is an urban adventure set entirely in the City and intended for a group of 3 to 6 players playing characters of 3rd to 5th level. If this is your first adventure, you can either use the pre-generated characters included with the *Talisman Adventures Fantasy Roleplaying Game* or have your players create new characters using the rules in that book. In either case, we recommend that you either advance starting characters to at least 3rd level (using **Character Advancement** in **Chapter 6** of the core rulebook) or reduce the number of enemies in most combat encounters by one or two.

If you're using this adventure as part of a campaign, you'll need to provide an incentive for the characters to stay in the City for a few days. The story provides one simple reason in the form of a festival taking place in the City, one in which just about any character might want to either witness or participate. Other possibilities are numerous and contextual depending on your players, but once the PCs are there, they'll become involved in the problems that occur on the first night. Examples include completing a delivery job, performing in the Town Square, seeking specific knowledge at the Academy, attending to holy business at the High Temple, joining a guild, or shopping for a special item.

SYNOPSIS

This story begins with the characters visiting the City during the Festival of Strangers, a week-long celebration during which every interaction with a stranger is expected to involve the exchange of minor gifts. To maximise the impact of the adventure's final encounter, the GM should try to learn something that each character fears or would have had nightmares about.

Act One: The characters enjoy the sights and sounds of the City during the Festival of Strangers. While visiting the Town Square, they see a building decorated with gargoyles, a visiting troupe of jesters (who unintentionally frighten a human child), and a few other bits of colour that won't affect the plot like those two will. Until nightfall, the player characters can drive what work or entertainments their characters wish to pursue.

At midnight, the City is suddenly attacked by especially terrifying gargoyles. The characters' assistance in defending the place is greatly welcomed, for the city watch, city patrol, and Night Guard are all overwhelmed and under-prepared.

Act Two: Investigating the attack reveals that things don't add up. The gargoyles seemed to come from nowhere, attacked without reason, and most curiously, had glowing red eyes. The characters can gain more information from Ohrzer's Magic Emporium (the location of the decorative gargoyles, which are mere stone), a friend of Ohrzer who has a phobia of gargoyles, and the two places in the City with experts on creatures like gargoyles: the Academy and the Menagerie.

From the friend of Ohrzer, the characters may learn that she had nightmares about gargoyles on the night of the attack, and that she had been gifted with a talisman earlier that evening. However, she has already given the talisman away this morning. If desired, the characters can then track down the chain of individuals who originally provided the talisman, as well as the chain who received it after her. The latter chain runs out before nightfall, but the origin chain leads to an evil sprite who, under questioning, confesses that the talisman was sent by his master to cause chaos in the City. At midnight on the second day, the City is attacked once more—this time by nightmarish jesters!

Act Three: The sudden appearance of the jesters is even stranger than that of the gargoyles, as jesters can't fly but they somehow bypassed the intact City Gate. After helping to defend the City again, the characters can investigate the cause of this attack. This leads to a child they saw at the beginning of the story who is afraid of jesters—and is in possession of the talisman. When the characters finally get within reach of the talisman, a red-eyed black horse manifests. This is the Night Mare, a creature that lived within the so-called nightmare talisman. The Night Mare attacks, joined by creatures pulled from the fears of each player character…

ACT ONE: THE FESTIVAL OF STRANGERS

The characters start the adventure in the City, either just arriving there or having been there for any amount of time (whichever better suits the Game Master's plans). Before we address why they are there, read aloud or paraphrase:

There's a buzz in the air, a palpable excitement about the beginning of the Festival of Strangers. This is a week-long celebration during which every interaction with a stranger is expected to involve the exchange of minor gifts.

Now help the players decide on the following details. Some of these will help you in staging the events of the adventure, while others will simply encourage backstory development and roleplaying. Skip any questions to which you've already decided the answer (such as if you have a reason in mind for the party to be visiting the City).

- **Why are you visiting the City?** Are you here to see the Festival of Strangers? Are you delivering something? Visiting a guild, perhaps to join? Do you need information about monsters from the Academy or the Menagerie? Seeking religious guidance from the High Temple? Are you shopping for a special item?
- **Where are you staying?** The Six Fates Inn is the most popular of several lodgings, and the City's numerous guilds sometimes provide beds for members.
- **Have you been in the City before?** When was that, and why? Did you grow up here?
- **Are you members of any of the City's professional guilds?** The City is home to the Alchemy Guild, Assassins' Guild, Beggars Guild, Chiurgens Guild, Crafters Guild, Entertainers Guild, Merchant's Guild, and the Rogues Guild.
- **Do you know anyone here?**

Now that these details are decided, continue setting the scene…

The sun is beginning to set as you explore the City. As you pass through the Town Square to see the sights, seek out dinner, or pursue some other goal, you can't help but notice the decorations most businesses and city institutions have put up for the festival. The statues in the Square of Kings have been given heart-shaped necklaces, the traditional gargoyles atop Ohrzer's Magic Emporium are decked out in yellow flowers, and the normally drab stone exterior of the jail has been covered in posters drawn by children. You also see unusual groups of people, such as the tribe of trolls, who stand out everywhere they go, and the troupe of jesters, who seem to delight everyone except for one little girl, who runs away crying. But don't worry, she is quickly comforted by a sweet treat, as are many of the festival goers who are enjoying tarts, strawberries, figs, small cakes, and other offerings from food vendors.

THE FESTIVAL OF STRANGERS

This popular annual event is a week-long celebration during which every interaction with a stranger is expected to involve the exchange of minor gifts. For the purpose of the festival, "stranger" is interpreted loosely: anyone with whom you have never spoken. Normal festival etiquette is to introduce oneself by name during the gift exchange. Common decorations for the Festival of Strangers include symbols of friendship such as flowers (especially yellow roses), knots tied in ropes or strings, entwined boughs, and interlocking hearts.

Each day, the first time each character gives a gift to a stranger, they receive 1 Light Fate. Keep this in mind since the adventure will take place over at least two days.

Consider adding occasional references to the festival throughout the adventure to keep it real in the players' minds—describe strangers approaching the characters while they investigate the mystery, and decorations being scattered during combat, and groups of unusual visitors to the City (fae, ghouls) here to enjoy this period of extra-welcoming spirit.

The following is a list of possible gifts that characters may receive (and re-gift) during the festival. Characters may purchase such items from a variety of general stores throughout the City, especially near the Town Square.

Beaver pelt
Bells on a string
Belt made of rope
Berries wrapped up in a leaf
Booklet of poems
Bundle of flowers
Candle
Castanets (one pair)
Chocolate coins
Cloth bracelet
Crown of leaves
Crudely carved walking stick
Deck of cards
Drawing of a faery
Drumsticks
Tiny duckling
A single egg

Envelope containing a note that says "I like you"
Fancy arrow
A feather
Hair brush
Hair clasp
Harlequin mask
Hymn book
Length of ribbon
Maracas
Mushrooms
Necklace of string
Night cap
Pair of gloves
Pair of socks
A painted stone
Pan flute
Piece of chalk

Potion that causes some minor useless effect (curling hair, changing eye colour, deepening voice)
Pressed flower
Quill pen
Scarf
Scroll containing a song
Sea shell
Sling
Spin drum
Spool of thread
Tabor drum
Toy figure carved from wood
Trading card for a famous gladiator
Vial of desert sand
Wooden spoon
Wooden top
Yellow rose

While taking in the sights at the Square, a friendly elven boy approaches the party and offers a gift to one of the characters. Choose a gift from the list in the sidebar **The Festival of Strangers** (or invent one of your own), and choose a recipient based upon whoever seems the most approachable (or whomever the GM thinks would be most entertaining to have receive a gift). The boy says, "My name is Matas. Good to meet you!" If the character gives Matas a gift in return, no matter how humble, the boy is happy and skips away, and the character receives 1 Light Fate. Otherwise, Matas frowns as he departs.

THE TRIBE OF TROLLS (OPTIONAL ENCOUNTER)

Also taking in the sights and sounds of the Festival of Strangers is a group of trolls visiting from their tribe far outside the walls of the City. If it fits the GM's wishes and the adventure's pacing, the player characters may witness an altercation between the trolls and a group of arrogant city patrol members.

You hear some sort of commotion ahead—raised voices. When you draw closer, you see a group of city patrol members confronting a tribe of trolls. One of the trolls stands over the wreckage of a produce merchant's stand.

"I SAID it was an accident," says the largest troll.

"And I say you're lying! You're all spending the night in jail!" screams the city patrol captain.

There are six trolls and seven city patrol members. The trolls are Juma (leader and toughest looking), Matuna (shaman and oldest looking), Kurzol, Napok, Kelraz, and Erodan (an adolescent eager to prove himself). The city patrol members are Santiago (the group's captain), Benjamin, Defne (a dwarf woman), Jacob, Martina, Lucas, and Gabriel (an elf). See page 81 for city patrol stats, and refer to Troll Warrior and Troll Shaman (for Matuna) in **Strangers, Allies, Followers, and Enemies** at the end of the adventure for more details on these characters—especially if a fight breaks out.

If the characters do nothing, the altercation escalates into a fight wherein the trolls defeat the city patrol members and then flee the City, knocking unconscious several members of the city watch on their way past the City gate. If the characters wish to de-escalate this situation and prevent the fight, they can try using such skills as **Deception (Wits or Insight)**, **Intimidate (Resolve or Brawn)**, **Persuasion (Insight)**, or whatever else the GM accepts at **Difficulty 13**. Any number of player characters can assist the one who is rolling, using their own choice of skills as usual. Use the following results as guidance on the outcome, adjusting as needed for the use of different skills.

DE-ESCALATING THE TROLL CONFLICT

Failure	The trolls and city patrol members are too eager to fight and cannot be persuaded otherwise. The fight begins.
Standard Success	Both sides agree to stand down, and the fight is averted. They are still distrustful of each other, so the city patrol attempts to follow and watch the trolls from a distance for the remainder of the festival.
Great Success	Both sides admit they were being hot-headed and that fighting would be against the spirit of the festival. They work together to help rebuild the produce merchant's stand.
Extraordinary Success	As Great Success, plus the adolescent troll wishes to become a character's follower. See **Adolescent Troll** in **Strangers, Allies, Followers, and Enemies** for more details.

The Rest of the Day

If the characters have business in the City (as possibly established in the introduction), this would be a good time for them to complete it. Otherwise, they are free to do whatever they wish until the next scene, which begins at midnight. The players can drive what work or entertainments their characters wish to pursue until nightfall. If the GM wishes to improvise a bit, let the players pick anywhere in town they would like to spend time (as detailed conveniently in this very book). Otherwise, feel free to fast-forward by declaring that the day passes uneventfully and the characters retire to their chosen lodging (such as the Six Fates Inn) after dark.

Midnight Attack

At midnight, the City is suddenly attacked by especially terrifying gargoyles. Any characters who are awake hear the commotion—the assault is happening all over the city. For any sleeping characters, the player must make a **Difficulty 10 Notice (Wits)** test to see if the sounds of the attack wake them. If no characters awaken, have a creature smash through a window or wall into where they are sleeping and treat everyone as having a Standard Success. (See below for how the characters identify the creatures.) If some remain asleep after others are up and fighting (perhaps separated because they aren't sleeping nearby), use a similar event to ensure no characters remain sleeping (to keep all the players involved).

Failure	The character continues sleeping.
Standard Success	The character wakes but is still groggy. All actions they take on the first round other than defend are at a −2 penalty.
Great Success	The character wakes and can act normally.
Extraordinary Success	The character wakes, can act normally, and can wake one other character. A character who is awakened gets to act normally. This can be applied to a character who is sleeping or groggy.

Read or paraphrase the following, changing details such as whether the characters were sleeping or not:

You are awakened by the sounds of combat in the street outside! When you look out a window or step outside, you see a city under siege by flying monsters! They're attacking the city guard, demolishing storefronts, and trying to bash into people's residences. It's difficult to get an accurate count amid all the chaos, but you'd guess there are dozens of the creatures.

Have all players who look outside (or otherwise encounter the attackers) roll a **Lore (Wits)** test against

Difficulty 12 to see if they know what the creatures are. Higher levels of success include the facts listed at the lower levels as well.

Failure	Flying grey monsters are attacking! Maybe some sort of fae folk?
Standard Success	All of the attacking creatures are gargoyles, winged creatures made of stone, wielding stone axes.
Great Success	Gargoyles are carved from stone and animated by arcane magic. They are normally only encountered in small numbers, in dungeons or other places where treasure needs guarding. You've never heard of them attacking the City (or even a village) *en masse.*
Extreme Success	The gargoyles' eyes are glowing red, and their rocky claws and teeth are at least six-inches long. These are not normal features for gargoyles.

If the characters avoid the fighting, have it come to them! A gargoyle might crash through a window to attack whoever is inside or throw a victim through the wall. Truly reluctant characters might receive a visit from a member of the town guard who knows of their reputation and begs for help in defending the City from this uncanny onslaught.

Gargoyle Combat

If the players join the fight, their assistance in defending the City is greatly welcomed, as the city patrol, city watch, and Night Guard are all overwhelmed and under-prepared. Use the **Gargoyle** stats from **Chapter 4** of *Talisman Adventures*, page 190. If the characters are near one of the locations in the box **Gargoyle Combat Locations**, that would be a good place to start staging the fight. There's no need to involve the characters in fighting every gargoyle—let them engage a few in an area or two of your (or their) choice and then conclude the fight before it becomes tedious.

Less combat-inclined characters can help out in other ways during the fight, perhaps inspired by the **Gargoyle Combat Locations**. For example, healers can help the acolytes from the High Temple in their efforts to rescue and heal citizens wounded in the attack, and crafty characters can repair parts of the City that might endanger others, such as the City Stables.

For any fight with the creatures, provide 1 attacking gargoyle for each character, perhaps adding or subtracting 1 based on your knowledge of the characters' combat capabilities. As an option, involve members of the city patrol, city watch, or Night Guard as temporary Followers for any characters, adding one gargoyle for each two such followers. These followers remain with the characters for the duration of the encounter or for the entire scene, at the GM's discretion.

Gargoyle Combat Locations

City Gate: Many of the City's defenders spread out from the City Gate to fight the invaders, as they were posted there as a matter of routine. If any characters ask, the guards say that the gargoyles did not come through the City Gate; indeed, nobody even saw them fly over the city walls. (More details about this are presented in Act Two, and the urgency of combat keeps anyone from talking much during the gargoyle attack.)

City Watch in Trouble: Several members of the city watch flee from dive-bombing gargoyles who have snatched away their weapons and their hats and now have plans for their heads.

The High Temple: Assisted by a few acolytes, the Light Priest is trying to de-animate the gargoyles by using a spell recorded in one of the Temple's rare tomes. The spell doesn't work, which confuses the Light Priest. Other acolytes assist the Gray Priest in trying to drag gargoyle victims to safety and provide healing. If the characters want to discuss this with the Light Priest, see **The High Temple** under **Investigating the Gargoyle Attack**.

Night Guard in Trouble: The characters see two battered members of the Night Guard searching a street for gargoyles and then see the three gargoyles perched above preparing an ambush.

Ohrzer's Magic Emporium: This is not a combat location, but if anyone thinks to check Ohrzer's Magic Emporium, which they noticed had decorative gargoyles when they passed it earlier in the day, they find its gargoyles still in their places, undisturbed. The Emporium is closed during the attack.

The Six Fates Inn: The City's most popular inn is also popular with the gargoyles, who have made it inside by both window and doorway and are chasing lodgers, terrorizing bar patrons, and destroying the kitchen.

The Town Square: A few merchants try to keep the gargoyles from destroying the merchandise in their stalls (foodstuffs, general goods, clothing), while the gargoyles pick up barrels and boxes and drop them on the merchants from high in the air.

The Wharves: Gargoyles are swooping down and throwing people into the water from the docks and even from the decks of ships. Though the sailors are generally good swimmers, an injury or two can leave them in dire need of rescue.

During combat, the gargoyles prefer to fly from target to target using their Flight benefit. These gargoyles do this more to be scary and chaotic than to protect themselves. In fact, the gargoyles in this combat fearlessly fight to the death, never attempting to flee. Bring them to life by describing the flapping of their stunted wings, their glowing red eyes, their extra long claws and teeth, and the way chunks of stone fly off them when a character lands a solid hit.

Here are a few examples of ways to breathe life into descriptions of the gargoyles during this encounter:

- A City defender's arrow glances harmlessly off a gargoyle's stone form.
- A character's solid blow shatters a gargoyle's wing, which crumbles into stone fragments. The creature is grounded but ignores the wound and keeps attacking.
- A gargoyle slashes through leather armour with its deadly claws.
- A pair of gargoyles chases helpless citizens down an alley towards a dead end.
- After a gargoyle attacks a player character, it flies away a short distance to ravage a member of the city watch.

Ending the Combat

When the GM and players have had enough fun engaging gargoyles in combat, the characters see the last of the creatures fall to a player's skillful attack (or a stranger's if the characters stayed out of the fight). Anyone engaged with or watching the gargoyles at the end of the fight may make a **Notice (Wits)** test against **Difficulty 11** to notice a final detail about them. Higher levels of success include the facts listed at the lower levels as well.

Failure	They're all dead. Mission accomplished.
Standard Success	After the last gargoyle died, it and all the other gargoyle bodies in sight faded away without a trace.
Great Success or Greater	The bodies vanishing suggests that they are not corporal beings, which doesn't match normal descriptions of gargoyles.

The various guards and any civilians around thank the characters for helping defend the City. The guards cease being Followers (for now) and split up to search for any more gargoyles and care for their wounded while other townsfolk begin repairing the physical damage from the creatures' attack. If the players are proactive and want to start investigating the gargoyles, the City folk ask them to wait until morning for any such discussions—or perhaps ask them to provide more healing, repair work, or patrolling.

ACT TWO: INVESTIGATING THE GARGOYLE ATTACK

The characters have a number of avenues of investigation open to them, should they choose to ask around about the gargoyle attack or gargoyles in general. This section covers the most likely people and places the characters might visit in their investigation.

We assume that such investigation takes place the following day, as most people the characters might want to talk to would be sleeping, healing, or otherwise busy recovering from the late-night attacks. If the characters instead insist on performing investigations immediately, the GM will need to modify some of this section to account for seeking out and talking to the people involved (likely accompanied by **Persuasion (Insight)** tests to get exhausted gargoyle-attack survivors to talk).

Remember that on each day during the festival, the first time each player character exchanges gifts with a stranger grants them 1 Light Fate.

TALKING TO CITIZENS

Most citizens know few details about an unusual monster like a gargoyle, so not many think much about the gargoyle attack other than that it was frightening, a cause for mourning those injured or killed, and a nuisance due to the need to repair or replace damaged property. However, asking around and talking to various citizens for a while can turn up some unusual observations that several people mention. (And remember to have citizens offer festival gifts to characters they haven't met before,

except in the case of citizens who may be distraught from losses taken during the attack.) Have anyone questioning citizens make an **Investigation (Insight)** test at **Difficulty 12**. Multiple characters can assist a single investigator if the players wish to team up.

RESULTS OF TALKING TO CITIZENS	
Failure	The citizens seem clueless about gargoyles and are obsessed with their own problems.
Standard Success	Nobody saw the gargoyles approaching the City from outside. Even though they fly, it seems odd that the creatures were within the City walls and on the attack before anyone realised it. Several people wonder where they came from. There's nowhere outside the City that is known to have gargoyle statues.
Great Success	There didn't seem to be a purpose to the gargoyles' attack other than wanton destruction and terror; they attacked people and property seemingly at random.
Extraordinary Success	The attack started right at midnight. Few citizens keep track of the time of day with greater precision than "midday" or "at dusk" or "when it cools down a bit," but some do, and the ones you talked to are sure the gargoyles came immediately after midnight.

Asking around about gargoyles also prompts someone to remind the characters that one building in the City features gargoyles: Ohrzer's Magic Emporium. (Yesterday when they were checking out the City the characters saw that the gargoyles on Ohrzer's were decorated with yellow roses.) See **The Gargoyles at Ohrzer's Magic Emporium** for more details.

TALKING TO THE CITY'S DEFENDERS

Discussing the attack with any of the City's guardians—including the city patrol, the city watch, and the Night Guard—can lead to similar results as seen in **Talking to Citizens**. This sort of discussion might take place at the City Gate or the jail (where **Sheriff Thurston Midge** can often be found), in which case describe the yellow flowers decorating the City Gate, a few posters advertising the Festival of Strangers on the City walls, and the miniature yellow nooses hanging from the bounty board in a simultaneous display of festivity and bad taste.

If the characters have a reasonably good relationship with any of the City's defenders, have one of them ask the characters to help them if another attack happens while they are still in town. And if the characters haven't thought of it, this defender might also ask if the characters will help augment the City's defences (see **Bolstering City Defences** if they agree to this or suggest it themselves). (Possible City defender contact: Gerald, grey-haired human veteran, wears several medals from past campaigns.)

THE HIGH TEMPLE

If the characters ask about gargoyles at the High Temple, the Light Priest talks about how he tried to use a de-animation spell to neutralize the gargoyles (as the characters may have seen in the **Gargoyle Combat Locations** box), but it didn't work. He refuses to believe that the flaw was in the spell or his casting and that this must mean these creatures are not truly gargoyles.

THE GARGOYLES AT OHRZER'S MAGIC EMPORIUM

If the characters check out the decorative gargoyles at Ohrzer's Magic Emporium, they find the establishment open during daytime hours or closed after dark. Ohrzer's is known throughout the Realm as an excellent source of magic items. The shop is located just off the town square, down a narrow alley along with a blacksmith, a dwarven market, and a few residential buildings. The residences facing Ohrzer's keep their windows shuttered ever since a recent magical crafting mishap briefly turned most of the nearby residents purple.

TALKING TO OHRZER BRITTLEAXE

Ohrzer Brittleaxe is the dwarven proprietor of the Magic Emporium. If it is during shop hours (basically when the sun is up), Ohrzer is present and crafting a ring of protection (see **Magic Items** in *Talisman Adventures* **Chapter 6: Rewards**). Otherwise, he is unavailable.

Ohrzer is a wiry dwarf with long auburn hair tied in braids and intense blue eyes. He wears a sleeveless tunic and humble cloth breeches. When characters visit him, he says, "Welcome to the Magic Emporium, strangers. I am Ohrzer Brittleaxe. Help yourself to stranger gifts on the table by the door. I'd give them to you myself but my hands are busy!" Ohrzer has no problem answering the characters' questions so long as they don't mind him continuing to work—and his attempts to sell them merchandise at a healthy festival markup.

Some possible questions, with Ohrzer's answers, include:

What do you sell here?

"Magical objects of all types… tools, protective rings and amulets, even weapons and armour. You worldly-looking adventurers could probably use an ancient elven bow—yours for only 250 gold!"

Are your gargoyles real?

"Mercifully no, they are stone imitations, crafted by an old friend of mine. But what I craft is magical items of wonder. Need a bottomless haversack? Only 150 gold!"

Who crafted the gargoyles?

"My friend Ebba Silverbough, best stone carver I know. We grew up together here in the city." (This might be a good time to mention the info under **Fear of Gargoyles**, below.)

Do you know anything about gargoyles?

"The common wisdom is that wizards bring them to magical life so they can protect their treasures and whatnot, but I've never encountered one myself and don't know if this is true. But speaking of bringing things to life with magic, you can take home this dancing sprite figurine for only 50 gold!"

Did you see the gargoyle attack last night? Where were you?

"I heard the commotion, sure, but I retreated to my cellar until things got quiet again. I'm an artisan, not a warrior! However, if you are a warrior, you may get good use out of a shield of defiance for only 350 gold!"

Will you contribute magical items to help defend the City in case of another attack?

Have the asking player make a **Difficulty 13 Bargain (Wits)** test. One other character can assist on this test.

Failure	*"Would that I could, but my supplies are low. If the City wished to purchase some of my items, of course, that would be a different matter!"*
Standard Success	*"Hmm. I suppose I could part with a few items without hurting my inventory too much."* He offers to donate three items worth up to 100 gold each from **Magic Items** in **Chapter 6: Rewards** of the *Game Master's Guide* in the core rulebook (not counting potions or elixirs).
Great Success	*"A very good idea. I would be proud to contribute."* Similar result to Standard Success, but he offers four items worth up to 200 gold each.
Extraordinary Success	*"Absolutely! I am ashamed I did not think of that myself."* Similar result to Standard Success, but he offers five items worth up to 300 gold each.

Fear of Gargoyles: When the players are finished asking questions, or the GM sees a good opportunity to inject this, Ohrzer adds that he hopes his friend **Ebba Silverbough** didn't see the Gargoyle attack since Ebba is terrified of actual gargoyles. "It took a lot of persuading to get her to craft the ones on my roof; she's been afraid of them since she was a child." Ohrzer does not know the reason for Ebba's fear.

Examining the Gargoyles

The shop features four stone gargoyles on its roof, one at each corner. Characters can gain access to them for a closer look by using a roof access ladder inside the shop (if it is open or they break in), climbing to the room from the outside, or flying. Climbing to the roof requires an **Athletics (Agility)** test against **Difficulty 13**. Up to two characters can assist another on this, and once one is on the roof, they can help others up without a test.

As described in **Festival of Strangers**, the gargoyles are decorated with yellow flowers draped around the gargoyles' necks like druid necklaces. They feel solid and seem to be normal stone statues. They show no damage other than signs of weathering consistent with years of exposure to the rainfall and climate of the City.

Examining the gargoyles shows no evidence of magical influence on the statues. The characters can, however, find the signature of the sculptor on the right rear paw of each: *Ebba Silverbough*. (See **The Gargoyle-Fearing Dwarf** if the characters wish to seek out this sculptor.)

The Gargoyle-Fearing Dwarf

If the characters go looking for the sculptor who carved the gargoyles atop Ohrzer's Magic Emporium, Ebba Silverbough (detailed in **The Gargoyles at Ohrzer's Magic Emporium**), they can find her easily. This is an opportunity to reward player creativity, so go along with whatever makes sense. They can find her using their own knowledge of the City (an Easy **Investigation (Insight)** or **Lore (Wits)** test, with failure resulting in wasted time before success), by asking around at the Crafters Guild, by asking Ohrzer, or similar investigations. The characters can track Ebba to her small house, to the sculpting workshop she uses at the Crafters guild, or whatever other place might interest the GM.

Ebba is a stout dwarven woman with a golden ponytail and thick spectacles. She is curious to learn why the characters are looking for her but eager to take a break from her sculpting. If asked, she confirms that she carved the gargoyles on Ohrzer's Magic Emporium (as detailed below).

Here are some other possible questions and answers with Ebba Silverbough, but make sure she mentions having a nightmare about gargoyles on the night of the attack:

Did you carve the gargoyles perched on Ohrzer's Magic Emporium?

"Yes I did. I've been friends with Ohrzer since we were kids, and I couldn't turn down his request for me to carve them, even though I have no love for gargoyles."

Why are you afraid of gargoyles? *OR* **What do you know about gargoyles?**

"When I was a child, my grandmother caught us raiding her supply of fruit tarts one too many times. The next day, she placed a stone gargoyle above the pantry door and told us, in graphic detail, what a gargoyle would do to children who tried to get past it to steal its treasure. The nightmares started immediately, and though I feel silly to say it, I still have them occasionally. But that's not unusual, is it? Aren't you afraid of anything?"

Have any of your sculptures come to life before?

"Never! Not to my knowledge, anyway."

Did you dream about gargoyles last night?

"I… I did. In fact, it was much as people tell me it happened last night. In my dream, the horrible creatures were flying all around the City, attacking everyone and everything they saw."

Did you see the gargoyle attack last night? Where were you?

"No, I slept through it. I wish I had awakened so I could help defend the City. At least, I like to think I would have overcome my fear to do so."

Did anything unusual happen to you lately? *OR* **Can you think of anything that would have made your nightmare come to life?**

"Hmm… on the evening of the attack, I WAS wearing a talisman I had received that day as a stranger gift. It didn't seem to do anything, so I hadn't thought much of it. I figured surely it's a minor talisman, but I thought it might bring me good fortune or something."

Who gave you the talisman?

"Let me think… I'm pretty good with names. It was Emil, a friendly dung cleaner I introduced myself to on my way home last night—in the spirit of the festival."

What do you know about this Emil?

"Nothing, really. He's human, brown hair, average appearance, cleans dung. He was cleaning up on Market Street when I met him."

Who did you give the talisman to?

"This morning I gave it to a gladiator I passed before breakfast, near the armoury. Oh I think I remember her name… Leonor."

What do you know about this Leonor?

"She is tall and golden-haired and powerful, and I wish I were like her."

Next Steps

If the characters learned about Ebba's talisman and wish to track it down (including trying to locate Emil or Leonor), proceed to **Tracking the Talisman**.

Tracking the Talisman

GM Note: If the characters miss the clues leading to Ebba and the talisman, perhaps have Ebba later seek out authorities (who then reach out to the characters) when she herself connects her dreams and possibly her (temporary) talisman with the attack she heard about—perhaps right before the next night's attack.

Characters who learn about the alleged talisman from Ebba Silverbough can trace it in two directions: the chain of people who had it before Ebba (the origin chain) and the chain of people who had it after (the destination chain).

Rather than detailing each person who had possession of the talisman, and where they traded it, we will abstract this with Investigation tests…

Keeping Track of Time

The GM may wish to keep track of how much time the characters spend in attempting to track down the talisman. One reason for this is that after dark, investigations will most likely shut down, as people go home and are not available for investigators to find (as tracking the people involved mostly means looking for people of certain descriptions, rather than going to an address). Another reason is that a second attack will start at midnight, which will interrupt any investigations.

The described activities allowing the characters to track the talisman include suggestions for how much time they will take (modified by success or failure). However, the GM is free to disregard tracking how long each activity takes if they wish, and they may instead choose to let the characters do as much as they'd like until the GM is ready to spring the next attack, at which time the GM can declare that the City has effectively shut down for the evening.

Tracking the Talisman's Origin

Characters who try to track the talisman's destination must roll an **Investigation (Insight or Wits)** test at **Difficulty 13**. An unlimited number of player characters can assist on this test, or everyone can roll separately. Each roll (other than assisting rolls, or tests done simultaneously) represents one hour of searching and talking to people, and failures use additional time to represent false leads and red herrings.

ORIGIN CHAIN	
Failure	The character fails to find the person Ebba received the talisman from. Alternatively, they find one or two (see **Where the Talisman Came From**) but not the person from whom it originated. The character wastes 1d6 hours from the search.
Standard Success	The character traces the chain of people from whom Ebba Silverbough received the talisman. See **Where the Talisman Came From**.
Great Success or Higher	As with Standard Success, but the character gets an instinctive reading on Ainley the Sprite that tells them Ainley will likely flee the area if spooked.

Tracking the Talisman's Destination

Tracking the talisman's origin works the same way as tracking the destination (detailed in that section previously).

GM Note: This investigative path will reach a dead end before nightfall, as one of the people in the chain cannot be found yet. This is done in order to present another nightmare attack.

DESTINATION CHAIN	
Failure	The character fails to find the person who received the talisman from Ebba. Alternatively, they find one or two (see **Where the Talisman Went Next**) but not the person it ended up with. The character wastes 1d6 hours from the search.
Standard Success	The character traces the chain of people who received the talisman after Ebba Silverbough, though it dead-ends at the docks. See **Where the Talisman Went Next**.
Great Success or Higher	As Standard Success, but a sailor at the docks (Sofia, a grey-haired but strong woman in red sailing garb) promises to contact the character if Nojus's ship returns early or she hears any other news about him.

Where the Talisman Came From

Here is the chain of individuals who owned the talisman before Ebba, followed by details for each. The chain is presented in the order the player characters would experience it, backtracking from each recipient. Depending on the characters' rolls to track the talisman and the GM's preferences, the GM can use this as a simple list to mention for flavour as the characters arrive at the end point, or they can let the characters visit each person in the chain.

If player characters ask for details about what other stranger gifts changed hands, either use the list in the sidebar **The Festival of Strangers** (page 104), improvise a gift, or have the townsfolk say (truthfully) that they don't remember. If they ask about fears or nightmares, none of these individuals have specific fears of gargoyles. None of them could tell that the talisman did anything at all.

Ainley (origin) > Noa > Logan >
Miraç > Elena > Emil > Ebba

Ebba received the talisman from…

Emil (human, average height, brown hair, wearing a soiled tunic and breeches): Emil is a dung cleaner who was working on Market Street when he gave the talisman to Ebba. Emil received the talisman from…

Elena (human, tall and lithe, wearing a well-made yellow dress): Elena is a dancer, and she gave the talisman to Emil after meeting him at a temple service. Elena received the talisman from…

Miraç (ghoul, smiling and gaunt, wearing a smart suit): Miraç runs a music shop, and he gave the talisman to Elena at his store. Miraç received the talisman from…

Logan (human adolescent, black hair, energetic): Logan was playing on Redbird Street when he gave the talisman to Miraç. Logan received the talisman from…

Noa (troll, long hair in a ponytail, wears leather merchant's garb): Noa is a merchant, and she gave the talisman to Logan at the bridge on Main Street. Noa received the talisman from…

Ainley the Sprite (sprite with curly blond hair, emerald tunic with gold trim, cap with a yellow feather sticking out of it). Ainley is the one who brought the talisman to the City, first giving it to Noa near the wishing well. Refer to **Ainley the Sprite** when the characters trace the talisman's origin this far.

Where the Talisman Went Next

Here is the chain of individuals who owned the talisman after Ebba, followed by details about each. Depending on the player characters' rolls to track the talisman and the GM's preferences, the GM can use this as a simple list to mention for flavour as the characters arrive at the end point, or they can let the characters visit each person in the chain.

If characters ask for details about what other stranger gifts changed hands, either use the list in the sidebar **The Festival of Strangers** (page 104), improvise a gift, or have the townsfolk say (truthfully) that they don't remember. If they ask about fears or nightmares, none of these individuals have specific fears of gargoyles. None of them could tell that the talisman did anything at all.

Ebba > Leonor > Zeynep > Nojus

Ebba gave the talisman to…

Leonor (human, tall, blond, and muscular, wearing leather armour). Leonor is a gladiator, and she received the talisman from Ebba near the armoury. Leonor gave the talisman to…

Zeynep (elf, stocky with short black hair and a guard's uniform). Zeynep is a member of the city guard, and she received the talisman from Leonor at the pawnshop. Zeynep gave the talisman to…

Nojus (elf, short and white-haired with wrinkled, leathery skin). Nojus is a sailor, and he received the talisman from Zeynep at the southeastern wharf. Unfortunately, the characters are unable to locate Nojus; people at the wharf who know him say he shipped out this afternoon for a sea-fishing journey on the *Dancing Dolphin* and isn't expected back for a week. (Pursuing Nojus is a dead end, so try to gently discourage attempts to pursue his ship, such as having no other ships ready to ship out today.)

Unbeknownst to the player characters, Nojus already gave the talisman to another recipient, Hanna Harper. They can learn this in **Act Three**.

Ainley the Sprite

The characters can track Ainley down at the Square of Kings (see page 117) based on their appearance: a sprite with curly blond hair, an emerald tunic with gold trim, and a cap with a yellow feather sticking out of it. When the characters locate the sprite, Ainley is sitting on top of a statue of one of the former kings, calling down occasional insults to passers-by. (*"Is that a shirt or did you knit your back hair?" "Madame, you might want to get checked for curses; I think you're turning into a frog." "Does anyone else smell that? Ah yes, the distinctive stench of street urchin!"*)

Roleplaying Ainley: The sprite loves teasing and insulting people and has no respect for anyone except their master, the Wraith Lord. Ainley's orders are to keep an eye on the talisman's progress (from a distance) until someone puts a stop to it, and then return to the Wraith Lord to report how it went. While spending time in the City waiting for the mission to be complete, Ainley intends to have a little fun spreading some harmless chaos. For full details on how Ainley will ask specific questions, see **Questioning Ainley** below. Ainley's full stats appear in **Strangers, Allies, Followers, and Enemies**.

As soon as Ainley guesses that the characters have tracked the talisman to them, they try to flee, flying away from the Square of Kings to attempt escape in the streets. The characters may pursue either on foot or in the air (for other flying characters). If the characters have no flying ability, perhaps Ainley has to fly under festival decorations strung across the streets or chooses to land to try and get lost in the crowd.

CHASING AINLEY

Depending on how involved the GM wants this scene to be, chasing Ainley can be resolved as either a single test or broken into combat rounds.

For resolving the chase with a single test, have one pursuing character roll an **Athletics (Agility or Brawn)** test against **Difficulty 14**. All the characters present may assist on this test, using any skills the GM considers appropriate (including Deception, to lead their quarry in a desirable direction, or Notice, to spot a shortcut to allow an interception). This can represent the party chasing Ainley together or splitting up to pursue in different ways—or whatever else the selected skills suggest.

Failure	Though the characters eventually catch Ainley and end the chase, everyone takes 1d6 damage from fatigue or mishap. Ainley is reluctant to talk to the characters (but does so without much trouble) and seems ready to flee at any time.
Standard Success	The characters catch Ainley and end the chase. Ainley acts reserved but answers questions when asked.
Great Success or Better	The characters intercept or surround Ainley quickly and with little trouble, and Ainley eagerly volunteers to tell the characters whatever they want to know.

To resolve the chase in combat rounds, let each pursuing character roll an appropriate test against **Difficulty 14**, likely using **Athletics (Agility or Brawn)**. There are no Failure/Success results; instead keep a tally of the Kismet Die results on successful rolls as a chase progress score, and when this score reaches 15, the characters have caught Ainley and ended the chase. Make sure to encourage the players to describe the results of their attempts, and use the following special Kismet Die results when they appear:

Mishap! Lose half the accumulated chase progress and take 1d6 damage.

Outstanding! Add 8 to the chase progress instead of 6.

Questioning Ainley

Below are the answers Ainley has to likely questions by the characters. Ainley puts up no further resistance after being caught and answers all questions truthfully (except for one, as noted).

Where did you get the talisman?

"Direct from the hands of the Wraith Lord. By the way, the Wraith Lord sends his compliments to all you clueless City folk!"

Who is the Wraith Lord?

"My master is a powerful immortal spirit who lives in a realm far beneath the City."

Why did the Wraith Lord send the talisman here?

"To spread chaos and weaken your City! My lord is unhappy with your City and its goody-goody adventurers. He plans to pay you a visit himself… eventually."

What does the talisman do?

"It contains a special friend of the Wraith Lord. I would tell you more, but why spoil the surprise, ha ha!" Note that Ainley will not reveal more about the talisman, even if threatened with death, as they believe the Wraith Lord's displeasure at "spoiling the surprise" will result in a worse death than any they could otherwise experience.

Why do you serve the Wraith Lord?

"He lets me keep the belongings of his vic—er, his visitors."

How do we find this Wraith Lord?

"You do not! The Wraith Lord finds you! If you are extremely unfortunate, that is."

Once they are finished talking with Ainley, the characters can decide what to do with the sprite: free them (Ainley is happy), ask the Sheriff to detain them (Ainley patiently waits for the master to intervene… someday), kill them (Ainley begs for mercy), or whatever they choose.

Conducting Research

If the characters wish to seek out more information about gargoyles or the talisman, they can do so in several places. The ones most likely to be helpful are the **Academy** and the **Menagerie**. If it looks like the players are unlikely to choose to visit both locations (or you only want to present one for time purposes), consider providing all the information from both places at the one they actually visit.

The Academy

The Academy is a massive building that takes up most of Noble Street. Long ago it was a school of higher learning run by wise elven scholars, but since they departed for more sylvan lands, it has transitioned into a centre of learning specifically focused on monsters and monster hunting. This is evident from the smell of decaying flesh and the alchemical mixtures used to turn monster hides into rugs, clothing, armor, and even parchment.

The grounds of the academy have been hung with yellow-and-white signs celebrating the festival: "Strangers Welcome" and "Happy Festival" and the like. Scholars and students of diverse ages and ancestries study on the manicured lawn and walk the halls of this classically-designed seat of learning. A central hallway leads to classrooms and libraries and meeting halls, and nowhere is safe from the odour of the tannery out back.

Inquiring about either gargoyle or talisman lore leads to a meeting with an elven woman everyone calls the Loremaster. She is, in fact, the City Loremaster and leader of the Academic Council of Wisdom, the Academy's governing body. (If the GM or the players wish to use a different Academy contact instead of the Loremaster, this will be fine; simply replace the references to the Loremaster in the rest of this section.)

Information About Gargoyles: The Loremaster can give the characters the following information without requiring a test. (To avoid repeating info they've already heard, this list notes where the characters might have already learned some of the information. However, sometimes a reminder can help, as it is easy for players to forget details they witnessed several scenes earlier.)

- In all past accounts of gargoyles, they are creatures made of stone that has been given life by arcane magicians. (Possible PC knowledge from **Midnight Attack** or learned from **The Gargoyle-Fearing Dwarf**.)
- Most reports of gargoyle esightings come from dungeons, tombs, treasure vaults, and such places that someone wealthy or magically powerful needs guarded. (Possible PC knowledge from **Midnight Attack**.)
- Gargoyles are rare, as each must be enchanted individually, and the process is expensive in terms of time and resources.
- No previous account has noted as many active gargoyles at the same time as we saw during the attack last night. (Possible PC knowledge from **Midnight Attack**.)
- Witnesses reported seeing the defeated gargoyles vanish when the fight was over. This does not match traditional lore regarding gargoyles, as it suggests that they are not corporeal beings. (Possibly observed by player characters in **Midnight Attack**.)

Information About Talismans: If the characters ask the Loremaster about talismans (most likely after talking to Ainley in **Ainley the Sprite**), she can give them general knowledge about talismans: that they are triangular relics created by the Great Wizard long ago, usually in the form of pendants, and they are imbued with powerful magic. Could one have caused the attacks on the City? Certainly, the Loremaster says.

If the characters speculate to the Loremaster in a way that connects dreams to talismans, she looks thoughtful and tells them that this could well be the work of a rumoured nightmare talisman. Legend says that this talisman will manifest the nightmares of whoever wears it. The Loremaster says that destroying the talisman would put an end to any nightmares that came from it.

The Menagerie

More of an exotic pet and livestock store than a zoo, the Menagerie features beasts both ordinary and supernatural. It is located in a warehouse just off Rats' Road and made up of dozens of cages, some small enough for a mouse, others sized to fit a drake (though no drake is currently in residence). Many of the cages are decorated for the Festival of Strangers with thick lassos with one end tied into a bow, and each occupied cage is labelled with the creature's name. The cages currently contain a few scorpions and rats, several wolves and great cats, two giant spiders, and a juvenile giant worm (with a metal plate at the base of its cage to keep it from tunnelling away).

A formidable-looking trollish woman known only as the Zookeeper manages the Menagerie, and she will be present any time the Menagerie is open. She wears a green explorer's outfit with boots and a coiled-up whip on her belt. Though she doesn't like talking about herself or how she acquires the creatures in her establishment, the Zookeeper is happy to talk to people, especially about animals. She normally deals with wealthy nobles, adventurers, and even well-behaved children, to whom she sells or rents out her creatures as beasts of burden or pets—but only to those she finds deserving of her monstrous friends.

GM Note: While the characters are talking to the Zookeeper, consider having her mention in passing that she hopes nobody is afraid of her giant spiders. This might get a player to confess a fear of spiders, which will be useful at the end, or simply keep alive the adventure's theme of fears and nightmares.

Likewise, the Zookeeper is happy to talk about gargoyles if asked. She can impart the following knowledge without requiring a test. (To keep the players from getting bored from repetition, this list notes where the characters might have already heard some of the information, so you can avoid repeating it.)

- The Zookeeper saw them firsthand and helped fight a few after her neighbours woke her to ask for her help.

- Gargoyles are tough, vicious, and smart—and good fighters.

- They have beady black eyes, not red ones like the creatures the characters met. (Possible PC knowledge from **Midnight Attack**.)

- They can use their wings to fly, though not especially well. They generally only fly short distances, perhaps a few hundred metres.

- Those gargoyles that attacked the City did not seem concerned about self-protection. This is odd, even for gargoyles, but not unknown, especially if they were animated by a mage who compelled them to fight to the death.

Bolstering City Defences

If they wish, the characters can help the City bolster its defences for another attack, if they (correctly) guess that a second one is coming. If they don't think of it, perhaps a member of the city watch can ask for such assistance—especially if the characters don't follow up on the gargoyle-fearing dwarf path. (Possible City watch contact: Gerald, grey-haired human veteran, wears several medals from past campaigns.)

Try to entertain whatever ideas the players put forth, so long as they make sense. In general, each completed defence enhancement adds a number of bonus dice the characters can use while defending the City (which will happen in **A Second Attack!**). Any of the characters can draw from this pool of bonus dice, so long as it makes narrative sense that they could be gaining the benefit of an associated defence enhancement. For example, if the characters trained some citizens as a militia and they fight alongside them, those characters can use the militia's bonus dice pool.

Completing a City Defence Enhancement

Any character wishing to do such work must spend one hour and roll a test using an appropriate skill. Ideas for possible enhancements and the associated skills to complete them appear in the **Example Defence Enhancements** table. The difficulty of this test is 13, which the GM can adjust based on how the players describe their plans for each enhancement. If the test is successful, the enhancement generates a number of bonus dice. Keep a note of the bonus dice available for each enhancement.

BOLSTERING CITY DEFENCES

Failure	The attempted enhancement fails. Describe how this manifests, such as the collapse of an archer tower mid construction.
Standard Success	The enhancement generates a number of bonus dice equal to the result of the Kismet Die.
Great Success	The enhancement generates a number of bonus dice equal to the result of the Kismet Die + 1.
Extraordinary Success	The enhancement generates a number of bonus dice equal to double the result of the Kismet Die.

EXAMPLE DEFENCE ENHANCEMENTS

Enhancement	Suggested Skill
Building archer towers	Artisan
Setting traps	Tinker
Arming a civilian militia	Bargain, Persuasion
Training City defenders	Melee, Missile Weapon
Enchanting defenders' weapons or armour	Spellcasting
Casting protective spells on allies	Spellcasting
Enlisting the aid of creatures from the Menagerie or even the Academy	Animal Handling
Organizing priestly healers from the High Temple or other temples wounded	Heal
Setting up efficient patrol coverage for the City's defenders	Notice
Hiring the visiting troll tribespeople to assist with defence; these can appear during combat as one or more Mercenary followers (from **Chapter 3: Followers** in *Talisman Adventures*)	Bargain, Persuasion
Persuading one or more guilds to help defend the City	Bargain, Persuasion, guild-related skill

Note that certain, seemingly sensible enhancements will not help in the upcoming second attack simply because the attackers will magically appear in town and will not have to physically pass the City's walls or gate. Thus, strengthening the walls or the gate or digging a moat will gain no bonuses. However, the characters have no way to know that yet (unless they learned from **Investigating the Gargoyle Attack** that no one witnessed a gargoyle actually entering the City), so allow them to put in the work if they choose.

A SECOND ATTACK!

At midnight on the second day, the City is attacked once more. Characters who are sleeping or indoors hear sounds of fighting in the streets similar to what they heard on the previous night.

Characters who are patrolling or doing other outdoor activities in the City at midnight see jesters suddenly appear—not as if they materialized (though they did), but stepping out from behind buildings and tents and people and immediately attacking. Anyone within view of the City Gate or the City walls sees no evidence of the jesters entering the City from outside; one moment before midnight, they're not there, but the next, they're everywhere.

Read aloud or paraphrase the following, adjusting as needed depending on whether the characters are outdoors or not.

For the second night, the streets are filled with violence! Tonight, however, instead of waking to confront dozens of vicious gargoyles, you find the streets filled with bizarre jesters! Not normal, innocent jesters either—if there is such a thing. These are taller than humans, so skinny they appear unhealthy. The jesters wear similar outfits in different motley mixes of colours: brightly-patterned coats, tight leggings suitable for dancing, pointed shoes, and three-pointed hats fitted with jingling bells. They each carry a sceptre that is topped with a small skull, itself wearing a miniature jester's hat. As you get a better look, you can also make out that each jester has pale white skin, glowing red eyes, and short, sharp, fanged teeth that flash in the evening torchlight as they cackle maniacally.

Similar to what happened in the gargoyle fight, the jesters are fighting with the City's defenders, chasing citizens, destroying property, and causing general mayhem.

FIGHTING THE JESTERS

If the characters engage the jesters in combat, see the **Enemies, Allies, and Followers** section at the end of this adventure for **Nightmare Jester** stats.

This time, let the characters' influence on the City affect how well-prepared the City's defenders are (the city patrol, city watch, and Night Guard) during the fight, and modify your description of the fight thusly. If the players have enhanced the City's defences (in **Bolstering City Defences**), make sure to mention how these enhancements come into play during the fight—and feel free to have the players make some suggestions. Remember to grant the players any bonus dice their enhancements generated.

If the characters begin the encounter near one of the locations in the box **Jester Combat Locations**, that would be a good place to start the fight encounter. As before,

JESTER COMBAT LOCATIONS

City Patrol in Trouble: Two members of the city patrol are trying to defend a butcher shop where a butcher and his family are cowering among the cured slabs of meat. The jesters have no interest in the food and are instead focused on stalking the people.

City Stables: Jesters have opened a gate at the city stables; the panicked horses threaten to stampede down Droppings Lane and into the rest of the City. A jester rides the lead horse.

The High Temple: Priests work to drag jester victims to safety and provide healing.

Residential District: Several jesters terrorize citizens along a residential road, smashing windows, kicking open doors, and throwing lit torches towards flammable materials.

The Square of Kings: Three jesters are gleefully toppling statues of former kings in the square.

The Town Square: Two jesters throw fruit at people from produce carts in the town square. For variety, they occasionally throw knives.

The Wishing Well: The characters see a jester trying to push a citizen down into the well, giggling as the victim tries frantically to keep from going over the edge.

the characters need not fight each and every enemy—let them engage a few in an area or two of your (or their) choice and then conclude the fight on a strong note before the players lose interest.

Less combat-inclined characters can again help out in other ways during the fight, perhaps assisting combatants, healing the injured, getting innocents to safety, repairing defences, and the like.

For each fight with the creatures, provide one attacking jester for each character, plus or minus one for variety. Remember to include members of the city patrol, city watch, Night Guard, or other defenders the characters might have enlisted—any of these can become temporary Followers for any characters, adding one jester for each two such followers. At the GM's discretion, these followers may remain with the characters for the duration of the combat, or even longer if it makes sense.

In combat, the jesters tend towards actions that would be funny if they weren't so deadly. They caper about, dancing and singing and joking, and punctuate these actions by using their deadly sceptre-like bauble for either a blunt or slashing attack. Remember to make use of their Bauble Attack and Maniacal Laughter Special Abilities. Like the gargoyles, they fight to the death, heedless of danger to themselves. When injured, blood splatters everywhere, and they laugh at their own injuries as much as those of their victims.

Here are a few examples of ways to breathe life into descriptions of the nightmare jesters during this encounter:

- A jester laughs gleefully as it chases a woman down an alley, holding a shining blade up menacingly.
- An injured jester sprays blood all around, laughing all the while.
- "Die, die, die, you're all going to die!" yells a jester standing on a roof.
- A jester bites a victim, grinning through clenched teeth while he tears away cloth and flesh.
- A jester dances and cavorts and does cartwheels nonsensically instead of attacking.

In addition to combat, here are a few other things the characters might try—and the potential results.

Examining a jester: The creatures appear to be tall, emaciated humans, but close examination shows their white skin is not makeup, and their pointed teeth and glowing red eyes are decidedly inhuman.

Talking to a jester: The jesters do not answer questions. They don't say why they've come, what they want, where they've come from, or what they are. They don't respond to persuasion or bribery or intimidation or even torture. They may taunt the characters, though, or laugh, or simply stare back with an inhumanly wide smile.

Act Two Experience

1 exploration experience if the characters engage with the Festival of Strangers (unless this was already awarded in Act One).

1 social experience if the characters talk to citizens about the gargoyle attack.

1 exploration experience if the characters visit the Academy or the Menagerie to investigate the gargoyle attack, or if they visit Ohrzer's for the same reason.

1 exploration experience if the characters track the talisman to its origin and/or as close as they can to its destination.

1 combat experience for overcoming Ainley the Sprite.

1 social experience for bolstering City defences.

1 combat experience for fighting the attacking jesters.

Act Three: The Talisman

Events escalate after the second night. The City has been attacked twice, and the characters likely know that a talisman is involved. Their investigations can go several different ways.

Remember that on each day during the festival, the first time each player character exchanges gifts with a stranger grants them another Light Fate.

Investigating the Jester Attack

This section covers some likely people and places the characters might visit to learn more about the jester attack. As with any investigation they might have done on the gargoyles, we assume that it takes place the following day, as most people the characters might want to talk to would be sleeping, healing, or otherwise busy recovering from the late-night attacks. If the characters instead insist on performing investigations immediately, the GM will need to modify some of this section to account for seeking out and talking to the people involved (likely accompanied by **Persuasion (Insight)** tests to get exhausted survivors to take some time to talk).

The Jester Troupe

If the characters remember seeing a troupe of jesters at the beginning of the adventure, they may seek them out to see if they were involved in the attack. They weren't, and in fact, the troupe has been confronted so often by angry citizens since the attack that they are leaving the City. If the PCs ask around, a citizen or guard will tell them this and that the troupe left through the eastern gate not long ago.

The characters can catch up with the troupe if they wish. The jesters look dishevelled and disheartened, and they are certain the characters have come to attack them. They explain they know nothing of the jesters who attacked, they don't know the jesters involved, and that they were just as frightened as everyone else.

Talking to Citizens

Many citizens are shaken by the jester attack, not as much because they were "evil jesters" but because it was the second attack in as many nights, which makes them think more will follow, and nobody knows why they are happening or how to make them stop.

Asking around and talking to various citizens for a while can turn up some unusual observations that several people mention. Have anyone questioning citizens make an **Investigation (Insight)** test at **Difficulty 12**. Multiple characters can assist a single investigator if the players wish to team up.

RESULTS OF TALKING TO CITIZENS

Failure	The citizens seem clueless about the jesters and obsessed with their own problems and fears of a third attack.
Standard Success	Nobody saw the jesters approaching the City from outside. As some may have noticed about the gargoyles, the jesters were within the City walls and on the attack before anyone realised it.
Great Success	There didn't seem to be a purpose to the jesters' attack, no objective at all, except for scaring and hurting people. Especially the scaring.
Extraordinary Success	The attack started right at midnight. Few citizens keep track of the time of day with greater precision than "midday" or "at dusk" or "when it cools down a bit," but some do, and the ones you talked to are sure the jesters came immediately after midnight.

TALKING TO THE CITY'S DEFENDERS

Discussing the attack with any of the City's guardians (city patrol, city watch, Night Guard) can lead to similar results as seen in **Talking to Citizens**. This time, the guards were being especially vigilant, concerned about another gargoyle attack, and did not see any jesters approach from outside the City.

This sort of discussion might take place at the City Gate or the jail (where **Sheriff Thurston Midge** can often be found), and if it does, describe the yellow flowers decorating the City Gate, a few posters advertising the Festival of Strangers on the City walls, and the miniature yellow nooses hanging from the bounty board.

THE HELPFUL SAILOR

If a character achieved a Great Success or Better when tracking the chain of people who receive the talisman after Ebba Silverbough, then the sailor Sofia promised to tell them if she heard news of the last person in the chain, Nojus, who had set sail before the characters could talk to him (all of which was mentioned in **Tracking the Talisman**). The morning after the attack, Sofia makes good on this promise.

She seeks out the character(s), either by finding them at their place of lodging or by hiring messengers to look for them in common areas of the City. Once she has found them, she (or a messenger) tells them that she doesn't know if this is important, but that she heard from one of the dockhands that Nojus gave away a talisman before

he left. He gave it to a little girl when they were picking up supplies in the Town Square yesterday. The girl is a young human with curly red hair and freckles, who was wearing a white dress.

If the characters try to locate the girl, see **The Jester-Fearing Child**.

THE JESTER-FEARING CHILD

If the characters have figured out that the attacks are being spawned from a person's nightmares—especially if they know that the talisman that can make such a thing happen—they may try to locate anyone who fears jesters. If the players don't remember that they saw such a person at the start of the adventure—the little girl who ran away screaming from a troupe of jesters when the characters were first starting to experience the festival—the GM can either remind them about her or let them ask around and encounter a citizen who knows such a girl. (Possible citizen: Venla, short elven woman, shabby clothes but cheerful attitude.) The characters can then locate the girl through the citizen who knows her or by searching the Town Square until they spot the child.

Alternatively, the characters might learn about the girl from the sailor Sofia after trying to trace who ended up with Ebba Silverbough's talisman (detailed in **The Gargoyle-Fearing Dwarf**, **Tracking the Talisman**, and **The Helpful Sailor**).

The child's name is **Hanna Harper**, an adolescent human girl with curly red hair and freckles, wearing a green dress. Hanna lives in a humble home on Crescendo Lane with her musician parents (Louise and Nora). When the characters approach the house, though, they spot Hanna having breakfast with her parents in a nearby courtyard frequented by members of the Entertainers Guild (which includes Hanna's parents). The courtyard is decorated with yellow flowers for the festival and consists of four tables arranged around the statue of a famous musician (let the players invent the musician and their history, if they like).

If the characters can give them an acceptable reason, Hanna's parents are fine with them asking their daughter some questions. Here are answers to some things the players might ask, which could also come from either parent.

Why are you afraid of jesters?

"They're creepy and act so strange! Not like regular people, like my parents and dwarves and those funny sprites and ghouls."

Have you ever been attacked by jesters before?

"No, what a horrible thought!"

Did you dream about jesters last night?

"I did! There were lots and lots of them and they were trying to scare people and hurt people. They had knives and glowing eyes."

Did you see the jester attack last night? Where were you?

"What? Jesters attacked? While I was sleeping?!" Hanna's parents heard the attack and learned details about it from neighbours this morning but did not tell Hanna about it because they didn't want to frighten her. Now the characters have done so—the monsters.

Do you have a talisman?

This answer depends on how quickly the characters find Hanna—or how quickly the GM wants to conclude the adventure. If they found her quickly (or the GM is ready to end the story), she still has the talisman they might have learned about from Ebba Silverbough (in **The Gargoyle-Fearing Dwarf**). Otherwise, she says she gave the talisman to a stranger before breakfast this morning. Use the list of talisman recipients in **Tracking the Talisman** as a guide and invent as many additional recipients as you like for the characters to chase down. When they reach the final recipient, proceed to **Triggering the Final Encounter**.

Who gave you the talisman?

"A nice sailor I met in the Town Square when he was shopping. His name was Norris I think. Or Jonas?" (It's Nojus.)

Triggering the Final Encounter

When the characters track down the talisman, this triggers the final confrontation with the instigator of the nightmare attacks. Proceed to **The Night Mare**.

The Night Mare

When the characters manage to track down the person who currently possesses the talisman (whether it is Hanna Harper or someone who received it after her), and they try to take it from that person, this triggers a final conflict. At the GM's discretion, this can happen even if nobody physically tries to take the talisman—what matters is that the spirit inside the talisman believes it is in danger of being taken, or that this is inevitable.

Suddenly the talisman glows bright red and a black horse leaps out of it, expanding to full size when it lands on the ground nearby. Perhaps even greater than full size, as this horse looks large and powerful enough for a troll to ride. It glares at you with its glowing red eyes and stamps one of its flaming hooves menacingly before speaking.

"What fertile ground this City has been, ripe with vivid imaginations to explore! I am the Night Mare, fools, and I don't appreciate you threatening my home. Unfortunately

for you, I know what fears live in your dreams and your hearts, and you will regret this intrusion!"

As the Night Mare is not interested in talking, combat ensues! See the **Enemies, Allies, and Followers** section at the end of the adventure for the **Night Mare's** stats. The Night Mare starts the fight by using its Nightmare Entourage benefit, summoning nightmare creatures

A Third Night?

If the characters have not managed to track down the talisman—or the GM wants more nightmare combat—then a new army of nightmare creatures attacks on the third midnight. Think of a fun type of nightmare creature to inflict upon the City, and remember to also come up with an NPC who has that fear and ended up with the talisman that night.

If the GM wants to make it more obvious what is causing the attack, they can introduce a character who mentions a specific, memorable fear (giant spiders, dolls, redheads) and have nightmare versions of that creature attack that night—because this character received the talisman, of course.

The Characters' Nightmares

Choose a nightmare adversary for each character. Interpret this as broadly as you like; for a character who seems fearless, it may have been a nightmare from childhood. For another, it might represent a recurring drea—or their greatest fear in real life even if they never actually dream of it.

If you like, you can have each player name a nightmare that would resonate for their character. If necessary, you can even motivate them with a Light Fate point in exchange for handing you the keys to their fears. (You might also remind the players that your intention is to create a meaningful scene, not to trick or "beat" them.)

For these nightmare adversaries, use the **Nightmare Minion** stats in **Enemies, Allies, and Followers**. As indicated there, don't use all of the stat block's Special Abilities—only use one or two to represent the abilities of the creature being simulated.

tailored to all the player character present (one for each). See the box **The Characters' Nightmares** for more information on these creatures.

Nightmare Combat

If this encounter happens at the Entertainers Guild courtyard where Hanna is, let the combatants make use of the setting—throwing chairs, ducking behind tables, flinging props sitting nearby for an upcoming play, toppling the statue, etc. If it takes place elsewhere (perhaps because the characters didn't look for her early enough to stop her from giving the talisman to a stranger), try to stage the fight somewhere interesting with plenty of room to manoeuvre. A few possibilities are at the wharves, the Scullery Pawnshop, or World's Finest Armoury (all of which are detailed in **Chapter 1: History of the Realm** of *Talisman Adventures*

During the fight, the minions each try to attack the characters who inspired them, while the Night Mare himself attacks anyone who seems to be doing too well—or whoever is closest to the talisman. Here are a few other ideas for spicing up this combat:

- The characters' personal nightmare creatures taunt them while attacking.
- The Night Mare attacks with his flaming hooves, potentially igniting any flammable surface for dramatic effect.
- An enemy threatens the owner of the talisman, purely out of malice.
- After a nightmare minion is defeated, the Night Mare summons a new, different one.

The Talisman: If the talisman is destroyed, this will banish the Night Mare from the physical plane. The Night Mare knows this and tries to prevent it. If the characters are smart and extra effective and manage to attack the talisman early in the fight, consider making the talisman tough enough to withstand three hits—and each time it is hit, it bounces (or even teleports) across the combat area, enraging the Night Mare and causing one of the minions to vanish. However, if the game is running long, or the GM wants to reward cleverness and doesn't feel an abrupt ending will displease the players, maybe the first hit does the job!

When the characters either destroy the talisman or defeat the Night Mare, read the following aloud (or paraphrase):

The Night Mare lets out an earsplitting screech and the talisman glows bright red before both of them vanish in a sudden flash of explosive light.

Any remaining Nightmare Minions vanish as well, and no traces of the nightmare creatures remain. The nightmare attacks on the City have ended.

Conclusion

Hanna and her parents (or a different talisman recipient if it didn't end up with Hanna) thank the

Rewards

The Magistrate of the City offers each character 50 gold for their assistance in ridding the City of the nightmare attackers. In addition, the High Temple gifts each character with their choice of any potion worth up to 20 gold.

characters for defeating the Night Mare, as do the people of the City when the news gets out that the characters have ended the nightly attacks. The City is able to sleep soundly again, and the characters can rest easy—until such time as the Wraith Lord resolves to punish them for their interference in his schemes…

Act Three Experience

1 social experience if the characters talk to citizens about the jester attack.

1 social experience if the characters talk to Hanna Harper about jesters.

1 exploration experience if the characters track the talisman to its origin and/or as close as they can to its destination (unless they already did so in Act Two).

2 combat experience for overcoming the Night Mare and his minions.

Strangers, Allies, Followers, and Enemies

The following section provides quick statistics for each of the Strangers, Allies, Followers, and Enemies encountered in this adventure.

Strangers, Allies, and Followers

This section details the NPCs that might help the player characters during the course of the adventure. A few of them can become temporary Followers, but unless the GM desires otherwise, they remain in the City when the player characters move on.

For stats for **City Patrol**, **City Watch**, and **Night Guard**, see page 81.

Troll Warrior (Ally or Enemy)

These trolls are visitors to the City from a wilderness tribe. Though they enjoy fighting, they do not kill without reason. They wear leather tunics decorated with animal bones and carry simple but well-made clubs.

Troll Warrior

Neutral
Threat: 14
Strength: 5   **Craft:** 2
Armour: 3 (leather tunic)   **Life:** 14
Attacks: 1   **Damage:** 1d6 (fist), 1d6+2 (club)
Speed: 6

Special Abilities

⚫ **Regeneration:** The troll immediately regenerates 1d6 Life.

Benefits & Banes

None.

Troll Shaman (Ally or Enemy)

The shaman from a tribe of wilderness trolls serves many roles, from spiritual leader to healer to sage advisor. They wear a light leather tunic, but for special occasions, add a robe and headdress made from feathers and bones.

Troll Shaman

Neutral
Threat: 14
Strength: 2   **Craft:** 5
Armour: 2 (leather tunic)   **Life:** 13
Attacks: 1   **Damage:** 1d6 (fist), 1d6+1 (staff)
Speed: 6

Special Abilities

⚫ **Regeneration:** The troll immediately regenerates 1d6 Life.

Benefits & Banes

Minor Knowledge of Nature Magic: The troll shaman knows three Basic spells and has a number of spell points equal to their Craft. They can cast one of these spells as an action. When a PC gets a Failure or Standard Success on an attack, the troll shaman can cast a spell as a reaction.

Adolescent Troll (Follower)

This young troll tribesperson is yearning to find their place in society, be that troll society or the larger world. To humans, they seem wild, but no one knows if their path will lead them to become a warrior, a shaman, or something different entirely. Many adolescent trolls feel the constant need to prove themselves in the eyes of others, which often comes in the form of combat.

Benefits

Combat Boost (Average): Spend 1 Loyalty. You can add the adolescent troll's Strength score to your damage from one successful attack.
Forager/Good Hunter (Strong): Spend 1 Loyalty. The adolescent troll grants you a bonus die when you're making a Hunting test.
Strength: 2   **Craft:** 2
Life: 12   **Armour:** 2 (leather tunic)
Max Loyalty: 5
Restore Loyalty: Once per day, you may restore 1 Loyalty for this Follower by feeding them treats worth 1 ration. Allowing them to get into a fight also restores 1 Loyalty.

ENEMIES

The following enemies are introduced for the first time in this adventure.

Nightmare Jester

These twisted versions of the entertaining type of jester are solid manifestations of nightmare. They wear clothing in the traditional jester style: motley-coloured, garishly-patterned coats; the similarly flamboyant tight breeches of a dancer; pointed shoes, sometimes curled at the ends; and the famed "fool's hats" with three points aimed in different directions, each affixed with a bell that jingles with the creature's every movement. The main things that distinguish a nightmare jester from the mortal kind are their pale white skin, unusually tall and gaunt build, mouthful of sharp teeth, and glowing red eyes. A nightmare jester also carries a twisted version of a jester's bauble, which is a sceptre with a head at one end topped with a small fool's hat. On a nightmare jester's bauble, the head is a skull, and the other end is a long, curved blade.

Nightmare Jester

Evil
Threat: 14
Strength: 3   **Craft:** 2
Armour: 1 (costume)   **Life:** 15
Attacks: 1   **Damage:** 1d3+3 (bauble sceptre)
Speed: 13

SPECIAL ABILITIES

Bauble Attack: The nightmare jester lashes out with its sceptre, either bashing with its skull end or slashing with its curved blade. When making a melee attack, their damage is doubled.

Maniacal Laughter: The insane laughter of nightmare jesters is terrifying to experience, whether it is an unsettling giggle or a startling guffaw. Before a character attempts their first attack against a nightmare jester in combat, they make a Fortitude (Resolve) test against Difficulty 14; on a failed roll, they cannot attack the nightmare jester that round.

BENEFITS & BANES

None.

AINLEY THE SPRITE

Ainley is a young sprite with curly blond hair, an emerald tunic with gold trim, and a cap with a yellow feather sticking out of it. They enjoy taunting and insulting everyone, and they serve the Wraith Lord in the hope of a future payout in wealth and power over the common people.

AINLEY THE SPRITE

Evil
Threat: 14
Strength: 2   **Craft:** 4
Armour: 0   **Life:** 12
Attacks: 1   **Damage:** 1d4+2 (dagger)
Speed: 8 (walk), 12 (fly)

SPECIAL ABILITIES

Taunt: Ainley has a stunning way of taunting people. Any single target of Ainley's insults who can hear and understand them makes a Craft test against Difficulty 14 to resist.

Failure: The target suffers 1d6+2 psychic damage and cannot attack Ainley for the next 1d3 rounds.

Standard Success: The target suffers 1d3+2 psychic damage and cannot attack Ainley for 1 round.

Great Success or Better: No effect.

BENEFITS & BANES

Flight: All sprites can fly at their normal Speed. This allows them to ignore difficult terrain.

NIGHT MARE

Creatures of legend, Night Mares are spirits that can reach into a person's dreams and bring their fears to life. The Night Mare in this adventure has been bound to the talisman by the Wizard, which compels him to manifest the greatest fear of whoever currently possesses the talisman (if anyone). Normally residing inside the talisman, the Night Mare generally only manifests in the physical world when enemies threaten to discover him. After taking physical form, he appears as a powerful-looking horse of grand proportions, large enough for a troll to ride comfortably. His hooves are constantly burning with a hellish flame, and when necessary, he uses them to attack enemies. However, he usually doesn't have to, as he has his nightmarish creations do his attacking for him.

NIGHT MARE

Evil
Threat: 15
Strength: 5   **Craft:** 2
Armour: 3 (thick hide)   **Life:** 15
Attacks: 4   **Damage:** 1d6+5 (flaming hooves)
Speed: 20

SPECIAL ABILITIES

Vision of Horror: The Night Mare surrounds itself with sights and sounds pulled directly from people's fears. One Follower of the GM's choice immediately loses 1d6 Loyalty. If the Follower's Loyalty is reduced to 0, it flees the party and is never seen again. The GM can spend additional Dark Fate to cause additional Followers to flee (2 Dark Fate per additional Follower).

Spawn Nightmare: When physically manifested, the Night Mare can bring nearby player characters' fears to life. It creates a nightmare minion for one of them.

BENEFITS & BANES

Nightmare Entourage: When the Night Mare is first encountered, it immediately creates a nightmare minion for each player character in the area. (This summoning doesn't cost Dark Fate; spawning additional nightmares later requires Spawn Nightmare, which does cost Dark Fate.) See the Nightmare Minion entry for information on presenting them.

Incorporeal: Nonmagical weapons cannot inflict their normal damage on an incorporeal creature; however, a character using a nonmagical weapon can still inflict an amount of damage equal to their psychic damage modifier. Magical weapons, spells, and psychic attacks affect a Night Mare normally.

Ignore Armour: A Night Mare's attacks always ignore armour.

Nightmare Minions

Note that a specific nightmare minion should only use one or two of the listed Special Abilities and boons, whichever ones are appropriate to its nature. For example, a nightmare sorcerer might only use the Spellcasting benefit, while a giant wasp could believably use the Venom Strike Special Ability and the Flight benefit.

Nightmare Minion

Evil

Threat: 14
Strength: 3   **Craft:** 3
Armour: 3   **Life:** 12
Attacks: 1   **Damage:** 1d6+3 (various attacks)
Speed: 10

Special Abilities

Formidable Strength: This Special Ability allows a nightmare minion to double its damage bonus (to +6) for a single attack.

Supernatural Attack: The nightmare minion unleashes a special attack on a target it can see. This attack is based on the minion's nature, which could include acid, fire, lava, force, lightning, psychic energy, or other exotic manifestations. The target makes an Athletics (Agility) test against Difficulty 15 to avoid the attack.

Failure: The target takes 2d6 damage. Depending on its nature, the attack may ignore armour, knock the target back 2d6 metres, or apply other side effects.

Success: The target takes 1d6 damage. Depending on its nature, the attack may ignore armour, knock the target back 1d6 metres, or apply other side effects.

Great Success or Better: The target takes no damage.

Venom Strike: The nightmare minion bites or stings the character and injects a deadly venom. The character makes a Difficulty 14 Fortitude (Mettle) test; on a failed roll, the character takes 1 point of damage (which ignores armour) on their turn until the character dies or the poison is cured.

Vicious Cut: The nightmare minion can be especially deadly with a weapon. When making a melee attack, their damage is doubled.

Benefits & Banes

Flight: If appropriate, the nightmare minion can take to the air on wings or simply through magic. During combat, the nightmare minion can move directly from one character to another as a normal movement.

Spellcasting: If appropriate, the nightmare minion has access to three Basic spells and spell points equal to their Craft. They can cast one of these spells as an action. When a PC gets a Failure or Standard Success on an attack, the nightmare minion can cast a spell as a reaction.

APPENDIX I: CITY ENEMIES AND STRANGERS

The following tables can be used for random encounters in the City. To generate a random encounter, roll 3d6 and consult the appropriate table based on the level of the PCs. In some cases, you may be directed to roll on a sub-table. You can use the number in parenthesis after the listed encounter to randomly determine the number of enemies or you can determine on your own, based on the composition of the party.

The tables are divided into City districts. Use the appropriate table for PC's current location.

These tables to use Strangers and Followers listed in Tales of the Dungeon, however an alternative from either this book is listed in italics next to these entries.

STRANGER AND FOLLOWER ENCOUNTERS

An Enemy encounter might indicate that the PCs encounter a Stranger. The GM can also use this table to introduce a fun but non-deadly encounter. As with all these tables, feel free to choose encounters, roll for them randomly, or use them as inspiration for your own Stranger encounters. Two tables are provided. The Outside a Dungeon Stranger Encounter Table can be used on the surface for the area just outside a dungeon entrance. The Inside a Dungeon Stranger Encounter Table can be used anywhere inside a dungeon. If the Follower result is received, roll again on the appropriate Follower Sub-table.

GOVERNMENT DISTRICT

LEVEL 1–3 DUNGEON ENCOUNTER TABLE

Roll 3d6	Encounter
3	Doppelganger (1)
4	Cutpurse
5	Corpse Collector/ *Night Guard*
6	Healer
7	Night Guard
8	Barterer
9	Barterer
10	City Patrol
11	City Patrol
12	Dungsweeper
13	Dungsweeper
14	City Watch
15	Named NPC
16	Pedlar
17	Mischievious Fiend/ *Follower sub-table*
18	Follower (roll on Follower sub-table)

THE SPIRIT QUARTER

SPIRIT QUARTER ENCOUNTER TABLE

Roll 3d6	Encounter
3	Doppelganger (1)
4	Cutpurse
5	Night Guard
6	Healer
7	Philosopher
8	Street Sage
9	Talismonger
10	City Patrol
11	City Patrol
12	Astrologer
13	Dungsweeper
14	City Watch
15	Named NPC
16	Sister of Fate/ *City Watch*
17	Redeemer/ *Follower sub-table*
18	Follower (roll on Follower sub-table)

THE AVENUE OF NUMBERS

AVENUE OF NUMBERS ENCOUNTER TABLE

Roll 3d6	Encounter
3	Doppelganger (1)
4	Cutpurse
5	Night Guard
6	Astrologer
7	Philosopher
8	Pedlar
9	Barterer
10	City Patrol
11	City Patrol
12	Dungsweeper
13	City Watch
14	City Watch
15	Named NPC
16	Prospector
17	Armour or Weaponsmith
18	Follower (roll on Follower sub-table)

THE ARTS QUARTER

ARTS QUARTER ENCOUNTER TABLE

Roll 3d6	Encounter
3	Doppelganger (1)
4	Cutpurse
5	Shady Dealer
6	Dungsweeper
7	Armoursmith
8	Pedlar
9	Barterer
10	Talismonger
11	City Patrol
12	City Watch
13	Instructor
14	Weaponsmith
15	Street Sage
16	Night Guard
17	Named NPC
18	Follower (roll on Follower sub-table)

RED LANTERNS

RED LANTERNS ENCOUNTER TABLE

Roll 3d6	Encounter
3	Doppelganger (1)
4	Grifter
5	Dungsweeper
6	City Patrol
7	Fugitive Fiend/ *Cutpurse*
8	Pied Piper
9	Barterer
10	Corpse Collector
11	Racketeer
12	Shady Dealer
13	Cutpurse
14	City Watch
15	Leper
16	Night Guard
17	Named NPC
18	Follower (roll on Follower sub-table)

ROSEWATER

ROSEWATER ENCOUNTER TABLE

Roll 3d6	Encounter
3	Doppelganger (1)
4	Grifter
5	Dungsweeper
6	Healer
7	Philosopher
8	Instructor
9	Barterer
10	City Patrol
11	City Patrol
12	City Watch
13	Sheriff's Deputy
14	Sheriff's Deputy
15	Dwarf Smith/ Weapon or Armoursmith
16	Night Guard
17	Named NPC
18	Follower (roll on Follower sub-table)

FISHTOWN

FISHTOWN ENCOUNTER TABLE

Roll 3d6	Encounter
3	Doppelganger (1)
4	Grifter
5	Dungsweeper
6	City Patrol
7	Pied Piper
8	Corpse Collector/ *Pedlar*
9	Barterer
10	Pedlar
11	Racketeer
12	Shady Dealer
13	Cutpurse
14	City Watch
15	Leper
16	Night Guard
17	Named NPC
18	Follower (roll on Follower sub-table)

Merchant's Cross

Fishtown Encounter Table

Roll 3d6	Encounter
3	Doppelganger (1)
4	Grifter
5	Shady Dealer
6	Racketeer
7	Cutpurse
8	Barterer or Pedlar
9	Barterer or Pedlar
10	Barterer or Pedlar
11	City Patrol
12	City Patrol
13	Armour or Weapon Smith
14	City Watch
15	Dungsweeper
16	Night Guard
17	Named NPC
18	Follower (roll on Follower sub-table)

City (Daytime) Enemies Encounter Sub-table

Roll 3d6	Encounter
3	Polymorphed Dragon (1)
4	Dark Acolyte (1d3+1) and Dark Initiate (1)
5	Crawling Slime (1d3)
6	Air Elemental (1)
7	Apparitions (1d6)
8	Gargoyle (1d3)
9-10	Giant Rats (2d6)
11-12	Bandits (1d6+2)
13-14	Wild Dogs (use Wolves) (2d6)
15	Fire Elemental (1)
16	Earth Elemental (1)
17	Brownie (1)
18	Ghost (1d3)

City (Nighttime) Enemies Encounter Sub-table

Roll 3d6	Encounter
3	Polymorphed Dragon (1)
4	Apparitions (1d6)
5	Crawling Slime (1d3)
6	Gargoyles (1d3)
7	Dark Acolyte (1d6+1) and Dark Initiate (1d3)
8	Vampire Bats (2d6)
9-10	Giant Rats (2d6)
11-12	Bandits (1d6+2)
13-14	Wild Dogs (use Wolves) (2d6)
15	Lemure (1d6)
16	Shadows (1d6)
17	Boggarts (1d6)
18	Ghost (1d3)

Sewers

Sewers Encounter Table

Roll 3d6	Encounter
3	Monster (roll on Sewer Enemies Encounter sub-table)
4	Tracker
5	Racketeer
6	Cutpurse
7	Fugitive Fiend
8	Mischievous Fiend
9	Deranged Alchemist
10	Pied Piper
11	Pied Piper
12	City Patrol
13	Corpse Collector
14	City Watch
15	Dungsweeper
16	Night Guard
17	Shrine Priest (Dark Initiate)
18	Follower (roll on Follower sub-table)

SEWER ENEMIES ENCOUNTER SUB-TABLE

Roll 3d6	Encounter
3	Putrid Zombies (1d6+1)
4	Dark Acolyte (1d3+1) and Dark Initiate (1)
5	Bandits (1d6+2)
6	Crawling Slime (1d3)
7	Skeleton (1d6+1)
8	Serpent (1d3)
9-10	Giant Rats (2d6)
11-12	Vampire Bats (2d6)
13-14	Lemure (1d6+1)
15	Apparitions (1d6)
16	Spectre (1d3+1)
17	Ghost (1d3)
18	Wraith (1d3)

LOWER AND MIDDLE-CLASS FOLLOWER SUB-TABLE

Roll 3d6	Encounter
3	Anathama Priest/
4	Jinx
5	False Prophet/
6	Witch Cat
7	Lost Soul
8	Disciple of Darkness/
9	Mercenary
10	Cat
11	Porter
12	Urchin
13	Dog
14	Torchbearer/
15	Haggler
16	Panhandler
17	Gremlin
18	Crow/ Raven

UPPER-CLASS SUB-TABLE 2

Roll 3d6	Encounter
3	White Maiden/
4	Theurgist or Light or Dark
5	Disciple of Darkness
6	Scout
7	Gremlin
8	Porter
9	Demagogue
10	Scribe
11	Servant
12	Physician
13	Mercenary
14	Falcon/ Hawk
15	Taleweaver
16	Temple Acolyte
17	Treasure Hunter
18	Champion

INDEX

CITY STREET

1 SQUARE = 1 METRE

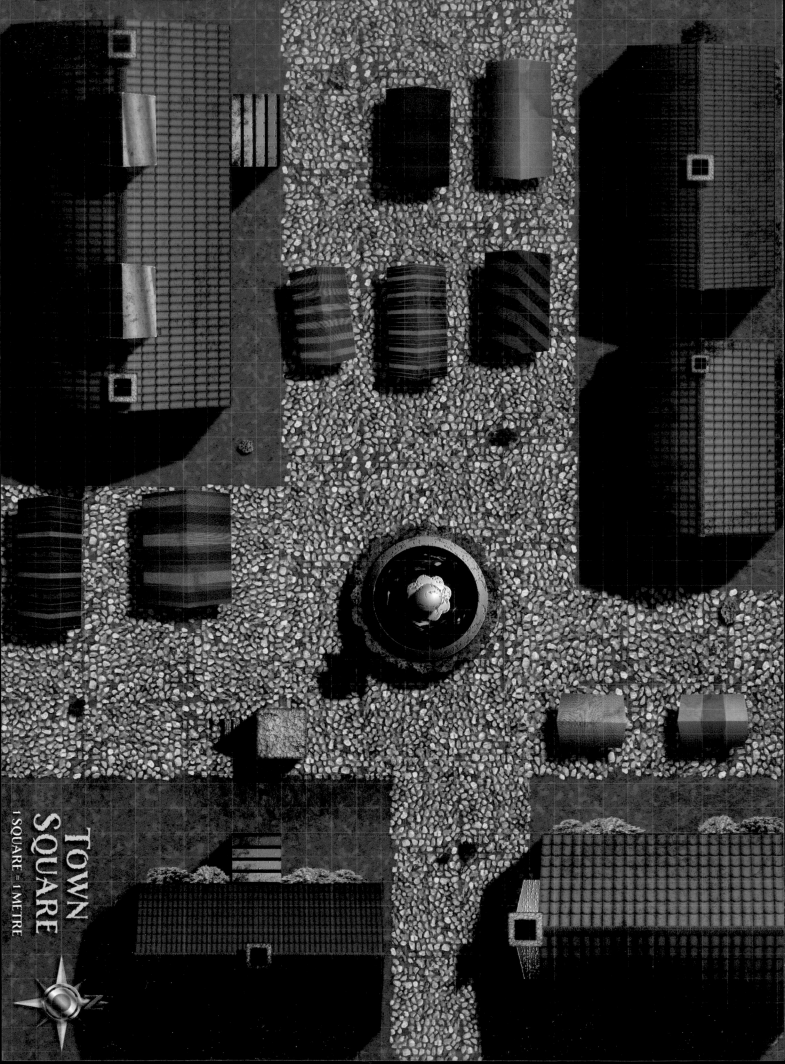

TOWN SQUARE

1 SQUARE = 1 METRE